Praise for *City Lights*

"Quite possibly I have missed a new generation of newspaper writers whose familiarity with and sensitivity to their urban bailiwick, as well as a gift for pungent and nimble prose, has made them an essential part of their cities' cultures—I'm thinking of Herb Caen, Mike Royko, Jimmy Breslin, and Murray Kempton. Possibly Dan Barry is a modern-day version of those types."
                                                           —*The Morning News*

"A glowing collection of essays that sparkles and illuminates as much as the city it endeavors to capture. . . . Readers will thank Barry for bringing these stories to their attention."   —*Booklist*

"Highly evocative."   —*Publishers Weekly*

"Terrific . . . he absolutely captures the diurnal kaleidoscope of this pell-mell place that comprises, in its immense diversity and Sisyphean tragedy, the constantly changing face of America."
                                                        —*The Virginian-Pilot*

"This is a great book to dip into, reading randomly, a column at a time. It's the book I'm giving to everyone I know who loves New York."   —Alice McDermott, *Commonweal*

Also by Dan Barry

Pull Me Up: A Memoir

Stories About New York

City Lights

Dan Barry

 St. Martin's Griffin 🦁 New York

www.stmartins.com

Design by Philip Mazzone

The Library of Congress has catalogued the hardcover edition as follows:

Barry, Dan, 1958–
    City lights : stories about New York / Dan Barry.—1st ed.
        p. cm.
    Collection of author's About New York weekly column in *The New York Times*.
    ISBN-13: 978-0-312-36718-3
    ISBN-10: 0-312-36718-X
    1. New York (N.Y.)—Social life and customs—Anecdotes. 2. New York
(N.Y.)—Social conditions—Anecdotes. 3. City and town life—New York
(State)—New York—Anecdotes. 4. New York (N.Y.)—Biography—Anecdotes.
I. Title
F128.55.B37 2007
974.7'1044—dc22

                                                            2007019668

    ISBN-13: 978-0-312-53891-0 (pbk.)
    ISBN-10: 0-312-53891-X (pbk.)

First St. Martin's Griffin Edition: April 2009

10 9 8 7 6 5 4 3 2 1

To those who gave me their time, and their stories

Contents

Acknowledgments

What follows is a painfully truncated list of all those to whom I am grateful. The editors at *The New York Times*, who allowed me to lease such valuable real estate in the world's greatest newspaper, especially Joseph Lelyveld, Bill Keller, Jill Abramson, Jon Landman, Susan Edgerley, and my brother in ink, Joe Sexton. The members of the Metro backfield and copy desks, who saved me so often from myself, especially Pete Khoury. Various *Times* photographers who always teach me how to report, and to see. A street parade of friends and mentors, including Al Baker, Jimmy Breslin, Betsy Causey, Dave Chmiel, Kevin Davitt, David Dunlap, Jim Dwyer, Kevin Flynn, Terry Golway, Christopher Gray, Pete Hamill, Kevin McCabe, Peter Quinn, Matt Purdy, Willie Rashbaum, Colleen Roche, Rick Simpson, Bob Sullivan, Maria Terrone, and Bob Weil. My agents, Todd Shuster and Lane Zachary. My editor on this project, George Witte, and all the people at St. Martin's Press. My father-in-law, Joseph Trinity, and all my in-laws, who should know better than to have accepted me. The Barretts and Horniks, the Seiberts and McShanes. My father, Gene Barry, who long ago imbued me with a love for New York, and my brother, Brian, and my sisters, Brenda and Elizabeth, and my mother, Noreen, whose storytelling I sorely miss. And, finally, my wife, Mary Trinity, and my daughters, Nora and Grace, the lights that guide me.

Foreword

by Alice McDermott

For those of us whose mid-century childhoods were spent in the New York suburbs, in the long shadow of "the city" (no need to specify which city, there was always only one), in the bland and history-less tract homes that had been purchased by parents who in previous and more interesting lives had been born in the city, raised in the city, educated, romanced, employed in the city, there will always be something inaccessible and enchanting about New York. No matter how well we come to know it in adulthood, no matter how diligently we try to amend that earlier exile by pursuing city careers, city romances, city addresses of our own, there remains for us something of the nose-pressed-against-the-window wonder of the permanent outsider. But we're not just any kind of outsider. Our wonder at the city is nothing like the slack-jawed astonishment of some new arrival from some far-flung place (the Midwest, for instance), but rather the proud, nearly-knowing, friend-of-a-friend, basking-in-the-reflected-glory wonder of the poor relation who has grown up just outside the palace gates.

As he made clear in his lovely 2004 memoir, *Pull Me Up,* Dan Barry is just such a proprietary outsider. A Long Island kid (Deer Park, to be exact) whose career as a journalist led him from the outer darkness of those suburbs, through Connecticut (the *Journal Inquirer*) and Rhode Island (*The Providence Journal*), and finally to that Gray Lady at the heart of the heart of the city, *The New York Times*, where for four years, twice a week, in columns of around a thousand words, he told his readers all about New York.

Easy comparisons abound—this trick's been tried before. Opening *City Lights,* a reader might be reminded of O. Henry's New Yorkers in *The Four Million*: "Being the last man living in one of the last flop-houses on the Bowery has its benefits." Or hear a trace of Jimmy Breslin's Queens-accented wiseacre wit: "For if Mr. Met could speak, he might release a banshee-like wail that lasts through the day and well into the night, long after the lights of Shea Stadium had stopped illuminating the latest crime committed in the name of baseball."

But Dan Barry sees the city with the wide eyes of a visitor (who but a visitor would write, "Here falls a well-dressed woman, and her dinner spills from a bag and onto the sidewalk. I hand her back her errant roll, and who knows why, but I say I am sorry"), a native's skeptical squint ("Funny, isn't it, how the life possessions of a man could vanish in Manhattan, just like that"), a tourist's delight, and a true son's healthy sense of self-deprecation. The resulting view is not like anything we've had before. It is wry but not cruel, poignant but not maudlin. It is a view informed by tremendous love for the city, the people, and the place, but without the annoying myopia that gives New Yorkers (think Steinberg's map, most Yankee fans, those of us who say "the city" as if there is no other) a bad name. Here is a writer who approaches the eight million residents of the greatest city in the world with a poet's eye for detail and a journalist's head for facts, but also with something that it seems has never been tried before: humility.

Because these columns were written between 2002 and 2006, in the aftermath, immediate and not so, of 9/11, it is perhaps not surprising to discover that loss serves as a recurring theme throughout. Some of these losses are a direct result of that terrible day: a description of the Circle Line's first trips around Lower Manhattan's altered landscape, or the tender moment when two young men whose brothers died in the World Trade Center are brought together by a mutual friend, for a drink at an East Side bar. But more of them still acknowledge the losses that are inevitable in the life of any city, of any life at all, the losses of time and tide, of old ways, old loyalties, of street-corner characters and ordinary landmarks and daily routines, of sounds and scents that once defined some part of the city, but are fading now, or already gone. There are columns about a ventriloquist's widow, an aging City

Hall reporter "famous for not suffering fools, especially editors who treated her as a second-class woman and not as a first-class reporter," the "mayor" of Central Park. There is a touching paean to the old Fulton Fish Market. Another column, remarkable for the quiet outrage that runs just beneath Barry's signature wit and gentle empathy, is about the closing of St. Brigid's Church in Tompkins Square.

But as with any chronicle of loss, there are celebrations, too, of what remains, what endures, what begins again: Barry records a swearing-in ceremony for new citizens at the Queens Plaza mall, and the moment when a group of Mexican laborers meet in the utility room of an apartment building on the Grand Concourse to discuss that most American of American dreams: a company of their own. He captures the bated breath and eternal hope of the aspiring dancer, "three weeks fresh from Pittsburgh," inside the Curious George costume at the Convention Center, the resilience in the face of city regulations, changing fashions, changing tastes, of the Afghan-born coffee-cart vendor, the dapper haberdasher, the Grand Sheik of the March of the Wooden Soldiers' tent of the Sons of the Desert, Staten Island's official Laurel and Hardy appreciation society. And he reminds his readers of the beauty, the beneficence, of the city's ordinary time: the deserted streets on the coldest nights of the year, the lone swimmer in the public pool in the last hour of summer, the daily, fleeting miracle of the bread line ("the Brigadoon of bread lines") at St. Francis of Assisi Church, a man's simple cross-town journey to a doctor's office.

In his memoir, Barry described himself as a young writer on the brink of that long journey out of the suburbs. "You retire to the basement to write for an hour or two on the baby blue Brother, next to the sump pump. . . . You have no idea what you will do with these bits and pieces. All you know is that you want to capture what you see with words, you want to preserve moments and then turn them upside down to see what truth lies beneath."

The at-the-window wonder that infuses these columns, then, is not solely a result of Dan Barry's Long Island roots. It is rather the native condition of the born writer, poet, artist, who must—who can fathom why?—capture what he sees with words, preserve moments, discover some truth. The truth is that our city is beautiful, changing, and like its eight million, like life, teeming with tragedy and comedy, hope and despair, resurrection and loss. Dan Barry understands that we are all permanent, if proprietary, outsiders amidst this overwhelming tumult of sights and sounds, stories, histories. That none of us can ever know this magnificent city completely. (See "A Forest Monk's Lesson in the New York Jungle," in which Donald Trump, waiting for an elevator in his own domain, is, all unknowing, observed by a Buddhist monk whose sole possession, a cloth bag, has just been stolen at the Trump Tower Starbucks.)

For anyone who loves New York, who has been enchanted by its tumult, its people, its stories, this failure is a matter of some disappointment. Noses pressed against the window, we would, if we could, take it all in, lose nothing. But the columns collected here remind us that there is compensation to be found. Turn to any one of them and you will find a New York moment captured, a New York sight, a New York sound, a New York smell preserved, a New York memory recalled, a New York life revealed. Turn to any one of Dan Barry's columns and you will find something fleeting and impermanent made secure against those inevitable changes of time and tide, real-estate developers, fashion trends, human folly, mortality itself, all by the grace of about a thousand words.

Introduction

The lunch-break workers dawdling in rumination along Fulton Street fail again to find any good reason not to return to their cubicles. Their hour of liberty ended, they yield the ancient Lower Manhattan street to tourists who impede sidewalk traffic as they photograph trace bits of Old New York. To consider these visitors a nuisance, though, is to miss the unifying inside joke: In New York, we are all tourists.

I pass my brother and sister tourists as I go down again to the river. At water's edge I climb the stairs to a secret city place, the easternmost, uppermost corner of Pier 17 at the South Street Seaport. The deck chairs are bolted to the wooden planks, as if to suggest, even insist, that here is an excellent place to sit awhile and reflect.

Across the ominous olive waters of the tidal strait called the East River, earthy Brooklyn returns haughty Manhattan's stare. The trees along its famous promenade form garish splashes of green against the background of brick brown and concrete gray. Below the stop-and-go stutter of the Brooklyn-Queens Expressway, an old warehouse bears large, faded letters that hint of a former purpose: TIONAL COLD STORAG. To the far right, a cruise ship docked in Red Hook looks massive, improbable. A column someday, I think.

To the left, the Brooklyn Bridge commands attention. Its crisscrossing cables shimmer like silvery cats' cradles; its granite towers rise from river and muck like the straddling legs of mythic Colossus. Lost in the spellbinding netting of those cables, I think of young Al Smith watching the building of this bridge from his Lower East Side neighborhood; of brash P. T. Barnum testing its strength with a parade of twenty-one elephants; of Walt Whitman and Thomas Wolfe and Bugs Bunny—of the thousands of people, many covered in vanilla-colored dust, streaming across its back in a collective daze after the towers collapsed.

This is how the New York mind works sometimes, now.

How strong the bridge seems today.

Brooklyn stories I've told, of Brooklyn people I've met, come to mind. The janitor, weary from a night spent cleaning the toilets of Wall Street titans, who ran across the street to catch a toddler thrown from a burning building; he hugged that child as if she were his own. The city worker who contemplated the ebb and flow of life as she operated a Gowanus Canal bridge; she prayed for that sick son of hers, recuperating back home. The basketball player, past thirty and barely five foot nine, who practiced and practiced because he planned to make the NBA; maybe he will someday.

I breathe the harbor-damp air, but it seems lighter, lesser. Glancing at the foot of the bridge planted in Manhattan, I remember why. That place-specific aroma; that perfume of fish guts and spilled coffee, of cheap cigars and melting sea-scented ice; that smell that slapped you in the face and shouted, Pay heed, son, you are at the Fulton Fish Market, here before your grandfather was born, here before Lincoln was president; gone. The aroma gone, the place, too, all to make more room for the expanding upscale mall called Manhattan.

Perhaps it was best for the market and its weather-whipped denizens to be moved to a new indoor facility in the Bronx in 2005; the iconic deserve shelter, too. Still, I wish New York had preserved that city-sea smell in, say, some interactive museum, along with the poetry of profanity grandly delivered under the Franklin Delano Roosevelt Drive, and the resounding *thwock! thwock!* of grappling hooks piercing waxed boxes of salmon and tuna, and the rumbling laughter that sounded like eruptions of phlegm, and the characters christened twice, before God and before Neptune—Shrimp Sammy, Porgy Joe, and the rest—and the call of South Street Annie as she wheeled her cart, peddling newspapers, cigarettes, and other things, hiya sweetie, hiya.

Goodbye, sweetie.

Behind the fish market, what was the fish market, Manhattan spreads west in sumptuous promise. I wonder about the people I have encountered in those high-rises and low-rises, in those shops, bars, buildings, and shadows. The young woman who worked as a mermaid; she would shimmy into a fin and plunge into a trendy nightclub's massive aquarium, where her blond hair danced like sea grass, and her troubled thoughts were rinsed free. The ventriloquist's widow who lives alone in an apartment with her husband's dummies—their "kids": Bruce, Cecil, Susie, Lulu, Uncle Sam, and Dr. Litchi, as in the nut. The old bank robber who spent thirty-five years on the lam, and, one day, while living in a five-by-seven room on the Bowery, decided to turn himself in; no one remembered the case. The recovering alcoholic who rose from the bowels of Penn Station to reclaim his name; the coffee vendor who asked of Manhattan only three feet of sidewalk, and was denied; the famous dancer, now in her eighties, who rents studio space in Midtown every week for the chance to glide again to "Stardust."

Every neighborhood, it seems, every landmark, conjures a moment in city time. Glancing north toward the Manhattan Bridge, for example, I think of an eleven-year-old girl named Quin-Rong Wu. She disappeared shortly after leaving her Henry Street tenement for her elementary school, just four hundred paces away, only to be found dead, days later, in the shadowy East River shoals beneath this bluish bridge. A decade later her murder remains unsolved, another cold case, and so whenever I see the Manhattan Bridge, I see a young girl walking to school.

Before me, another Circle Line tour boat moves south toward New York Harbor, the divinely situated body of water that made this a city above all others. The boat will pass from my view, curve around the bottom of Manhattan, and head up the Hudson River to its dock on the West Side, a few blocks from the New York Times building. I think of the Circle Line excursions of my childhood, and I think of a Circle Line trip with some friends in late August of 2001, and I think again of the day two weeks after that, when the Circle Line fleet ferried thirty thousand shaken people away from a broken New York to the secure shores of New Jersey.

The Circle Line returned less than a month later to taking

sightseers on a half loop around Lower Manhattan, and I boarded
one of the first cruises to hear how fresh catastrophe had been incorporated into the tour guide's patter. As the boat eased south, a guide
sporting epaulets pointed out the Empire State Building, Greenwich
Village, TriBeCa—"triangle below Canal," he confided. Then the
captain cut the engine, and the boat glided in silence past the smoldering pyre.

The tour guide's words intruded like loud whispers during a
Mass's moment of silence. "That's the American Express tower, which
took a real big hit. . . . Such a tough sight to see . . . It's amazing how
many buildings were not affected. . . . Just all the devastation and
horror . . . According to the mayor, the cleanup here might take up to
a year."

Camcorders whirred, cameras clicked, someone cried. And a couple from Dublin kept their camera packed at their feet because, they
later told me, they thought that taking photographs would approach
sacrilege.

Now, watching another Circle Line keep to its schedule, soon to
pass the ground zero absence on Manhattan's lower west side, I think
about what it is I have been doing for well more than three years.
I have been a tourist, a paid tourist, writing "About New York," after.

In the course of this blessed assignment, of filing two columns a
week, I have tried to shed my cocky, New York sense of ownership
that comes from having been born in New York and having lived in
and beside it for most of my life. There are people who will tell you
that they know a place in the West Village that serves the best—the
best—cupcake in New York. There are people who will advise you to
never—*ever*—take the Van Wyck Expressway. The subtle implication
is that because they know where to get a cupcake, because they know
to avoid some traffic congestion in Queens, they therefore *know* New
York.

Sitting here, at water's edge, I realize that I know enough now to
say I don't know New York, no matter how many years I have gazed
at the city lights. What I do know, and what I hope this collection reflects, are a few of those flash moments that are universal and yet distinct to these five boroughs.

The way the dust clings like conversation's residue to the wishbones at McSorley's Old Ale House. Or the way the Staten Island ferry

groans at your feet as it lumbers through these green-dark waters. Or the way a rainy day in Manhattan summons a chorus of sidewalk salesmen to sing, *'mbrella, 'mbrella, 'mbrella*. And once that rain has lifted, and that song has ended, the way you sense the sun shining upon a new city, a different city, an ever-evolving, ever-vibrant, wounded, resilient, seductive, and thoroughly unknowable City of New York.

PART I

Robert Stolarik

New York, Starring New York

NOVEMBER 26, 2003

From an Alabama Sousaphone, a Fanfare for the City

They deserved New York. Those who have willingly donned the maroon-and-gold uniforms of the Pinson Valley High School marching band, who have lived to the tweets of their director's whistle, who have played so much upbeat music that they can bring pep to "Avé Maria." Yes, these children of Alabama deserved to participate in that glorified commercial known as the Macy's Thanksgiving Day Parade.

But none deserved New York more than their five sousaphone players, including Andrew Parsons, sixteen. His lot in band life is to lug around a heavy instrument that looks like a tuba straining to be a boa constrictor. While others frolic among the high notes, he and his four mates boomp-boomp-boomp in the low. Andrew likes that.

Those boomps were an integral part of what won his band its brass ring: selection as one of the nine high school bands in this year's parade. Hundreds of practices followed, as did car washes, cookie dough sales, and other fund-raisers to pay for the 950-mile trip to New York.

They left Alabama on Sunday evening, 261 students, parents, and teachers packed into five chartered buses. They breezed through Washington on Monday and got to their hotel near Newark Liberty International Airport around midnight. Andrew shared a two-bed room with three other boys; he slept on the floor.

The band practiced its routine again in the hotel parking lot yesterday morning, somehow blending "Old Man River," "Jingle Bell Rock," and "Big Noise from Winnetka" into a toe-tapping medley. The band director, Jeff Caldwell, who stays up nights thinking about band precision, blew his whistle and told everyone that they looked and sounded great.

Then the people from Pinson Valley piled onto the purring buses for a day trip to Manhattan. Like many around him, Andrew had never been to New York, although he had been to St. Louis once. He had his name tag around his neck and his camera in his pocket. He took a window seat, not far from where his parents sat.

As the buses pulled out, Andrew set aside his performance anxieties—about remaining four paces behind the mellophone players and four ahead of the percussionists—to focus on Manhattan. The first stop was to be lunch at the South Street Seaport.

"Never heard of it," he said as Jersey whirred past. "What is it?"

Over the next few days the Pinson Valley band will have the same New York experience as that of most of the other parade bands. Accommodations at a New Jersey hotel (it's cheaper); meals at Planet Hollywood and the ESPN Zone; Thanksgiving dinner on a chartered boat; a Broadway play; and visits to South Street, Times Square, and ground zero.

"I'd like to see where they were," he said of the twin towers.

The buses hit congestion on the road to the Lincoln Tunnel, which meant that the Pinson Valley tour included protracted views of a McDonald's, a Taco Bell, and some auto junkyards. Andrew pointed at an industrial parking lot and said, "We have stuff like that in Birmingham."

The buses inched along, eating away at Andrew's excellent adventure. "Is traffic always like this?" he asked. He was gently told yes.

Then the lead bus pulled into a Wendy's restaurant parking lot, a stop that was not on an itinerary that had been months in the planning. Soon all five buses were in the lot, waiting for a woman who had hustled inside. Andrew stared out the dusty window and asked whether they were already in New York. He was gently told no.

Some students passed the time by wondering what they might have for lunch in the seaport's food court. Their meal coupons listed options that ranged from California rolls to Nathan's hot dogs. "What's souvlaki?" one of the students asked.

The woman returned, and the five buses eased back into the congestion. But traffic quickly cleared up, and soon there appeared the Manhattan skyline across the Hudson River, dominated by the largest building that many of them had ever seen.

"Oh, wow!" said students and parents as cameras and video cameras clicked and recorded. Andrew was on the wrong side for this panorama, so he hurriedly handed his camera to his mother. Too late, though.

At the Lincoln Tunnel toll, a few students puzzled over a sign that said camera use was prohibited inside the tunnel. "They don't want you to find a way to blow it up," Andrew explained.

As the buses drove into the tunnel's dusk, a parent explained that they were traveling under the Hudson. Then came sunlight, and tall buildings, and quiet. Andrew Parsons, a sousaphone player from Alabama, had made it to the show.

OCTOBER 15, 2005

Over Asphalt Rivers, the Source of the Three-Dollar Umbrella

Umbrella.

Say it fast, as one peddler did in Times Square—umbrella-umbrella-umbrella—and there's music playing. Say it soft, as another peddler did at Herald Square—ummm-brell-laa—and it's almost like praying.

Umbrella. Umbrella. Will we ever stop saying umbrella?

In the steady rainfall that seems to have begun in 2003, the drenched denizens of New York have walked the streets under half bubbles that separate them unnaturally from the heavens. Our guardian angels above cannot distinguish one mortal from the next; all they see are what look like beach balls, bobbing and slogging along asphalt rivers.

But where do all these umbrellas—or bumbershoots, if you prefer—come from? Especially those cheap black umbrellas, you know the ones, with the incomplete question mark for a handle and the silvery pop-up button so poorly made that it surprises you every time it works? The ones that wind up in garbage-can nests, looking like splayed crows?

This is not a frivolous question. These curious objects force eight million islands into engagement. They change the way we walk the streets, because you assume responsibility for three times your normal airspace by using one. In the sidewalk's umbrella sea, do you raise yours, lower it, tilt it—or offer the first thrust in an eye-threatening game of chicken?

The lobby of Macy's offers a study in how we carry umbrellas like weapons. People flowing into the store aim theirs to the ground, shake them free of rain bullets, and tuck them away, as if in holsters. People leaving the store wince as they pull the trigger, as though shooting a blunderbuss they don't entirely trust.

But who is arming the people of New York with these explosive devices?

For the answer, follow the peddlers. "Umbrella, umbrella, umbrella," they sing in their mellifluous Midtown chant, above the swish of passing cars, the finger-roll thump against canopies, the loud yet barely perceptible roar of rain meeting pavement. Follow them as they wheel their empty tarp-covered carts south on Sixth Avenue, toward what is called the Flower District. In this October rain, in this floral place, it is not crocuses that sprout but umbrellas, opening like bulbs turned upside-down.

In Thursday's pouring grayness, several peddlers knelt on wet pavement outside a wholesale store, slicing cardboard boxes, removing umbrellas made in China, and muttering about bad business.

Bad business? With all this rain?

"Everybody has an umbrella now," explained one peddler. "No good." He rose and wheeled his crammed cart east on West Thirty-first Street, past an Irish pub's dripping, flickering neon sign.

Another peddler, all but lost inside a New York Jets poncho, arrived just as the store closed. His name was Antoine, and he said that he rises at four in the morning to hear the weather forecast so that he knows whether to peddle umbrellas or socks.

"I'd rather sell socks," he said.

Antoine was cagey about where he sells his wares: Midtown, he said, which he defined as the eight-mile stretch between West Eighty-sixth and Fulton streets.

He was just as cagey about where else he buys his umbrellas, although one name slipped past his lips. "Imperial," he said, "West Twenty-eighth Street."

Down in yesterday morning's wetness to West Twenty-eighth Street, where pumpkins adorned a flower shop window display, and where Oscar Rodriguez stood outside another wholesale store, chanting the season's theme song to the rain: "Umbrella, umbrella, umbrella."

He said that when he arrives at the store at seven-thirty on rainy mornings, the peddlers are lined up, waiting to buy a dozen for ten dollars—which they then sell piecemeal for whatever they can get. "Depends on the area," he confided. "White people pay more."

Finally, to a dreary storefront with a sign saying wholesale trade only: Imperial Umbrellas. You have to be buzzed into its drab show-room, where the multicolored umbrella display somehow added no color, and where the fluorescent light's buzz provided the only music.

Several peddlers in wet clothes stood before a worn desk, behind which sat a small man with white hair and hound-dog eyes: Solomon Korn, for thirty years a Man To See in wholesale umbrellas.

As the peddlers placed their orders, Mr. Korn and an employee in the back engaged in an umbrella-model duet.

Employee: "Mr. Korn, Mr. Korn. One dozen W, two dozen 58-58, one dozen 22S?"

Mr. Korn: "One dozen W, two dozen 58-58, one dozen 22S. Give him the black, with the cover."

The peddlers counted out their wet dollar bills and handed them to Mr. Korn. He smoothed away the crumpled dampness as best he could, and laid the bills neatly in a side drawer. Then the peddlers grabbed their cardboard boxes and left to make some more wet bucks.

Mr. Korn sells high-end and low-end umbrellas. He sells those cheap ones that end up like dead crows in the garbage for nine dollars a dozen, which means the peddlers pay seventy-five cents an umbrella. "They sell them for three dollars if it's raining," he said with a shrug. "Two dollars if it's not."

His profit on each dozen of the cheap ones, he said: fifty cents.

Outside, the sky released another torrent. "Rain, we need; rain, you live by rain," said Mr. Korn, who uses only the cheapest models, and only when he absolutely has to.

"I hate umbrellas," he said.

APRIL 10, 2004

Where Lost Are Found, So Was a Child

Another funeral Mass at Our Lady of Loreto Roman Catholic Church had ended by late morning, and now this worn place of worship was all but deserted. Save for one inconspicuous person on a pew in the far back, near the wicker baskets used for Sunday collections.

The visitor was so still that at first the pastor mistook him for a doll. But the blinking of eyes confirmed the presence of life. A baby: dressed in a red outfit, wrapped in a towel, and tucked into a green knapsack, but—at about six hours of age—entirely naked to Brooklyn and the world.

"He never cried," said the pastor, the Reverend Fredi Rosales.

The police radio's report of an abandoned child was quickly revised once officers from the Seventy-third Precinct in Brownsville reached the church: Make that abandoned newborn. The updated information summoned a troop of officers to walk up the church's cracked concrete steps, past the massive red doors, and into the cool, dark vestibule.

Yep. A newborn. Abandoned on the first of April, beneath a faded roster of parishioners' names, those who had once donated statues and crucifixes and were now long gone from Brownsville. Except for the dangling umbilical cord, the infant seemed to have been cared for in the brief hours between birth and abandonment. He was wearing that red outfit, Lieutenant Kathleen Caesar recalled. "And he was totally clean."

While her driver raced to a hospital, Lieutenant Caesar leaned into the backseat to help two emergency service officers tend to the baby. The officers clamped his umbilical cord and waved the nozzle of an oxygen tank before his face. "But the kid wouldn't cry," she said.

Back at the century-old church, beneath the stony gaze of Saint Peter and Saint Paul, detectives photographed the vestibule and dusted for fingerprints. They trailed after a bloodhound that followed a scent down the steps, past the storefront emblazoned with the words "God Is Love," to a train station a couple of blocks away. That is where the scent ended.

They wanted to find the baby's mother mostly to see if she needed help, although it was unclear whether she had followed the laws protecting those who leave newborns at a hospital, firehouse, or some other "safe haven." Was a church vestibule the proper place to leave a child? Should she have alerted someone?

The welfare of children weighed on the minds of the officers of the Seventy-third. A day earlier, two gunmen had shot up a family sitting in a car, killing a two-year-old boy. "The thought came to my mind," Lieutenant Caesar said. "Here you have a baby killed, and then a baby born. It's a blessing in a way. I'd rather find a baby on a bench, alive, than in a Dumpster, dead."

With the infant now at Brookdale University Hospital and Medical Center, officials at the city's Administration for Children's Services were searching their foster-care list for parents in Brooklyn who had also expressed interest in adoption. The agency was quite familiar with the process; this was the twentieth time since January of 2001 that it was required to deal with an abandoned newborn.

With city officials searching for a proper match, the baby squirmed in anonymity in the pediatrics unit, where the nurses nourished him with bottles and hugs.

"They'll give the baby extra cuddling, extra attention," Ruth Richman, a hospital spokeswoman, said. "It's so the baby has that safe feeling."

One day this week, Father Rosales, a short, roly-poly man, visited the baby he had found in the vestibule. The nurses told him to admire the infant from behind the glass window, he later said, but he insisted that he wanted to see the newborn in person. The nurses relented.

Then, with hospital tap water contained in a disposable cup, he baptized the baby.

"I baptized him and I named him Fredy Alfred," he said. If the name has a certain ring, that is because it is also the given name—but for one letter—of a certain pastor in Brownsville.

On Wednesday, a Family Court judge in Brooklyn granted custody of the child to William C. Bell, the city's commissioner of children's services.

And on Thursday evening, a city caseworker walked out of the hospital with the baby in her arms, and drove him to the home of a foster parent who would like to adopt him one day. Within the year, if everything works out.

Who knows what awaits the Infant of Our Lady of Loreto—whether the name Fredy Alfred will stick, whether the birth mother will resurface. All we know is that he was born on April Fool's Day, was baptized during Holy Week, and is a child of this city.

JANUARY 17, 2004

At 1 Degree, a Metropolis Is Also Frozen in Time

Beginning around midnight and lasting for a few fleeting hours, the official temperature of Manhattan dropped to 1 degree. By four in the morning, the temperature had doubled—to 2—but that brief 1-degree period granted a curious distinction to the day: It tied the record for the coldest January 16 in city history, a mark established in 1893.

In one sense, this seems the slimmest of connections between days separated by 111 years. In another sense, though, there was odd comfort in knowing that this very cold was felt on this very day in this very city at a time when a Tammany Hall lackey named Gilroy was mayor, and the economic calamity known as the Panic of 1893 was but months away.

This fleeting bond between two eras that bracket the twentieth century was explored during a rough circumnavigation of the island of Manhattan in the morning hours when the temperature clung to 1. True, the experience was more often seen than felt, through the salt-encrusted windshield of a black sedan. But that sedan sometimes rocked to the rhythms of gusts, just one of the many ways that nature reiterated its timeless point: that even a great metropolis must give deference.

By 12:30 A.M., ice-sharp winds from the northwest were dodging the edifices of Midtown to send streetlights swaying like buffeted piñatas, as if to suggest how easily nature can toy with us. It was as good a hint as any to stay indoors, and yet here came a deliveryman on a bicycle, wobbling down Lexington Avenue, while on his handlebars he balanced a box containing someone else's pizza.

The Gothic building that once housed the Bellevue Psychiatric Hospital loomed over the intersection of First Avenue and East Thirtieth Street; though ancient in appearance, it had yet to be built in 1893. A city shelter now, it was providing beds at this moment to several hundred men, a chilling thought made all the colder by the knowledge that behind the building were refrigerated trucks with the unidentified and unclaimed remains of World Trade Center dead.

On First Avenue near East Fifty-sixth Street, a steam pipe jutted like the Cat in the Hat's hat from the middle of the mostly deserted street; white plumes poured out, as though the only heat to be found at this hour was emanating from the earth's molten core.

It was not a night to strike up casual conversation with the few spirits darting in and out of the elements. A worker at a Department of Sanitation depot on the Upper East Side gave little more than a grunt as he shoveled rock salt onto a glazed sidewalk. A deliveryman for Poland Spring quickly shared that some of the water in his truck's hold was indeed frozen solid, and then he rolled up his window as fast as he could.

Occasionally these breath puffs of human interaction reflected an unshakable trust in the urban machinery. Just north of a Harlem park named after Marcus Garvey, who turned six in 1893, a man stood rock-still in a bus shelter whose transparent shields shivered in the wind. "It's coming," he said of his bus. "I see it coming."

Exchanges like these were few, though, because it takes two to talk. Other than the dodges of taxicabs and the crawl of the occasional police car, the only movement came from the knotted, garbage-filled bags that scuttled across streets to the whims of the winds that had liberated them.

Along a deserted northern stretch of Riverside Drive, where the roadway rises to meet the western hillocks of Manhattan, the winds whistled across the Hudson River to rattle the chains that hung Marley-like from a West Side Highway billboard, and to cause an unsettling banging sound—rope against flagpole?—at ghostly Grant's Tomb. The tomb was under construction in 1893.

"It's one degree and clear in Midtown," a radio news broadcaster said, delivering an assessment that was truer than he might have realized. At two-thirty, the gaudy video graffiti that moves across the buildings of Times Square—the network plugs, the zipper news, the chewing gum come-ons—played to an audience of none.

The black sedan grumbled south, past the ice-coated plastic flaps of greengrocers; past a single, underdressed woman hugging herself on a corner in the meatpacking district (what was she waiting for?); past ground zero, set aglow like New York's eternal flame.

At three in the morning, with the temperature at 1 and the wind-chill factor making it feel like minus 20, the bottom of this crowded, swarming island was as desolate as the surface of Mars. Two visitors violated the stillness by trying to walk to the Hudson River at Battery Park, but were given the bum's rush by the muscular wind. It pushed them back to that black car like a bouncer who would not take no for an answer.

The wind was not as forbidding near the ferry terminal, at Manhattan's southern tip. But the water was: A murky gray, it chopped about the harbor, taunting anyone who might wonder how it calls some to its icy embrace, and not others.

Above New York Harbor hung a crescent moon that dangled like the smile of the vanishing Cheshire cat. It was three-thirty and 1 degree out. Time for anyone still out there to come in from the cold.

JUNE 15, 2005

Getting to Here from There, with a Scoop of Rum Raisin

Two dozen children gathered yesterday on Level 3 of the Queens Center mall, between the Häagen-Dazs and the Pretzel Time, near J. C. Penney. They squirmed in red seats, smiled for photographs, and munched on crackers from a modest buffet. This was a big day, a joyous day, a day of formal welcome to the United States of America.

They faced a lectern embossed with the mall's Q logo and flanked by two flags: the American flag, of course, and the official flag for the Department of Homeland Security. Häagen-Dazs, Pretzel Time, and the Department of Homeland Security, all at the Queens Center mall.

The children were born elsewhere—in China, perhaps, or Guatemala, or maybe Romania—and adopted by American citizens, which automatically granted them citizenship in this country. But their parents wanted a more formal celebration than the simple receipt of a certificate of naturalization in the mail. So the federal government and a mall obliged.

Two soldiers, one carrying another American flag, marched past Pretzel Time to stand in front of the lectern. Dawn Simon, the mall's marketing manager, told the crowd that this was the sixth citizenship celebration at Queens Center in Elmhurst, and that at this very moment, one P.M., dozens of other malls around the country were also celebrating Flag Day.

She asked everyone to rise, salute the flag, and say the Pledge of Allegiance. The patriotic recitation echoed down the corridor of commerce.

As a chorus of children sang about "the land of the free and the home of the brave," a clerk at the Häagen-Dazs counter told people to move along, because the manager said they were impeding the paths of customers. With no customers in sight, people stayed where they were, until two mall security guards, or maybe the Department of Homeland Security, arrived to make room for phantoms craving rum raisin ice cream.

Another speaker, a woman in a dark suit, asked "our newest citizens" to please stand and take the Oath of Allegiance, which begins: "I hereby declare, on oath, that I absolutely, and entirely, renounce and abjure all allegiance and fidelity to any foreign prince, potentate, state or sovereignty of whom or which I have heretofore been a subject or citizen."

The young citizens recited this and other parts of the oath, including a vow to bear arms on behalf of the United States when required by law; to perform noncombatant service in the armed forces when required by law; and to perform "work of national importance, under civilian direction," when required by law.

"Congratulations!" said the woman in the dark suit, and then she walked away from the lectern. When she was asked for her name and affiliation, she gruffly directed the questioner to look it up in the brochure. The brochure identified her as Ladawn Flores-Benjamin, acting/supervisory district adjudications officer, United States Citizenship and Immigration Services, Department of Homeland Security.

For any other questions, she said, ask someone from Queens Center. Which meant that a federal official was referring questions about a citizenship celebration to people who work for a mall.

Then, one by one, the children heard their names called and made their way to the lectern. Elizabeth Marie Buckley, three, from Guatemala. Jonathan Robert Mattner, nine, from Mexico. Jake and Mark Dowling, thirteen and fourteen, from Romania. The four Leacock sisters, from Guyana.

They returned to their seats clutching their certificates of naturalization, government documents that declare in the poetry of bureaucracy one's bond to this land. Cherished pieces of paper, they say: I came from there, and now I am here.

The children were also clutching gift bags, courtesy of the mall. Along with those sacred certificates, they received a small teddy bear, a plastic cup, a noisemaker, free soap from one of the stores, and two coupons. One coupon offered 20 percent off their next purchase of fashion accessories, and the other offered "hot" summer tank tops, two for twenty dollars, or four for thirty dollars.

In a way, the setting for this celebration was infinitely more appropriate than some dreary government office. Here, on Level 3 of the Queens Center mall, the children could learn that in the United States, you can't always stand wherever you want; in front of the Häagen-Dazs, for example. That government officials are not always helpful; the woman in the dark suit, for example. And that great emphasis is placed on marketing and acquisition.

But Jamila Leacock, nineteen, seemed focused on a larger lesson. She now had the certificate proving she was a citizen of this great country, where, she said, "the sky's the limit." She had no plans to shop, by the way. She said she was going home, to Canarsie.

SEPTEMBER 3, 2003

Everyone Out of the Pool (That's You!)

Eight hours remained until James Gomez could give the signal to begin draining the massive Astoria Pool. Eight hours until a few valves could be opened to release 1.3 million gallons into the East River, where the churning Hell Gate waters would rinse away any lingering hint of summertime splashes and butterfly strokes.

It would be a long, long eight hours. On this Labor Day—the last day of summer, at least for the Department of Parks and Recreation—a steady rain pocked the pool's ice-blue surface. The temperature clung to the low sixties, and the looming sky carried an overcooked oatmeal cast.

This was not a pool day.

But you never know; someone might show. Shortly before the

opening hour of eleven A.M., the lifeguards gathered in their shack on the far side of the pool. The bathroom attendants went to their stations. The workers who monitor water quality took a reading. And Mr. Gomez, the pool manager, looked out upon his dampened domain and marveled at what is the largest public pool in New York.

"It's for the masses," he said.

When the Works Progress Administration built eleven city pools in the mid-1930s, all under the steely gaze of the urban planner Robert Moses, it reserved its grandest scheme for the Astoria Pool in Queens: 330 feet long and 165 feet wide; a diving tank 16 feet deep; an Art Deco pavilion; and two mushroom-shaped fountains to support mammoth torches. This last touch reflected the pool's elevated status. The Olympic swimming trials were held here in 1936, and again in 1964.

The rub of time has taken some of the pool's luster. The diving tank hasn't been used for years—not worth the risk of injury—and the fountains shoot water, not fire, when the lifeguards want to clear an area.

Still, the Astoria Pool remains a municipal wonder, a place that can provide joyous respite for a capacity crowd of 2,178 people—all while the Triborough Bridge, the Hell Gate Bridge, and the Manhattan skyline provide a majestic backdrop.

The rules are many. No goggles, no water pistols, no running, no—well, Mr. Gomez said, it is easier to remember what is permitted. "Bathing suit, towel, sandals or slippers, and a plain white undershirt," he said. "Everything else is not allowed."

As the rain fell, and as the staff waited for someone, anyone, to show, Mr. Gomez sat in his scuffed office and talked about how he came to be manager of the city's largest pool, whose waters were graced by the immersion of his concrete-block frame only once this summer.

He said that parks and recreation work came naturally to him; he is descended, he said, from "a long line of parkies." He said that he started his parks career nearly twenty years ago by working the "bag and stab" cleaning details under the Coney Island boardwalk. Golf course worker, maintenance man, heavy-equipment operator, supervisor; at forty-five, he has done it all.

He said that he was proud of the pool's reputation as a no-nonsense place—proud, too, of its history, some of which he has learned from the old-timers who come to reminisce. He volunteered that 98,173 people had visited the pool this summer, all without serious incident.

Two young pool workers shuffled past the manager's desk. "What's up, Gomez?" said one. "What's up, Gomez?" said the other. "Not much," Mr. Gomez replied, aptly.

Just then, someone gave a heads-up. The pool had a customer, its 98,174th. Mr. Gomez went out into the rain to investigate.

A young woman he had never seen before tucked her dark hair under her bathing cap and waded into the gargantuan and otherwise empty pool. While nearly two dozen pool employees watched, including a gaggle of lifeguards, she began to swim laps. Back and forth, back and forth, alone, in the largest pool in New York City.

Her name was Despina Alexiadou. A twenty-eight-year-old exchange student from Greece, she had been in this country all of four days. Noticing the pool while out on a jog, she inquired about the admission fee. It is free, always free, she was told. Welcome to New York.

Later, in the misty dusk, Mr. Gomez would give the signal, and the summer of 2003 would swirl and disappear. But Mr. Gomez and his colleagues may well remember the image of that lone woman gliding through their waters, a woman new to this city.

And what she will remember, Ms. Alexiadou said, is how she felt as though she were swimming in the sea.

FEBRUARY 18, 2004

At McSorley's, Dusty Bones Conjure Ghosts

Consider the wishbones as you drink from your mug. As you sit at a wooden table with cheese and onions fresh on your breath. As you stand at the bar, jostled by college students in baseball caps who are old enough to vote, old enough to die in war, and now, at twenty-one, finally old enough to drink.

As all around you, stories spill onto the sawdust floors of McSorley's Old Ale House, just as they have for 150 years this week. Stories about Lincoln and about Dempsey, about ghosts who stroke the house cats and about that mounted fluke behind the bar, blackened by decades of smoke and steam. Most stories last no longer than the day's sawdust; some linger awhile in the beer-pungent air; a few get better with age.

So consider the wishbones, about two dozen of them, dangling upon an old gas lamp at the far end of this Bowery bar, all but one of them covered with dust so thick and dark that it looks like moss.

They appear out of place at McSorley's, where there are so many artifacts adorning the walls that the distinct beauty of each item dulls in the frequent retelling of the bar's history. The wanted poster for "the Murderer," John Wilkes Booth. The tribute to another assassinated president, William McKinley. The handcuffs of Harry Houdini. In such company the wishbones seem insignificant, even grotesque.

But the wishbones do belong, including that one without dust. Hovering as if in suspended animation, they have invited generations of patrons to ponder their meaning. Are they just remnants of dinners long since digested, or do they represent something else, like wishes never granted?

Here is one story, as recorded by the writer Joseph Mitchell more than sixty years ago. The founder, John McSorley, had a "remarkable passion for memorabilia," and he saved the wishbones of holiday turkeys. The "dusty bones," Mitchell wrote back in 1940, "are invariably the first thing a new customer gets inquisitive about."

Mitchell, a fine man, knew some things but not everything, says the current owner, Matthew Maher, who began working at McSorley's nearly forty years ago. The wishbones actually date to World War I, he says, when departing doughboys enjoyed one last meal, then hung the bones above the bar to symbolize their hope—their wish—that they would make it back home.

The men who returned from France would take down their small trophies, then drink to those now represented only by poultry bones dangling from above. There the bones have stayed, he says, through all the wars since the war that was to end war, their significance lost to most.

It is a poignant story, but is it true? Or are we in the territory of invented tradition, myth—what the Roman historian Sallust was referring to when, roughly translated, he wrote: "Now these things never happened, but always are."

The question is asked of Geoffrey Bartholomew, barman and bard. In his collection, *The McSorley Poems* (Charlton Street Press, 2001), the first poem, "The Wishbones," suggests that either story could be "the bone truth."

In the requisite shirt of white, Mr. Bartholomew leans across the ale-wet counter to acknowledge that he did not know for certain the provenance of those bones that have been part of his workplace for more than thirty years. Still, he says, John Smith, the bartender who trained him, is the one who shared the doughboy story, and John Smith—"His picture's on the wall here somewhere"—began working at McSorley's sometime around the Great Depression.

"And John didn't say much," Mr. Bartholomew says, as if to distinguish his mentor from the common spinners of barroom blather.

What Mr. Bartholomew does know is that the wishbones are sacred. Every so often a beery patron will reach up and—"and I'll grab his wrist and say, 'Don't touch,'" he says. "We get very territorial about it."

Even so, last fall a patron managed to knock a wishbone into a sink, washing away nearly a century's worth of cobwebs. The bartenders returned the bone to the gas lamp, where it dangles in alabaster distinction from its dusty mates.

Perhaps this cleaned but ancient wishbone will come to be a bar's odd tribute to another generation of soldiers who never returned: ours, in Iraq, some 540 so far, including several from New York City. Riayan Tejeda from Washington Heights, for example, and Rasheed Sahib, from Brooklyn. And Linda Jimenez. And others.

Consider the wishbones as you drink from your mug. Consider, too, the last line of Mr. Bartholomew's wishbone poem: "Godspeed to all ghosts."

What Lies Beneath, or Doesn't

The divers from the Police Department tried again yesterday, immersing themselves in the wintry dark waters of the lake at Prospect Park. And, again, they failed to find the body of a man who decided to take a Sunday morning stroll across thin ice.

A search for a body trapped beneath ice seems like the awkward kind of tragedy that is more likely to occur someplace else, someplace colder; upstate, maybe, or in New England. But in a man-made lake in Brooklyn? In water about six feet deep? It all seems so out of place.

Then again, these are among the very elements that make the event seem almost distinctly, eerily New York. In a popular park in a heavily populated part of the city, a man shakes free of the urban crush to cross his personal tundra, which then rewards his independence by swallowing him up.

Or not. No one has filed a missing person's report in the week since, and there are conflicting reports about whether he managed to reach shore. Will the police eventually find a body? Or will the man become the subject of Brooklyn lore, a Prospect Park phantom, spotted for certain at summer's dusk by boys and girls aching to be scared?

The answer has yet to surface. The police, who suspect that he did die, have no recourse but to continue their search. And visitors to the park can only stand at the lakeshore and read significance into the many shoe prints—of recovery workers and, who knows, the man himself—that will remain imbedded in the lake's surface until the next thaw.

"I don't ever recall a situation like this," Liam Kavanagh, a deputy commissioner of parks and recreation, said. "Usually the victim is recovered within hours of the incident."

On maps of Brooklyn, the sixty-acre lake looks like a wispy blue whale nestled at the park's southern corner. Since its construction in the late nineteenth century, the lake has gone through cycles of grandeur and neglect, and is now a clouded refuge for frogs and ducks, a place for children to fish with rolled-up balls of bread on their hooks.

On Sunday morning, some dog walkers spotted a young man in brown clothes walking on ice toward the center of the lake, parts of which were not frozen. Some people shouted at him to come back— What, was he crazy?—while others hurriedly dialed 911. He fell through the ice, pulled himself out, and then fell through again.

Several witnesses told the police that he screamed for help before disappearing for the last time, although one witness planted some doubt by saying that the man had made it to shore and walked away.

Rescue divers from the police and fire departments spent Sunday searching waters so murky that they could do little more than hunt by hand. The police divers have returned several times since then without luck. Sometimes their scuba equipment freezes up; sometimes the water surface above them begins to ice over.

After three hours in the morning bite of yesterday's cold, the police divers set aside their manhunt and drove away, allowing the lake to keep its secret for at least another day—and casting this corner of the park in an unsettling winter light. Did this jogger huffing his way past, or that horseback rider bouncing along, know that lodged beneath the lake's icy layer there might be the body of a man dressed in brown?

The January sun threw the skeletal shadows of barren trees upon the gray ice, while Canada geese rising from the water honked in farewell. Along the lake's southern shore, yellow strips of plastic bearing a familiar phrase, POLICE LINE DO NOT CROSS, fluttered from trees and lampposts.

On the western shore, two park officers sat in the warmth of their idling truck and stared out at the lake, which looked like a gray-white meadow interrupted only by a wide circle of unfrozen water. That is just one reason the city ought to fence the lake off in winter, one of the officers said.

They said their job was to keep people from venturing onto the ice, which happens regularly, despite the dozens of signs that say DANGER, KEEP OFF AT ALL TIMES. It might be people emboldened by liquor or subdued by depression, or pet lovers dashing after their seagull-chasing dogs.

"Next thing you know, you're in there," the officer said.

And across the lake, on the eastern shore, there sat a single police car. Any time a passerby ventured close to the pallid body of suspended animation, the police car emitted a wah-wah of warning that told the living to keep moving.

AUGUST 31, 2005

Treasure on an Island Called Staten

You could imagine them calling from the other side of the closed library door. Babar and Madeline, Dr. Salk and Dr. Seuss, Henry and Beezus, Frank and Joe Hardy, Eleanor Roosevelt, Sitting Bull, and maybe a triceratops or two, all calling from the quiet, empty children's section: *Read about me, please, and me, and me.*

Read, they plead, read—because, as we all know, there is no greater agony than to be a character in a book unread.

And who knows? Maybe, through some supernatural gift of childhood that dissipates with age, young Robert Clark Bailey heard these plaintive calls as he opened a plate-glass door yesterday to become the first patron of the renovated Great Kills Branch of the New York Public Library on Staten Island.

Although several weeks short of four and several inches short of the checkout desk, Robert still seemed to understand. He breathed in the new-book air, gazed at shelves crammed with virgin volumes, realized that he had just stepped foot on Treasure Island, and let out a shout, as if to reassure Babar, Beezus, and the rest that their pain was about to ease.

As he walked up the marble steps to the children's section on the second floor, Robert passed a framed black-and-white photograph of what looked like a toolshed. It was, in a way, if books are tools. The shack was the original home for the Great Kills library in 1926, and Robert's great-grandmother Florence Ripley was its first librarian.

When the shack could no longer accommodate the clamor for books, the New York Public Library opened a state-of-the-art branch on the site in 1954, with a dedication ceremony attended by Mayor Robert F. Wagner. In the first two days, enough books were borrowed to average one volume for each of the several thousand households in the neighborhood.

In city life, though, only a nanosecond separates state of the art from state of exhaustion. A larger, fancier branch—with parking!—opened in nearby Richmondtown in 1995, which led to questions about the need for the Great Kills branch. But the neighborhood rallied and Great Kills survived, albeit with poor lighting, inadequate air-conditioning, and only one of its three floors open—which meant that *Sense and Sensibility* was nearly cheek-by-jowl with *Spot Bakes a Cake.*

"Children's books, young-adult books, adult books," Hishi Velardo, the head librarian, recalled, chopping the air to show how close. "It was very crammed."

Two years ago, the public library closed the Great Kills branch for renovations, to be paid for with $1.5 million in city money secured by the local councilman, Andrew J. Lanza. Ms. Velardo went to work at other public libraries on Staten Island, and various book characters joined Little Bear in a kind of literary hibernation.

Until shortly after noon yesterday, that is, when young Robert Clark Bailey shouted in glee and clambered upstairs beside his mother, Susan Bailey. Advance word had reached the library staff that he loved trains, so three picture books about trains were waiting for him at one of the impossibly small tables.

As he sat there, proudly announcing what he saw in one of the books—"freight car, oil car, steam engine, caboose"—one could not help but wonder where the boy's interests might lead him next.

Maybe one day he will wander over to the picture books section and take a stroll down Mulberry Street with Dr. Seuss, or share in dress-up with a pig named Olivia, or go to a birthday party with Eric Hill's dog, Spot. If he does attend that party, maybe he too will ask why Spot has a pet's name, while his friends—an elephant, a monkey, a hippo—are named Tina, Steve, and Helen. (Could lead to yet another book about the dog: *Spot Goes to Therapy.*)

Maybe he will graduate to the series books, near the window, and join Frank and Joe Hardy in the case of *The Tower Treasure* or *The Secret of the Old Mill.* The case of *The Missing Chums,* alas, was missing.

From there, who knows. To Oz, to Wonderland, to the Chocolate Factory. To the science section against the far wall, for *Experiments With Magnets.* Or to the biography section nearby, to meet Pablo Picasso, Jimmy Carter, or Rosa Parks.

These decisions all lay in the future, as did the moment, a half-hour from now, when Robert would help to cut a red ribbon in front of the library, and dozens and dozens of people would file in to breathe in that new-book air.

For now, though, he was busy riding a freight train.

NOVEMBER 10, 2004

Daily Bread, Every Day for Seventy-five Years

By the time you read this, the St. Francis Breadline will most likely have vanished for the day. It is one of the daily apparitions of Manhattan: there and then not; flesh, blood, and hardship, then nothing.

Paul Johnson, restored by a sandwich or three, will have resumed his job hunt. Laymon Brice, who says his wife kicked him out a few years ago, will have returned to his tiny Times Square room. Omie Singer, known to this bread line since the 1950s, will have cold hands because she lost her gloves. Gone until tomorrow, when the line forms again before sunrise.

The Brigadoon of bread lines, it operates less in deference to the sensibilities of morning commuters than in keeping with Franciscan simplicity. Here is a sandwich. Here is some coffee. God be with you.

Seventy-five years ago last month, the stock market crashed and the Great Depression began. Gabriel Mehler, a Franciscan brother at St. Francis of Assisi Roman Catholic Church in Midtown, saw a need and began a bread line that was soon attracting thousands every day, all seeking sustenance until better days.

Brother Gabriel, who came to be called the Angel of the Bread Line, died in 1940, but the daily ritual did not. A succession of Franciscans took up the job, including Brother Albert Aldrich, now seventy-five and living in Providence, Rhode Island. For twenty-two years he helped to uphold and refine the few rules of the seven-day-a-week operation that is neither a soup kitchen nor a drop-in center, but an ever-moving shuffle.

"Ladies go first," Brother Albert recalled, citing one rule. "Always, always."

By Monday's chilly dawn, nearly sixty men and ladies had formed a line on West Thirty-first Street that snaked toward nearby Pennsylvania Station. Some slouched along the building's brick face, eyes rheumy, coats inadequate. Others chatted around their shared need of food, but never about it. Everyone waited for the seven o'clock tolling of the church bell, which announces the first Mass of the weekday, but is interpreted by some as the moment when a certain side door will open.

"When the bell rings, that's when it starts," Mr. Johnson said. He wore his knit hat pulled tightly over his head, and talked about the spring, when he will be picking up garbage again at the tennis center in Queens. Until then, he said, "I'm in a holding pattern."

The bell finally chimed, the door finally opened, and the sharing of bread and water began again. Out came boxes of ham-and-cheese sandwiches, bought from the Manganaro's Hero-Boy shop on Ninth Avenue. Out too came four silver urns, along with sleeves of plastic foam cups.

Ladies first. Then Mr. Johnson, in his role as the "marker," grabbed two sandwiches and headed to the back of the line. This way, the friars know that when the marker reaches the front of the line—for a third sandwich if he wants it—everyone who was here by seven has been fed, and a separate row of latecomers can fall in.

Two friars in robes, the Reverend Vincent Laviano and the Reverend Brian Jordan, walked the line, greeting the familiar and the new, reminding everyone not to block the steps leading to the morning's first Mass. They watched for people trying to cut the line, which can lead to arguments, which can lead to violence, which is why soft-speaking Brother Albert remembers himself as a strict disciplinarian.

"Oh, but I was an awful son of a gun, a tough guy," he said. "I walked the line and I demanded order. And if I didn't get it, whish, I'd take the coffee in."

This day required no such measures, only the occasional verbal nudges of Father Jordan. "Don't block the line," he called out. "You're with Bush now; move to the right."

Mr. Johnson, fifty-six, finished his coffee, crushed the cup in his hand, and said that he had to get back to his seventy-five-dollar-a-week room in Hell's Kitchen. Some man might be calling about a quick-and-dirty job in Jersey.

Mr. Brice, seventy-four, a retired truck driver with some miles on his face, ate his sandwich and recalled that his penchant for buying new cars had led to his current wifeless predicament. "I was thinking I was big," he said. "But I was only being a damned fool." He headed uptown.

Ms. Singer, seventy, a retired fashion worker who said there was nothing she couldn't make—jackets, pants, nothing—examined her sandwich, marveled at the five slices of meat and the four slices of cheese, and declared it to be "beautiful." She headed downtown.

Within thirty minutes the people had scattered and the bread line had vanished, leaving no trace save for a coffee spill or two to consecrate the pavement.

JANUARY 7, 2006

Where Fallen Trees Go in the Not-So-Silent Night

Tens of thousands of discarded Christmas trees now sag in green heaps at this city's curbside, joyless, desiccated, done. With boughs limp and trunks planted amid black bags of debris, they signal that January is here; deal with it.

You wish these scented, faintly irritating reminders of Christmas Just Past would simply disappear. The thing is, they do.

Shortly after midnight yesterday, with Manhattan nestled all snug in its bed, a large white truck pulled away from a depot along the Hudson River and set out for the mostly deserted streets of the Upper West Side. Its red and yellow lights twinkled in festiveness or in warning, depending on your mood. In its cab sat Gary Baer and Marcos Ortiz, elves in Department of Sanitation green.

Tree duty isn't so bad, said Mr. Baer. "You go home smelling good."

"Except the needles get in your pants and hair," said Mr. Ortiz.

Mr. Baer, thirty-three and burly, spent Christmas with his wife and two children on Staten Island. Mr. Ortiz, twenty-four and fit—he used to be a personal trainer—enjoyed the day with his wife and in-laws at home in Brooklyn. Around what kind of trees did they celebrate?

"Artificial," said Mr. Baer.

"Me too," said Mr. Ortiz.

Now, far from homes where Christmas trees slide needle-free into storage, these two men began to prowl the darkened streets of foreign neighborhoods for the holiday detritus of others. It was January 6: the Feast of the Epiphany; Three Kings Day; Little Christmas; the end of the season.

They found their first two trees at the corner of West End Avenue and West Sixty-fifth Street, lying on the ground as though overcome by too much cheer. A third leaned against a brick wall, exhausted. A fourth slumped outside a firehouse. The sanitation workers did not pause to imagine the Christmas carols and children's smiles these trees might have conjured. They just grabbed the withering cones by the trunks and heaved them into the truck's maw.

Mr. Ortiz pulled a lever, and the truck began to eat the trees with grim purpose, the way one might eat a stale Christmas cookie. It made a lot of noise as it chewed.

A truck like theirs can compact several hundred trees into its hold, although the number depends, oddly enough, on the borough. A Sanitation Department survey once determined that Queens and Staten Island have the largest trees, probably because those boroughs have many single-family homes. Manhattan, island of cramped high-rises, has the smallest, meaning more trees to a truck.

The two men shook the needles from their clothes, climbed into the cab, and continued to play their mop-up roles in the city's annual Christmas pageant.

Every year at this time, sanitation trucks trawl city streets for pines and firs that have gone from being the center of attention to being the focus of anger—space-eating nuisances—in a matter of days, even hours. Last year the city collected 156,000 of them for its Christmas Tree Collection program.

The city will not, however, collect the Rockefeller Center Christmas tree, which this year is a nine-ton, seventy-four-foot-tall Norway spruce. The private contractor who carried the monstrous evergreen in will have to carry it out.

Trees of more modest size are compacted in the holds of trucks and taken to the Fresh Kills landfill on Staten Island, or to Randalls Island, where they are fed into wood chippers. Their dusty remains are mixed with collected autumn leaves to create compost that is used in the city's parks, ball fields, and community gardens, transforming their purpose from the aesthetic to the practical.

But Mr. Baer and Mr. Ortiz do more than simply pick up and toss. They have to make sure that people have stripped their trees of the tinsel and lights that would make them ineligible for composting. Trees that cling to vanity—that insist on glittering from curbside—are destined for the dump.

The white truck turned left onto West Sixty-sixth Street, then right onto Freedom Place, a short road that runs beside the cavernous Trump Place complex for the affluent. Several mounds the color of money awaited them.

Within these mounds, a Citarella bag; a large red ribbon; a tree ornament featuring a gold spoon, fork, and knife; strands of tinsel that sparkled in the lamplight; and a large tree wrapped in a string of lights. "Wherever there's high-rises, there's lots more lights," Mr. Baer said, briefly assuming the pose of sanitation sociologist. "See, now that has to go in the garbage."

The tree hunt continued, up one street and down another, through a quiet, Christmas-sated city. Lift and toss, lift and toss, pull the compacting lever. Lift and toss, lift and toss, pull. By dawn the two men will have collected 452 trees.

At one point deep in the night, when few creatures were stirring, the white truck pulled up to another mound of discarded trees.

Mr. Baer reached into the pile and pulled out a wreath adorned with candy canes. He studied it for a moment before yanking the candies off and tossing the wreath like a green Frisbee into the hopper.

The gesture said: January.

OCTOBER 6, 2004

A Dark Stain That Returns All Too Often

As another Manhattan morning came into crisp October focus, Nina Felshin walked with purpose toward a Dominican restaurant that she believes has the finest café con leche in the city, bar none. What a fine way to toast this glorious Sunday.

Something near the intersection of Amsterdam Avenue and West Ninety-sixth Street caught her eye and took her breath. The windows of the MidWest Cleaners had been defaced overnight with expletives scrawled in garish orange paint. But the symbols beside these offensive words all but rendered them invisible.

Swastikas. Three of them.

"It felt like a violation," Ms. Felshin recalled.

Others soon paused to take in this Sunday morning greeting of hate. An Asian woman, on her way to church, promised to pray. A black man, waiting for a bus, took out his MetroCard and began scraping away at the words and symbols on the storefront window.

It'll come off, he said. It'll come off.

Ms. Felshin walked away, got her coffee, carried on with her morning. But those swastikas had clouded her sunny day. She is Jewish, but the symbol has meaning beyond Nazism, she said. "It represents, more than ever, the general hatred for people who are not like yourself."

With those symbols burning in her mind's eye, she returned several hours later to the dry cleaner's, which was closed for Sunday. Someone had scrubbed away the epithets, the anti-Semitic slogan, and the three swastikas. Traces of a washrag's swirl could still be seen on the dark-tinted windows, and the scraping had been so forceful that some lettering—the O in One Day Service—had fallen victim. There also remained some orange paint, including the single word: You.

Ms. Felshin did not know who had cleaned the window; nor did the dry cleaner's manager, James Yi. As soon as he opened his doors at seven, on Monday morning, customers streamed in. "Jimmy, do you know what happened?" "Jimmy, the message said this, and this. And there were swastikas!"

Mr. Yi, who is Korean-born, could not believe that his business had been singled out. "A Nazi symbol," he muttered to a visitor that morning. "A swastika."

He wondered aloud about disgruntled customers who might have done such a thing. A week ago, a regular customer again complained loudly that the collars of his shirts were not being pressed properly. When Mr. Yi defended his work, the customer mocked his accent— "I don't speak English so good"—and stormed away.

The same day, Mr. Yi had to inform another customer that a silvery button missing from her dry-cleaned jacket could not be found, but that he would be glad to replace the button and not charge her for the dry cleaning. She picked up a heavy stapler and threw it down hard.

"Very stressful," Mr. Yi said as another bing-bong rang out, signaling that another customer had walked in with another mound of dirty laundry. People often do not understand stains, he said. "Sometimes it comes out, and sometimes it doesn't come out."

He recited again what had appeared on his storefront's window: the epithets, the anti-Semitic phrase. "But most important," he said, still shaken, "is the Nazi symbol."

So far this year, the Police Department's Hate Crimes Task Force has opened files on 226 criminal cases of bias or hatred. They include the usual expressions of intolerance: the assaulting of gays, the harassment of Muslims, the spray-painting of "K.K.K." But Detective Kevin Czartoryski, who spent six years with the task force, said that in more than one third of those cases, the offense centers on that ancient, simple symbol whose sudden appearance anywhere strikes the heart like a fist.

"It's that one symbol that symbolizes hatred, bigotry, and persecution, even to death," said Abraham Foxman, the national director of the Anti-Defamation League. "It's a very selective graffiti. You can make circles and squares and triangles. But all you have to do is the swastika, and it communicates eighty years of hate."

There it has been this year, scrawled on the side of a building in Brighton Beach, on the doorstep of a private Jewish school in Woodhaven, on the walls of a subway station in the East Village, on the hood of a car in Sheepshead Bay, in a playground in Williamsburg. On the windows of a Korean-owned dry cleaner's on the Upper West Side.

Mr. Yi took a razor blade to those windows and spent two hours finishing the job that his good and anonymous neighbors had begun. Stain removed.

OCTOBER 9, 2004

Maintaining Enough Levers to Carry a Vote

Democracy in this city weighs heavily on the mind of a regular guy from Throgs Neck, and he feels all 29,164 tons of it. That is the collective weight of the city's 7,291 voting machines, those hulking booths that magically appear in school gyms and parish halls whenever the electoral clock tells us it is time again to choose our president, our mayor, our surrogate judge.

The tired gray machines look as though they could have doubled as lockers for the Mets of Casey Stengel, a fitting resemblance in that they date back to the early 1960s. And their twenty thousand aged parts—springs, rollers, spindles, cotter pins, lightbulbs—must interact seamlessly for the proper tallying of that prized but often neglected possession of the citizen, the vote.

But whom does the city call when things happen to these ungainly mechanical wonders? Things like an awkward fall off the delivery truck, or a voter's muscular casting of a ballot. During last month's primary a Bronx man exercised his voting rights so enthusiastically that he broke the booth's metal handle, then continued his exercise by running away.

And whom does the city call when overzealous supporters of one candidate enter the booth and remove the small black levers beside the names of their candidate's opponent? Why, the same person who keeps barrels of those black levers at the ready, and who appreciates these machines, these Shoup 3.2s, the way that some car buffs appreciate their '68 Mustangs? That regular guy from Throgs Neck, John P. O'Grady.

"They're my babies," he says.

Mr. O'Grady, forty-two, works out of a Board of Elections office in Lower Manhattan that isn't much larger than a few voting booths. He arrives at 7:30 in the morning, often doesn't return home until well after dusk, and works seven days a week in the months leading up to the general election. When people joke that he and his board colleagues work only two days a year—the primary and the election—he does not laugh.

"I want to strangle them," he says without a smile.

He has tried to brighten his surroundings with photographs of the family he rarely sees, and with aromatic candles whose fragrance helps to calm him down. "They smell nice," says this facilitator of democracy. "Some days are very stressful, I gotta tell you."

The funny thing is—actually, it's not that funny—Mr. O'Grady joined the Board of Elections in 1991 as a computer analyst who would help New York replace those Shoup 3.2s with a modernized voting system. That system was installed—never.

Fourteen years and countless machine breakdowns later, the capital of the world still relies on Mr. O'Grady's mechanical babies, for reasons ranging from political quarrels to differences over how to improve the system. Federal law requires modernized systems—maybe with touch screens—by 2006, which means, as the board's executive director, John Ravitz, puts it, "Our backs are against the wall."

Or against the Shoup 3.2.

These matters are beyond Mr. O'Grady's concern for now. He and his eighty-five technicians and supervisors have to concentrate on having all those voting machines tuned up, adorned with the proper ballots, and delivered to more than thirteen hundred polling sites throughout the city for the general election on November 2.

"We have to get it done," he says. "I can't postpone an election."

Mr. O'Grady leaves his office for the board's warehouse in Queens, where technicians are preparing 1,717 machines. The warehouse sits above a Toys "R" Us in a huge building in Middle Village. Downstairs, PlayStation 2; upstairs, the electoral equivalent to Etch A Sketch.

Every borough presents its own challenges. For example, in Queens, 117 polling sites require machines that present the candidates and ballot questions in four languages. The reconfiguration takes time, Mr. O'Grady says.

He walks past the rows and rows of Shoup 3.2s, which stand side by side like the six-foot toys in *March of the Wooden Soldiers*. He pauses to admire the complicated guts of one machine, then gives it a reassuring pat.

On the Wednesday before Election Day, Mr. O'Grady will begin trucking 7,291 machines to polling places across the city, with the stern message that they be treated with tender loving care.

Then, on Election Day eve, he leaves the office early—at six P.M. He returns to the Bronx, shares dinner with his family, watches a little *Monday Night Football*. Then this facilitator of democracy attempts sleep.

MARCH 31, 2004, WEDNESDAY

A Forest Monk's Lesson in the New York Jungle

The stolen bag did not contain much in the way of material value. But its sudden absence greatly distressed the Buddhist monk who had been victimized, and so the police were summoned to the scene of the crime: a Starbucks at the opulent Trump Tower on Fifth Avenue.

A police officer in a softball jacket sat down to take the statement of the tall man in a brown robe, whose decaffeinated coffee, no milk, was turning cold. Routine questions elicited complicated answers. For example, the victim's name was Venerable Kassapa, but Venerable is a term of respect, not a first name.

"I'm a Buddhist monk," the robed man confided. "In case you're wondering."

"I knew," the police officer said gently. "I've been around."

This is a simple tale that is not so simple, about a monk, a theft, and New York–style redemption.

Venerable Kassapa, forty-one, is a forest monk in Sri Lanka. He usually lives alone or with a few other monks in rock-shelter huts, where he depends on the charity of villagers. He eats one proper meal a day, does not carry money, and devotes much of his celibate life to meditation, contemplation, and the study of Buddhist texts. People often bow before him.

He sometimes travels to other countries and often speaks to very small groups about Buddhism. For the last few weeks he has been in the New York area, his trip sponsored by the New York Society of United Sri Lankans.

On Monday afternoon he sat on a stone bench in front of the Plaza Hotel and recalled how, as a young boy in London, he became disillusioned with the world. "I wanted to find a way out of discomfort and uneasiness," he said. "A way out of suffering."

His mother's struggle with an illness may have prompted his brooding; he is not sure. But he is certain that the factors leading him to a Buddhist temple at the age of thirteen included these: his mother's interest in transcendental meditation, and his own interest in a popular television program of the time, *Kung Fu*.

When he asked one of the temple's monks whether they taught martial arts as well as Buddhism, he recalled, the monk laughed. "Here we don't tend to the body," the monk told the boy. "We tend to the mind."

At fourteen, he became a novice monk and moved to Sri Lanka; at twenty, he was ordained. "And I've never, ever, regretted making this move," he said.

With the sun slipping behind the Plaza, Venerable Kassapa agreed to take a stroll for a cup of coffee at the Starbucks in Trump Tower. Walking down Fifth Avenue in his simple cloth robe, a simple cloth bag clutched in his hand, he was a character out of context: a six-foot-four study in self-denial, ambling along the boulevard of acquisition.

"I am a beast out of its habitat," he said.

He passed under the "You're Fired" advertisement that adorns

Trump Tower and moved through the marble lobby, seemingly unaware of the effect his presence had on others. As an escalator raised him up to a floor redolent of coffee, he was asked whether he knew the name of Trump. "I've heard of him," he said. "He's a very wealthy man."

Venerable Kassapa sat at a small table and accepted a cup of decaffeinated coffee. Soon he was sharing what he described as his "vision" for the United States: that this great country, filled with energy and potential, would one day lead the world into a brave new era of truth and harmony.

Shortly after suggesting that American power "can be harnessed for harm or for good," he noticed that his cloth bag was missing from the chair beside him. He felt no anger when he realized that the bag had been stolen, he said later. Only shock, because such things do not happen to contemplative monks.

"This is very bizarre," he kept saying. "Nothing like this has ever happened to me before."

Security officers were summoned, and then two police officers from the Midtown North precinct. They glided up the escalator and walked directly toward the monk. He was easy to pick out.

One officer went off to check garbage cans, while the other interviewed the monk. Finally the time came to detail what was in the bag. No money, of course ("I don't use money," the monk said), but an eclectic list of items duly recorded by the officer.

Among the articles inside the cloth bag: a white plastic bag; a cell phone that someone had lent to him for his New York visit; a bottle of water; some white thread that he gives to people as a blessing; and many pieces of paper. On these were written the names and telephone numbers of his supporters around the world.

"I would really appreciate it if you could do as much as you can," the monk said to the officer. But the officer leveled with the monk. "A lot of times, with nothing of value, they just throw it in the trash," he said. "It could be in Brooklyn, it could be in the Bronx."

The officers left Venerable Kassapa to contemplate his loss, especially the bits of paper bearing the names and phone numbers of all those friends. "This is a raw lesson in life," he said, the kind of thing that "I first became a monk to overcome."

He descended the escalator, peered briefly into a garbage can—just in case—and then paused to study Donald Trump, who was standing at the elevator bank, talking on a cell phone. "I've never seen a billionaire before," he said.

Outside, on Fifth Avenue, the forest monk expressed a keen desire to go to that Manhattan forest called Central Park. "I need a little bit of a breath of fresh air," he said, and then he was gone.

That could have been the conclusion to the monk's New York tale. But destiny would not allow it.

Late Monday afternoon, Riccardo Maggiore found a white plastic bag at the entrance to his hair salon on West Fifty-sixth Street, just off Fifth Avenue. Yesterday morning his wife, Eileen, did some sleuthing. And before noon, plans were under way to return the plastic bag—though not the cloth bag—to its owner, a forest monk.

There wasn't much inside the bag. A cell phone. Some white thread. And what Ms. Maggiore described as "a million pieces of paper."

JULY 29, 2006

Outside Arms of Parents, in Fate's Hands

A monthly calendar, courtesy of a gas station on Jerome Avenue, hangs in the kitchen of a spare apartment in the Bronx. The fourteen pencil strokes upon its face represent fourteen successive days this month that one family got past without incident.

But the space reserved for Saturday the fifteenth remains unmarked, as do all the July days that follow. That is because Saturday the fifteenth is the day the youngest in this family, a fussing bundle of boyhood called Bryce McMillan, all of twenty-three months, fell out a seventh-story window.

Some stories about children leave us wishing. We wish we could have stopped Tiffany Gunaratne, nine, from chasing after her dog on Staten Island, so that car would not strike her. Or have warned Jennifer Moore, eighteen, disoriented in West Side darkness, not to share a cab with that stranger now charged with killing her.

We wish we could protect all children. But since this is impossible, we wish for miracles.

That Saturday morning began like many others in Bryce McMillan's short life. His mother, Tarkeshia Wilder, headed off to her Parks Department job. His father, Brian McMillan, went to help an elderly relative. And Bryce and his sister, Amanda, whiled the day with relatives in the Highbridge Gardens public housing project.

Amanda, nearly eleven, was watching an Aaliyah video while her brother bounded about. "Then, um, I turned around," she recalls. "And he wasn't around."

The children's great-grandmother, Nancy Wilder, and great-great-grandmother, Dianna Nelson, began calling out: Bryce! Bryce!

Ms. Nelson focused on a bedroom window that faces the Major Deegan Expressway. It hadn't had a window guard for quite a while. Instead, a pillow usually rested on the sill so that people could lean in comfort while observing the rush and flow below.

But the pillow was gone.

Amanda quietly repeats the words that her great-great-grandmother screamed: "The baby's out the window!"

Bryce had slipped from the safety of family and footing and into the bottomless air, space reserved for birds and angels. The arms of a nearby sycamore tree did not catch him, so he plummeted.

This boy who had been born three months premature, weighing barely three pounds. This boy who had so defied the odds that at twenty-three months he weighed thirty pounds, big enough to be mistaken for a three-year-old. This boy falling.

Past the fifth floor.

Past the fourth.

Past the third, falling so fast you'd have seen only a babyish blur.

Past the second.

Past the first.

Past the ground-level lobby.

All told, past six windows, each one featuring a window guard.

He fell and fell and did not stop until he hit a small swath of grass, close to an old fallout shelter sign and around the corner from another sign saying keep off the grass. Thirty pounds of Bryce meets the green earth of the Bronx.

But here is the miracle. According to his family and the police,

Bryce went overboard clutching that pillow, and dropping through the air like a body surfer without wave support. When he hit land, the pillow softened the impact.

According to his mother, his great-grandmother rushed to his side and said, "Bryce! Bryce!" And, with eyes opened, he breathed in and out, releasing a sigh that sounded like, "Uh-huh."

Amanda looked down to see her baby brother on a pillow on the grass, then went to a room to cry. Someone told her to call 911, and she did.

Tarkeshia Wilder wailed when she heard what had happened; Brian McMillan passed out. They rushed to Lincoln Medical and Mental Health Center, where they waited for the verdict of scans and tests.

Mr. McMillan caught a peek of his son beneath ganglia of tubes and wires. "It didn't look too good, to my eyes," he says.

Finally, a doctor came out, put his arms around the teary-eyed parents, and explained that Bryce had suffered only a broken leg, a bruised liver, and a bruised spleen. This is one lucky boy, he said.

"It's a miracle," Tarkeshia Wilder says.

Bryce is now at Jacobi Medical Center, charming nurses, eating food from McDonald's, and waiting for some congestion to clear so that he can be sedated and fitted with a cast.

Then he will return home, where that calendar on the wall will remind his parents how time flies, and sometimes babies.

NOVEMBER 17, 2004

Legs and Mind, Wandering New York

With no great desire to arrive early at your destination, a walk across Manhattan on Monday becomes more of a meander, a strolling silent plea for distraction. This city is quite generous that way; no matter which way you look, you see snippets of the cinematic features that are the lives of other people, and for a moment or two you forget the melodrama that is your own.

The walk begins at Broadway and West Sixty-eighth Street and heads east, past the Loews multiplex, past apartment buildings and storefronts, into the diversion of Central Park. At the entrance sits a man with his head tucked into the folds of his soiled coat, one hand on his skeletal companion, a shopping cart. But the way he has adorned it, with rows of overstuffed plastic bags, each one a different color, suggests an attention to detail normally seen in storefront displays at holiday time.

Out the park's other end, and the destination draws nearer. But a friend beside you provides further distraction with his New York stories, and he knows more than most: of misbegotten boxers and ballplayers long forgotten, of Gotti, of Giuliani, of kids of color dying in Iraq. You nod, you say yes, you lose yourself in his words.

Before you know it you have reached the doors to your destination, a hospital, and because you are early, you do not go in. The city falls silent for a moment, or maybe you just do not hear for a moment. Then the sounds return: the angry words croaked into a cell phone by a woman sitting on a nearby bench, surgical gauze taped across her throat; the footsteps of a healthy-looking man carrying a brown envelope large enough to hold X-rays; a doctor's white coat whishing past.

They are the sounds of three separate movies playing simultaneously in this multiplex of a city, this grand distraction.

In you go and, four hours later, out you come, thankful for the special effect of fresh air. The East Side darkness has you imagining that you are in your own film noir, and you recall the moment in *Out of the Past* when Robert Mitchum's girlfriend asks him whether anything is wrong. His answer: Maybe not.

Tuesday offers another eight million reels in eight million movies. The people of New York constantly, even generously, provide one another with distraction, but rarely do we think of ourselves as cast members in the same never-ending film. Your role today: just another man going to a doctor's office in Midtown.

A crowded E train pulls into Pennsylvania Station, and you have the sense that the gods of Gotham have finally chosen to smile upon you. The subway car that opens its doors right in front of you is empty; so many seats to choose from, all awaiting the honor of bearing your weight.

You board, the doors close, and immediately you realize why the train is empty: A homeless man is sleeping in the corner of the car, and his many problems have revealed themselves in a smell bad enough to bring tears to the eyes.

You don't ask yourself what Jesus would do because you don't want to hear the answer. You just move to the next car at the Forty-second Street stop.

In the waiting room of the doctor's office, you sit among other actors in private New York films, including some that may end soon, which makes you feel uncomfortable and sets you to looking about for more distraction. A woman wearing a baseball cap to cover her bald head slumps in a chair while her husband negotiates with a clerk about dates for the next appointment, and the next. A man whose hair is beginning to grow back, but who needs a cane to get around, jokes with staff members, because he knows how the injection of laughter can lift a melodrama.

Someone calls your name. In you go and, two hours later, out you come, thankful again for the fresh air.

Eight million movies continue to unwind as you board the long escalator at East Fifty-third Street that leads down to the E train. As you slowly descend, you look at the faces of the people slowly ascending toward daylight. Out of central casting, every one of them, for that blockbuster about a city.

Here, in the bowels, a thickset man named James Qi plays a keyboard and pits his rumbling baritone against the hiss and sigh of passing subways. He inhales the close, subterranean air and transforms it somehow into a hypnotizing rendition of "Ave Maria." People nod and toss crumpled dollar bills into a black bag at his feet, and so do you.

Tracking Shadows Under the Snow and Cardboard

Snow an inch high and climbing covered the mound of beaten luggage that leaned against the church's door like some forgotten late-night delivery. Only the steady descent of white flakes broke the city stillness.

Then a flap of cloth flipped up from somewhere within the mound, releasing a puff of perfume and revealing the face of a woman, lined and with hair like gray straw: the night's Madonna of the Elements, huddled at the stone hem of St. Monica's Roman Catholic Church on East Seventy-ninth Street, a stumble step or two from First Avenue.

"Leave me alone," she called out from the mound. "I'm fine, I'm fine."

She was, in a way. The two men from the Bowery Residents' Committee, an outreach program, wished her well and moved on to the next person sleeping outside on a cold and snowy Monday night in February, with intimations of a blizzard in the wind. In New York City, there is always a next person; just look.

The weather forecast had been so dire that the Department of Homeless Services postponed its annual "homeless street count," in which two thousand volunteers were to try to quantify the unquantifiable: the number of people in this city's five boroughs who live on the streets—who rock to fitful sleep on subways, who linger in Penn Station, who find subterranean refuge.

Last year the count was 2,694, a figure that did not include Queens or the Bronx.

That the weather might be too foul for the city to count those living in its February foulness seems absurd at first. But Linda Gibbs, the commissioner of homeless services, explained that she had to consider the safety of the volunteers. In a few days the city will try again to conduct its count.

The postponement did not change anything on the street Monday night. The men and women of the pavement continued to huddle beneath idiosyncratic castles of cardboard and tarp, and the men and women of the outreach—on contract with the city—continued to offer help in finding warmth, counseling, a better way.

To that end, a blue Bowery Residents' Committee van prowled Manhattan's slushy streets, its passengers peering through fogged windows to spot scaffolding and doorways that might give shelter.

Andrew Apicella, the director of the agency's outreach program, drove. Muzzy Rosenblatt, the executive director, sat in the back. And Jason Tarnowski, an outreach worker, tapped data about every encounter into a laptop computer, which helps the agency to track general trends and specific histories.

There is plenty to type. Just before meeting the gray-haired woman in her church-step cocoon, they had answered a 311 call about "someone in a box" in front of the Church of St. Stephen of Hungary on East Eighty-second Street, beneath a stone inscription, *Venite Adoremus Dominum.*

That someone, a man, declined help with a choice epithet. Mr. Apicella and Mr. Tarnowski said good night, having assured themselves that, if nothing else, the man's shelter—rigged with green tarp, cardboard, and a bungee cord attached to the church's door handle—reflected experience with sleeping in the wet and cold.

"You can tell a lot by the designs," Mr. Apicella said.

There are other things that Mr. Apicella knows, after more than a decade of outreach work. That many of the mentally ill tend to congregate on the quieter East Side, where they think they will be left alone, while panhandlers prefer the busier West Side. That the best times to encourage someone to seek treatment are in the early evening hours, before bedtime, and around dawn, when they wake and pack up. That once ensconced for the night, they want to be left alone.

This proved the case with Victor, buried in snow and sleeping bags on the steps of St. Monica's, a dozen feet from that woman. When told that someone might be checking on him later in the night, he said, "If I'm asleep, don't wake me."

The van stopped in front of St. Jean Baptiste Church, at the corner of Lexington Avenue and East Seventy-sixth Street, to check on a coffin-sized shelter that included plastic wrapping and a green umbrella. The voice of a woman rose up to say that she was fine, fine.

The van continued south on Fifth Avenue, as men shoveled in front of luxurious apartment buildings where they work opening doors, as orange curtains billowed in Central Park, as a radio broadcaster announced that it was "thirty-one degrees and snowing in New York."

In front of the Petrossian restaurant stood a large man holding an umbrella and wearing an unzipped coat not much thicker than a windbreaker.

Snow had transformed half his face and most of his black hair into a mask of white. "I'm OK, man," he said with a hint of menace. "I'm OK."

With the three-to-eleven shift drawing to a close, the van headed to the agency's outreach base on the Bowery. A few minutes later the van headed back into the night, this time with members of the eleven-to-seven shift, Gabriel Carter and Michelle Washington.

They stopped in front of the Paul Smith men's fashion store on Fifth Avenue and West Sixteenth Street, where another of life's odd juxtapositions was taking place. A man inside the store was working on a window display, separated by a pane of glass from a man who had made his bed on the sidewalk.

The man on the sidewalk said that his name was Kerry, that he was forty, that he had been sleeping in this spot for a month, that he was "certifiable," and that he could never forgive his mother. Mr. Rosenblatt sat by his side, nodding, listening, and gently urging him to get help.

"This is about you, not your mother," Mr. Rosenblatt said.

After a discussion that gave Kerry an opportunity to vent, he promised to consider visiting the agency's office. "Lafayette Street, huh?" he said as Mr. Rosenblatt rose to leave.

The van continued on, as did the snow. Well after midnight, the outreach workers stopped in front of a clump of a man outside the Duane Reade store on Eighth Avenue in Chelsea.

He sat on a wet cardboard box marked Little Bunnies diapers, with a bottle under his overcoat and a five-dollar bill clutched in his freezing right hand. The outreach team concluded that he was at risk.

After a circular conversation in which the man insisted he was fine, Mr. Carter called 911. Two police cars and a Fire Department ambulance arrived a few minutes later, but not before the man had gotten to his feet and walked north toward Penn Station, a silhouette in snow, and then, nothing.

FEBRUARY 1, 2006

People Cringed, But Twelve Cameras Never Blinked

Twelve security cameras bear witness at the White Castle on Webster Avenue in the Bronx. Mounted high in unobtrusive places, they create a multiframed silent film of life unfolding in a place of transience, a fast-food pit stop.

The cameras are meant to see all. Early Saturday morning, they did.

By now the city knows that on that morning, in this White Castle, several young men pummeled an apparently intoxicated off-duty police officer named Eric Hernandez. They kicked and beat him until he managed to crawl out the door.

Once outside, he held his gun over a sixth man whom he mistakenly believed to have been one of his attackers. A uniformed police officer arrived, ordered him to drop the gun, then shot him three times when he did not. Officer Hernandez remains in very critical condition, and so far the police say they have rounded up four of his six assailants.

The police have zeroed in on the painfully long minute of violence preserved on videotape. But the twelve cameras also captured many small moments that more fully present the everyday Bronx ballet, brutally interrupted. We see the post-attack posturing of young men, but we also see the sobbing of a White Castle worker, as she sits alone in the back, shoulders hunched, wiping away tears.

The tape begins at 4:27 A.M., showing in a dozen frames the world of a White Castle approaching the weekend dawn.

In the dining room, young people eat and flirt, while a man in a gray cap, sitting alone, rests his head on a back table. Behind the counter, workers make hamburgers, pour sodas, and pass white bags out the drive-through window. Outside, cars pull into the parking lot, pause, and pull out.

Life as captured by these stop-action cameras has a herky-jerky quality, as though every character on this small, unnaturally bright stage pauses to contemplate every move.

At 4:40, some young men join the crowd. The police later christen a few of them Striped Shirt, Blue Sweater, White Hat, and Gray Hoodie, the alpha male in the group. A few minutes later they are joined by another man, in a shirt that says STOP SNITCHING NOW. He becomes Stop Sign, and when arrested, he does not live up to his motto.

The men strut about the dining room, horsing around, ordering food, and, witnesses later say, complaining about being shortchanged in soda. Meanwhile, in the corner, the man in the gray cap has raised his head briefly and placed it back down.

At 4:50:20, a strapping Officer Hernandez walks in—a heartbreaking entrance, given that what awaits him in five minutes is already known to the viewer. Dressed in a white coat and a blue baseball cap, he drops his keys twice. The young men watch.

Gray Hoodie addresses him; the police later say he is strongly suggesting that Officer Hernandez buy everyone a soda. Verbal parries and thrusts follow. Gray Hoodie does a dance and removes his coat. His companions seem to take positions. The officer walks out with his food, but returns twice, as if to respond to things Gray Hoodie has said.

At about 4:55 Gray Hoodie lunges for Officer Hernandez, which prompts five others to join in. As they throw the officer to the ground, and kick him and punch him and throw food at him, seven White Castle employees stare out a window in disbelief. One walks away, her hand to her face.

Striped Shirt reaches for some food, eats what looks like a French fry, and returns to kicking the officer. At the same time, a White Castle supervisor reaches for a telephone. The man in the gray cap does not look up.

After Officer Hernandez crawls out the door, where events continue to conspire against him, the attackers strut and gloat. One attacker slaps the officer's baseball cap on Gray Hoodie's head; a trophy.

By 5:01, Gray Hoodie has left, the officer's cap in his hand. Gone, too, are his companions. The workers come from behind a locked door and into the dining room, where now only the man in the gray cap sits, still. They look out the window.

A police car, lights flashing, pulls into the view of one of the twelve cameras. Soon a police officer rings the parking lot with the yellow tape that says something bad has happened. Soon the workers are back at the grill, back at the drive-through window.

But one worker, a middle-aged woman, takes a break. She passes a detective and sits down in the back. And from 5:11 to 5:13, she weeps.

JANUARY 7, 2004

Dress Is Formal, But the Food?
Cold and Slimy

There is a touch of swank to the place. But then the man in green appears with the afternoon's repast in two buckets, and what had seemed like a cordial gathering turns into last call at a bad Waldorf soiree. For penguins, apparently, nothing beats the feel of a nice cold smelt sliding down your gullet.

The man in green, Rob Gramzay, knows this better than most humans. Officially, he is the Central Park Zoo's "senior wild animal keeper for polar birds and polar mammals." Unofficially, he is Manhattan's penguin guy, responsible for the well-being of this island's forty-two chinstraps and twenty-three gentoos.

He has other charges, of course, including but not limited to thirteen puffins, three polar bears, two screech owls, and old Breezy, the blind sea lion whose repertory of tricks once wowed them at Coney Island. But the penguins are especially dear to his heart, in part because they seem always to be gently mocking those on the other side of the zoo exhibit's glass partition: waddling about in comic self-importance, beaks raised as if detecting an aroma nowhere near as pleasant as a bucket of smelt.

On the penguin side of this partition, the chilled air reeks of fish and wet feathers, and the braying and splashing of its inhabitants resound off the gunite shores. But Mr. Gramzay has spent so much time here that he barely notices. By now he knows every one of the sixty-five penguins by name and habit: Nicky hangs out with Dr. Bob, his mate; Geppetto prefers herring to smelt; Georgey gets so excited at mealtime that she stands tippy-toe.

Mr. Gramzay grabs a fistful of smelt—in this case, a smelt called capelin—from a bucket and begins feeding the penguins by hand, while an assistant with a clipboard keeps track of what Duffy eats, what Squawk eats, what Nipper eats. Sometimes the braying grows so loud that the humans have trouble hearing each other; sometimes they have to beckon the penguins with whistles and shouts.

"Frankie, you going to come and eat!" calls the man in green, who at forty-two looks like an older and wiser Richie Cunningham.

Mr. Gramzay, who has lost the taste for smelt that he enjoyed as a youth in East Detroit, earned a bachelor's degree in zoology and worked for four years at the San Antonio Zoo before joining the renovated Central Park Zoo in 1988. Some of the penguins have been at the zoo longer than he has, he said, "so there's quite a relationship there."

The zoo at Central Park is one of the few where penguins are fed by hand. This up-close attention has helped the captive penguins to live longer and grow in number. It has also tightened the bond between man and bird, though not to the point where Mr. Gramzay feels the pangs of a sympathy molt.

Still, he has engaged in penguin gossip with other zookeepers about who nipped whom, and about the nest-swapping habits of a certain couple that had many a beak flapping (OK, it was Georgey and Terry). He has occasionally traveled with penguins or their eggs, transporting them to zoos as far as Germany.

He has even dreamed about penguins, often during the breeding season, when he worries about the safety of newly hatched chicks. In one dream, he imagined himself in a Florida motel room with all sixty-five penguins. He doesn't remember fretting about room-service charges, though he does recall warning his roommates, "You're going to make a mess."

Mr. Gramzay smiles when recalling his dream. It may seem silly to others, but he finds true companionship with these penguins, true connection in their cold, odoriferous domain.

There are times outside the partition when he is not having the best of days, times when he is focused more on the life cycle of human beings than on the mating cycle of polar birds. Several years ago, for example, he was consumed with the illness and death of his partner, Rich Almanza; they had lived together for more than a decade. But time has passed, and now he is eighteen months into another relationship.

Bad day, good day, it doesn't matter; the penguins must be fed. And when he steps into their domain, Custo and Schatzi often greet him with slight bows, and he remembers again what it is he does for a living, and he thinks, "This is really cool."

After forty-five minutes, all sixty-five penguins have been fed. The man in green reaches for his empty pails and walks toward the door that leads to the other side. Many of the penguins wave their stumpy wings, as if in applause.

MARCH 25, 2006

Once Again, a Killer Makes His Pitch

The man entered the conference room and exchanged hellos and good mornings with his three visitors. These pleasantries were brief, a kind of clearing of the throat. The light of a January day in upstate New York seeped past the barred windows.

"How many years have you been in?" one of the visitors asked.

"It will be forty-two in March," he answered.

"Yep. Forty-two," answered the visitor, who then got right to it. "On March 13, 1964, in Queens County, you stalked and repeatedly stabbed Kitty Genovese. She was pronounced dead on arrival at Queens General Hospital. Numerous stab wounds were found on her back, on her front of her body; her hands were also found to be lacerated, which indicated some defensive wounds."

The visitor then noted that the man had once revealed a compulsion to rape and kill women. "Pretty heinous thing, Mr. Moseley," he said.

"I agree," answered Winston Moseley.

The visitor, a State Board of Parole member named Edward R. Mevec, went on to recall Mr. Moseley's escape from custody in 1968 and the crazed two-day crime spree of rape, kidnapping, and robbery that followed. "Any indication as to why you did what you did?" he asked.

"Yes," Mr. Moseley answered. "I have thought about it, and it really had to do with my parents."

This man is serving twenty years to life for killing Kitty Genovese, whose cries for help went unheeded on a darkened street in Kew Gardens, and whose miserable death forced the nation to reflect on the fraying of the bond we share with one another. She was twenty-eight when she died at the bottom of a stairwell; he is seventy-one now, and will almost certainly die in prison.

Still, a civil society has its customs. Every two years, Mr. Moseley appears before the parole board to plead for liberty, now and then tweaking his argument. He once apologized for inconveniencing the victims of his 1968 rampage; another time he explained that for the victim, "it's a one-time or one-hour or one-minute affair, but for the person who's caught, it's forever."

This time, in addition to blaming his parents, he also noted that when he escaped in Buffalo back in 1968, he demonstrated restraint. "I'd like you to take that into consideration, that none of those people were killed," he said. "I could've killed all of them, but I was done with that."

"All these events occurred many, many years ago," he added.

Since then, Mr. Moseley has earned a college degree, participated in various prison programs, including "aggression replacement training," and claimed to have tried to quell the violence during the rioting at Attica in 1971. He has been disciplined only three times in twenty years, the last time in 1997, for possession of a weapon.

But he remains the man who killed Kitty Genovese.

"You remember what you did?" one of the parole officials asked.

"I remember, sir."

He went on to make his pitch, explaining that killing Ms. Genovese was a way of killing his mother, with whom he had a "love-hate relationship." He talked more about the restraint he had shown in not murdering anyone during his escape.

"Interesting," a parole official said.

Someone asked him if he was the oldest inmate at Great Meadow, a maximum-security prison seventy miles north of Albany. No, he said, but he had the oldest inmate number (64-A0102), which signals that he has been incarcerated since 1964. During that time, he said, he had seen gangs emerge and interest in rehabilitation wane.

But the conversation had to return to Kitty Genovese, and it did, beginning with his arrest a few days after the murder for an unrelated burglary charge.

"And how did they put it together that you . . ."

"I told them."

"Why did you tell them?"

"I don't think I wanted to live with the guilt of that."

The short hearing drew to a close. Mr. Moseley expressed his willingness to see a parole officer two or three times a week if he was released. He thanked his visitors for being reasonable because, he said, "I know this is a hard matter to deal with."

"You'll get a written decision in a few days," Mr. Mevec said.

"Thank you, sir."

"OK," Mr. Moseley said.

"Take care," someone said.

A few days later the parole board notified the killer of Kitty Genovese that he was an "out-of-control predator," and that his request for freedom had again been denied. His next appearance is scheduled for 2008, when it will still be 1964.

Here's Looking at You, Dr. Zizmor

No matter where you sit or stand, his eyes find you. He stares at you with a blank expression that in its very blankness judges you. Especially your face; your wrinkled, sagging dishcloth of a face.

Before you boarded the subway, you were feeling pretty good about yourself. Now, his eyes seem to say, you have something on your face. There.

There?

No, no. There. Yes, there. What is that?

Well, actually, it's—just my face.

I see, the eyes of Dr. Zizmor say. I see.

In *The Great Gatsby*, the eyes of Dr. T. J. Eckleburg stared out upon the ashen urban landscape from an old billboard in Queens. Dr. Eckleburg's practice had long since vanished, but his gigantic blue eyes, framed by enormous yellow spectacles, continued to watch in seeming judgment the striving, hapless denizens of 1920s New York.

The successor to the good Dr. Eckleburg is the good Dr. Zizmor, who gazes down at us now from subway car advertisements everywhere. Promotions for night school and safe sex come and go, but what lingers in the mind are the repeated suggestions of flawed being, as conveyed through the ads of Dr. Jonathan Zizmor, dermatologist.

He first began to scrutinize our facial imperfections a quarter-century ago through ads that promised "Now You Can Have Beautiful, Clear Skin." The eyes in his smiling, baby-chubby visage bore like laser beams into our skulls to read our innermost insecurities—about acne or moles or stretch marks or the risqué tattoo that seemed like such a good idea down at the beach that time.

One reason these ads continue to draw the eye is the art of their artlessness. Instead of featuring a sleek, nameless model promoting a national brand of beer, they present us with the image of a local doctor who is exceedingly average-looking and more than glad to take a look at that rash.

The ads also seem to celebrate typographical errors, which contribute to a look of having been cobbled together by someone who doesn't work in graphics or advertising—which, it turns out, is the case. That someone is Dr. Zizmor.

For example, the ads usually feature a rainbow-colored background that brings to mind the trippy Sammy Davis Jr. hit, "The Candy Man." ("Who can take a rainbow, wrap it in a sigh, soak it in the sun and make a groovy lemon pie.")

People who deconstruct Zizmor sometimes interpret the rainbow to mean we are a city of many skin colors. Truth is, fifteen years ago the doctor's six-year-old daughter was fiddling with the computer, came up with a rainbow—and he liked it.

Finally, the ads cast a spell because they combine Dr. Zizmor's judging stare with language rooted in the tradition of the very finest direct-mail come-ons. One of the ubiquitous Zizmor ads currently featured in your local or express—his face appears, it is said, in every fifth car—includes a yes-or-no quiz to ponder as you rock and sway in self-consciousness. "Is your skin loose? Do you have more than one chin? Has your skin lost its firmness and tightness? Do you think you look older than you should for your age?"

The ad suggests that you also give yourself a test when you get home. Stand before a mirror, place your hands on the sides of your scalp with thumbs extended, and then raise the skin of your cheeks using only your thumbs. "If this makes you look better," the ad says, have we got a procedure for you.

To prevent you from hurting yourself in this exercise, the ad includes a how-to illustration. It shows a woman with wrinkles and a double chin who looks like dowdy Shelley Winters, *The Poseidon Adventure*, 1972. But when she presses her hands against her face, the woman becomes fresh-faced Debbie Reynolds, *Singin' in the Rain*, 1952.

There is no change, though, in the face of Dr. Eckleburg; make that Dr. Zizmor. Ageless and omnipresent, he looms over us as we go from here to there, his expression conveying neither pain nor joy, his eyes zeroing in on the bags under our eyes, the creases over our brow.

Occasionally, the real Dr. Zizmor, who looks older than he does in his ads, takes the subway. One would think, one would hope, that Dr. Zizmor would then be subjected to the scrutiny of Dr. Zizmor.

But he never seems to be in a car that features one of his ads, he says. "You can go nuts looking for these things."

JANUARY 14, 2004

At 99 Cents, Mystery Sells Cheap

Another customer, perusing the odd items of yet another 99-cent store in this city, selects a synthetic black belt from a rack and wonders aloud whether it is long enough to complete the loop around his formidable girth.

Yes! And with room to spare.

"How much is this belt?" he asks, his smile suggesting that he already knows.

"Ninety-nine," answers the proprietor, Rocko.

Yes! The pleased belt sampler calls two aisles over to his wife, who is admiring some 99-cent socks. "Baby," he says with triumph, "I got my belt."

His reaction, in turn, pleases Rocko, who believes in the economic promise of his business, the American 99 store, in the Allerton section of the Bronx. Leave it to others to scoff at the exotic provenance and eclectic selection of his merchandise. He is meeting a community need, he says, and he is doing it straight up.

"This store here is one of the true ninety-nine-cent stores," he explains. "When you come here, you know that everything is ninety-nine cents or less. It is what it is. A lot of the others, they sell ninety-nine-cent items, but they also sell merchandise that's more than ninety-nine cents. Their signs say 'and up.'" Rocko spells that last word aloud—"U-P"— to punctuate his penny's worth of a point.

The stodgy five-and-dime store of the past has been replaced by the wacky 99-cent store of the present. The essential attraction of discounted stuff is the same, but today's 99-cent stores seduce customers with the added allure of cheap mystery. Where does this stuff come from? What new item that I never knew I needed will appear on the shelves this week? And how do the owners squeeze out enough pennies to make a profit?

Rocko, a stocky man tucked into a University of Kentucky sweatshirt, takes a break from unpacking boxes to provide a 99-cent primer. His real name is Kasho Ramdin, he is thirty-three, he moved here from Guyana in 1990, and he has a wife and two young sons whom he rarely sees. That is because he works seven days a week amid boxes of odd-brand cereals ("Forelli's Frosty Corn Flakes"?), rows of scented candles ("Opium"?), and, and

"Glue traps for mice?" a woman asks.

"In the back, along the wall," he answers.

He says that he used to work in electronics sales, until his older brother explained the potential in discount stores. Now their family operates three stores in the Bronx, including this one on Burke Avenue, a few steps away from an elevated subway line.

Rocko emphasizes that he is not one of those 99-cent magnates who saves pennies by exploiting workers. He is a hands-on boss, he says, one who works every day but New Year's Eve; who believes that "if you put in now, you get back later."

Most of the merchandise comes from distributors who sell the excess of stock intended for other countries; those boxes of Close-Up toothpaste, say, which "*verskaf berkerming teen tandbederf*" (provides protection against tooth cavities). Some items, like those six-inch ceramic ducks in sailor outfits, come from cheap-labor operations in China. And some things come from wholesale auctions; those cans of Carpet Wizard, for example.

On average, he pays about 65 cents for what he sells for 99 cents. Some products, like laundry detergent, cost him more, but those essential items draw customers to the store. Once they're inside, he reasons, who knows what might catch their eye? Perhaps those 99-cent men's blazers that somehow made their way to the Bronx from England.

"Hi, Sweetie Pie," says a woman, a regular customer. "You got more bath mats?"

Rocko says that he works hard to create an inviting environment for his multiethnic clientele, going so far as to rotate the style of music that emanates from the store's sound system. "In the mornings we play religious music for one hour," he says. "Then Spanish. Then reggae. And in the evening, calypso."

"I can't play my own stuff," he adds. "Heavy metal and hard rock."

This attention to customer service paid off during last summer's protracted blackout, he says, which prompted many stores along Burke Avenue to yank down their steel gates. His store remained open, selling flashlights and an inordinate amount of scented candles. "I had nothing stolen," he says. "Matter of fact, my customers were helping me out."

A woman asks about brooms. A man cannot find the flashlights. Some delivery people are unloading socks and undergarments. Rocko has to get back to work.

"A lot of my customers say, 'Why don't you go up in price?' " he says. "But I maintain, no. I want to be a ninety-nine-cent store."

MARCH 22, 2006

Obliged to Pause in Its Tracks, Manhattan Takes Note of the Manhattan of Beasts

Word had come from the other side of the East River by police radio crackle: They're in. Now, in the midnight freeze, a welcoming party of the enchanted and the less so stared into the Manhattan maw of the Queens-Midtown Tunnel, waiting for the improbable.

Elephants.

Normally, only creatures of the genus Vehicular Traffic inhabit this

small asphalt plain on the East Side. They leave the savanna of
Queens, emerge from the tunnel, and follow their behavioral instincts:
uptown, downtown, crosstown.

But this was a once-a-year night, when the traveling circus of
Ringling Brothers and Barnum & Bailey tries again to compete with
the everyday circus of New York. It parades the elephants through the
tunnel and along Thirty-fourth Street to Madison Square Garden, where
they live and perform for three weeks.

A rube might ask why the elephants must come through the tunnel, requiring the closing of one of its two tubes. The circus has its
own mile-long train, after all. Instead of parking in a rail yard in
Queens, couldn't that train pull into Penn Station, directly below the
Garden?

Well, let's break it down.

First, commuters on the 7:04 out of Ronkonkoma are rarely in
a good mood to begin with; imagine how they'd feel about boarding
an escalator behind Juliette the elephant. Second, the best publicity
comes wrapped in the gauze of tradition, and this tradition dates back
to 1981, when development overtook the West Side rail yards that
once accommodated the circus train.

All of which explains why overtired children and childlike adults,
anxious circus employees and angry animal-rights activists, along with
various police officers and photographers, now gathered on this asphalt
plain, freezing, fussing, facing Queens.

Among them was Michael Shea, a veteran bridge-and-tunnel officer assigned to the Queens-Midtown, like his father before him. He
had worked the three-to-midnight shift, but when he heard the elephants were coming through again, he seized the offer of overtime.
"It's a good thing," he said of the elephants, and perhaps of the overtime as well.

His police radio's chatter told the tale of the elephants. How Jew-
ell was being taken by truck over the 59th Street Bridge; "not a big
fan of the tunnel," a circus spokesman later explained. How the other
elephants were mustering at an elephantine pace in Queens. How,
nearly an hour later than planned, they were lumbering toward the
entrance and—they're in.

Imagine what these natural miracles experienced as they walked
more than a mile through this man-made miracle snaking under the

East River. The echoing clop of their massive feet. The sleek walls of off-white Depression-era tile. The soft lighting befitting a strange dream about a journey.

At 12:46, the police radio said the elephants had reached Marker 21.

"Almost halfway through," said Officer Shea.

At 12:54, Marker 49.

"Come on, ya freaking animals," said a freezing photographer.

Then, at 1:03, a grayish smudge emerged to blot the light at the distant tunnel's mouth. Elephants in Manhattan.

Karen and Juliette, Nichole and Minyak, Bonnie and Kelly Ann—and Sara, at four, the baby. They ambled up the road, trailed by a pair of zedonks—half zebra, half donkey—some horses, and various trainers and assistants. Cheers rose to warm a cold and cheerless city corner.

The elephants seemed diminished at first by their urban surroundings. But as they drew closer they became larger, larger, until at last they somehow belonged—so much so that their grayish skin blended like camouflage into the asphalt and concrete around them.

In a few minutes they would be hustled west along Thirty-fourth Street, across Lexington, Park, and Madison, past Macy's and at least three Duane Reade drugstores, while cabs and cars paused in deference. Their massive ears would snare the hoorays of the enchanted and the boos of those who believe the circus mistreats its elephants and other animals—a charge the circus denies.

And beginning tomorrow, they would star in the Big Top of cities, repeatedly performing a hip-hop act called "Wave That Trunk," while children of all ages marveled at creatures never seen through the scratched windows of the D train, or on the sands of Jones Beach.

How the elephants feel about all this, no one can tell for sure, though their eyes, small marbles set in massive skulls, always manage to convey a mood short of happiness.

But they are veteran performers by now, professionals—even Sara, the baby. Fresh from the tunnel, they paused, took their cues, and greeted Manhattan with a little dance.

PART II

Angel Franco

Vanishing New York

A Last Whiff of Fulton's Fish, Bringing a Tear

It smells of truck exhaust and fish guts. Of glistening skipjacks and smoldering cigarettes; fluke, salmon, and Joe Tuna's cigar. Of Canada, Florida, and the squid-ink East River. Of funny fish-talk riffs that end with profanities spat onto the mucky pavement, there to mix with coffee spills, beer blessings, and the flowing melt of sea-scented ice.

This fragrance of fish and man pinpoints one place in the New York vastness: a small stretch of South Street where peddlers have sung the song of the catch since at least 1831, while all around them, change. They were hawking fish here when an ale house called Mc-Sorley's opened up; when a presidential aspirant named Lincoln spoke at Cooper Union; when the building of a bridge to Brooklyn ruined their upriver view.

Take it in now, if you wish, if you dare, because the rains will come to rinse this distinct aroma from the city air. Some Friday soon, perhaps next month, the fish sellers will spill their ice and shutter their stalls, pack their grappling hooks and raise a final toast beneath the ba-rump and hum of the Franklin Delano Roosevelt Drive.

And on the Monday, they will begin peddling their dead-eyed wares inside a custom-made building in the Hunts Point section of the Bronx, to be named the New Fulton Fish Market Cooperative, and the old Fulton Fish Market—that raucous stage of open-air overnight commerce—will be no more.

The fish market's closing should come as no surprise, though it does. From the beginning, New York questioned the location of this rough and odoriferous trade. In 1854 a city elder wondered whether "a more advantageous disposition may not be made of that valuable property by the removal of the Fish Market." And in 1859 another sachem suggested moving the market uptown, in part because the ebb and flow of the East River was, as *The New York Times* delicately put it, "not sufficiently strong to carry off the offal."

Offal and the official's concomitant complaint of a blanket of mag-gots on the water were not issues in the decision to move the market finally to Hunts Point (a plan that dates back at least to the mid-1950s). Instead, the creeping conversion of Manhattan into a monstrous mall for the affluent played a role, as did the grudging realization that the market had become impractical, anachronistic. Fishermen haven't un-loaded their catch there for more than a generation.

Before it leaves us, then; before it lives only in news footage and movies like *Splash:* one last look at a part of the city taken for granted, save by fish people, nighthawks, and urban anthropologists. One long, last inhalation of the exquisite Fulton Fish Market bouquet.

Three in the morning, and forklifts clatter over rutted pavement, unloaded trucks sigh in escape, and workers pierce wax-coated cases with grappling hooks—*whup! whup!*—as they move fish from here to there.

Some lights of the market stand before the silvery truck of a man who calls himself Steve the Coffee Guy. Beansie, the union official, is there, smoking a cigar, and Richie Klein, a burly fish salesman, savor-ing a cigarette, and Joe Tuna, on his forklift, drinking tea. When Joe Tuna glides over curb and cobblestone, his meaty biceps jiggle so much that the tattoos move like cartoons.

They wear rubber boots and soiled sneakers that never cross the thresholds of their homes; clean jeans and fish-bloodied shorts; polo shirts and T-shirts, some torn in the back by the tips of the hooks slung over their shoulders.

In winter, the East River winds blow through you no matter what you wear, so Steve the Coffee Guy will warm himself with a propped-up propane heater, in homage to barrels of flames that once flickered wickedly along South Street. On this summer's night, though, the muggy air clings like lotion to the skin, and coolness is found at the coffee truck's icy bed of soda, over which hangs a dated photograph of a beautiful young woman in shorts, briskly walking.

The rumor, or the hope, is that it's South Street Annie, also known as Shopping Bag Annie, that shrunken woman with wild gray hair who strolls the market calling, "Yoohoo!" Selling cigarettes and newspapers from her red-wire cart, she is coarse, ribald, ubiquitous: the flawed mother of fish town. A worker confides that on his first day in the market more than a decade ago, he was instructed to kiss one of her pendulous breasts—for good luck.

In the market, superstition demands that you watch out for stray animals and broken people. The men take care of her, enduring her rants, her feigned grabs at their crotches. The *New York Post* costs a quarter; the men give her a dollar. The *Daily News* costs fifty cents; they give her a dollar, maybe two.

Thank you, sweetie, she says. What a guy.

Burly Mr. Klein grabs his coffee and walks over to Stall 31, where he and a partner run Third Generation Seafood in what is known as the New Market Building; the old building was demolished after a chunk of it fell into the river in 1936. He passes crates of croakers, porgies, and "day-boat" Montauk fluke, which means it was caught less than twenty-four hours ago.

He pauses to watch one of his fillet men, Wilson Quirizumbay, slice a tuna carcass so close to the bone that only maroon wisps of flesh remain. "They have a feel for the bone, and for the knife," Mr. Klein says. "The skill is in the yield. He's gonna give me seventy percent."

In the next stall stands Vincent Tatick, of the Joseph H. Carter Fish Company. His father ran Frank Tatick Fillet under the old Sweet's Restaurant. Both are gone now, and here is the son, twirling a grappling hook as though it were a child's toy. He wears a dark-green shirt, dark-green pants, and a camouflage headband, sports five pencils and a pack of Parliaments in his breast pocket, and keeps a Marine Corps knife on his hip. Rambo among fish.

Mr. Tatick has no opinion about the market's move, he says, other than: What is, is. But he wonders about leaving behind the nuns at St. Rose's Home, on the Lower East Side, who nursed his father in his final two years. During that time, the Taticks agreed that it would be nice to give the nuns some fish, twenty-five pounds' worth, every Friday.

When his father died, Mr. Tatick says, "I didn't know how to say, 'Sorry, the deal is off.' So I never said anything."

That was more than forty years ago, he says. "I still give them fish."

This is just one story among thousands, tens of thousands, to rise from the fishy swirl, only to dissipate from memory with the passing of time and old fishmongers.

All those market fires, including the devastating blaze of 1878, possibly caused by rats munching on matchsticks. That strange, huge turtle brought to shore in 1900. The dream that a customs official had during Prohibition, leading to the discovery of two thousand bags of whiskey hidden among tons of fish in the hold of the schooner *Caroline*. The dead fisherman found hanging over an ice machine in 1939, leaving nothing but a last known address of the Seamen's Church Institute, 25 South Street.

Many of the stories centered on characters who worked hard for their nicknames: Iceberg Tommy, who settled his nerves by immersing his feet in ice; Shrimp Sammy, who promoted the freshness of his shellfish by eating them raw; Porgy Joe, who strolled the market with two live crabs clinging to his ears by their claws. Men of the water, now dust.

There was Alfred E. Smith, governor and presidential candidate, who often bragged of earning his degree from F.F.M., for Fulton Fish Market, the educational institution of his fish-peddling youth. And Joseph Lanza, a mobster who controlled the market for decades— whether in or out of prison—and whose sobriquet of "Socks" referred to his penchant for punching those who refused to pay him for the right to sell fish.

A hearing in 1931 became one of the first tutorials in the true ways of the market, thanks to the testimony of several uncomfortable witnesses, including a fish-store owner named James McAleese.

"A man called up and told me to send down forty dollars by my buyer, or the carriers would not deliver fish to my truck."

"Why did you pay it?" he was asked.

"Because I wanted my fish."

The mob and the market became so intertwined, with tribute to wise guys as common as a buck to Annie, that a government investigation of some kind always seemed under way. Successful crackdowns have considerably reduced the mob's presence, but still: One section of the city's administrative code begins with the assertion that the fish market "has for decades been corruptly influenced by organized crime."

More than the ghosts of characters, though, more than the whiff of the mob, there lingers in this city corner a palpable, connective air to who we once were; what we saw; what we said. The eels wriggling free along Fulton Street. The hook fights among fishmongers. The ice-coated masts of sloops in winter. The fedoras, the aprons, the scales of fish justice. That market man who, on one summer's night in 1872, called out an order:

"Lively, Jim, ten baskets of lobsters."

On this night, one of the last, it is Frank Minio who calls out. "Lemon sole is one-thirty-five today, and the large is one-fifty. I got one day-boat gray sole left, three-fifty."

Mr. Minio is bald, muscular, and in full command of his domain, a business on the west side of South Street called Smitty's Fillet House. A college graduate, he had planned to "pursue theater," as he puts it, but his father died in this very stall twenty-seven years ago, and, well, it's a family business.

He says he looks forward to some aspects of the move to the Bronx: not freezing in winter, for example, and not paying for so much ice in the summer. Still, he wonders, couldn't the city have built an enclosed market here, alongside exhibitions that celebrated New York's inextricable connection to the water?

"It's been done this way a long time," he says, before moving toward a man poking at the cheeks of fish. "Good morning," he says to the bold customer. "One-sixty on the pollock."

The sky begins to lighten. Below a for-sale sign on an old brick building, circa 1830, a fat man eats a turkey-on-a-roll near a gray mound of grouper. A skinny man shovels ice, shoosh, onto some snapper the color of the pinkish dawn. Someone calls out, "Frank-e-e-e!"

Another forklift clatters past. South Street Annie appears, selling fresh news. Behind her, the Brooklyn Bridge, looking almost new.

MAY 7, 2005

One Heaping Order of Memories, to Go

The Munson Diner just up and left Manhattan this week. No farewell blue-plate special, no second cup of joe. It waited for the light to turn green, made a left on Eleventh Avenue, and rumbled away from a city that had lost the taste for its meatloaf and gravy.

The diner did not take its leave until three-thirty on Thursday morning, as if to say to nighthawks everywhere, This one's for you. Passing under the stage lights of mostly deserted streets, its silvery chrome dazzled, its beveled glass winked, and echoes of diner lingo spilled imperceptibly upon the pavement.

The place closed late last year after six decades of serving eggs lookin' at ya, and the property owners had no interest in short-order cooking. Word spread one hundred miles northwest to Liberty, New York, where some entrepreneurs thought an authentic Manhattan diner could lend retro charm to their upstate town. But the deal did not include free or easy delivery.

Enter Mel Brandt, a specialist in diner relocation from Lancaster, Pennsylvania, whose hands are so grease-stained and callused that they look like gloves. The jobs just blur together: disengaging Russell's Diner from Massachusetts one day, the Ideal Diner from Delaware the next. "Basically the same procedure," he growled. "But still different."

Distinguishing the Munson job was Manhattan, a place that Mr. Brandt found disorienting. But after spending days prying the building from its Hell's Kitchen foundation, he felt comfortable enough by Wednesday to eat his take-out lunch at the diner's darkened counter, using abandoned shakers to salt-and-pepper his chicken. Ike and Mike, those shakers used to be called.

By two the next morning, he and his crew—Paul, Eli, and Omar—had things set for the move. At the southwest corner of Eleventh Avenue and West Forty-ninth Street, a hole gaped where the diner had been, and on the flatbed of an idling truck sat a mostly intact, well-secured diner, with counter, stools, and a menu marquee still offering meatloaf for $6.50. A sign on the plate-glass door promised the tastiest sandwich in town.

A waiter from another diner, Roger Cruz, stopped by to pay his respects. He lived around the corner, he said, and ate here many nights. "Eggs and French toast, four in the morning," he said, looking into the hole. "Would sober me up before going to bed."

Mr. Brandt, fifty-seven and looking it, tended to last-minute details while waiting for the state-certified escort cars that would lead him and his sleek cargo up Manhattan and across the George Washington Bridge. He wasn't quite sure of the route through this foreign terrain, though. "Eleventh and Tenth and Amsterdam?" he asked. "Does all that make sense to you?"

Shortly after three, Mike Aprile and Pete Liota, partners in the Staten Island company S&M Vehicle Escorts, pulled up in vehicles adorned with yellow sashes saying "Oversize Load." The ride to the bridge shouldn't be too bad, Mr. Liota said. "You just got that hill in Harlem, from One Twenty-fifth to One Thirty-fifth. By City College there."

The sight of a diner festooned with flashing orange lights and practically floating in air caused a passing police car to pull over. "Where they taking it?" one of the officers asked.

"Liberty."

"Where?"

Finally it was time. Mr. Brandt walked over to his escorts, and all he did was nod. Mr. Aprile nodded back and said: "Rock and roll."

The light turned green. An escort vehicle turned onto Eleventh Avenue, followed closely by Mr. Brandt's truck, lugging a fifty-foot-long diner that was fourteen feet wide and looking as if it might still be open for business. Sensing that this was not an everyday occurrence in baffling New York, Mr. Brandt beeped his horn in exultation.

The Munson Diner grunted up the avenue at thirty miles an hour, turned east on Fifty-seventh Street, then north onto Amsterdam, lumbering and trundling, as taxis rode beside it like a Secret Service detail in yellow. Lights glowed green in deference as it continued on, receiving a silent blessing from the Cathedral of St. John the Divine at 111th, an invisible diploma from City College at 136th.

Potholes and road bumps surely knocked free the diner's clinging ghosts, and released into the cool uptown air all those contained whispers of late-night plots and early-morning coos. Warm that up for you? That'll be two bits. See ya, doll.

The diner paused at the foot of the bridge, waiting for a Port Authority police car to lead it across the span. The black sky turned soft blue. The city stirred and yawned, but was not quite awake when a streamline diner slipped across the Hudson River, bound for Liberty.

JULY 30, 2005

A Prayer for a Church Unsaved

When Edwin Torres joined St. Brigid's more than thirty years ago, it seemed a good fit, like dry lips to a brimming chalice. Here was a young man from Puerto Rico, hungering. And here was an old Catholic church, born of hunger.

Irish shipwrights built St. Brigid's in 1848 as spiritual shelter for those brothers and sisters who survived steerage on famine ships. Its twin steeples rose over Tompkins Square in proud declaration to nativist New York: we Irish—we Catholics—are here to stay.

By the early 1970s, when Mr. Torres first knelt in its coolness, the church was like a creaking ship that had willed its way through many storms, its twin masts of steeples long since removed. But if you lifted your eyes toward the ceiling, you would see small sculptured faces looking back—the images, it was said, of shipwrights who had built the church and who now could be imagined saying: steady as she goes.

Mr. Torres devoted himself to St. Brigid's. He served as a catechist, sang in the choir, worked as an usher, volunteered as handyman, available whenever the boiler gave out. He witnessed the baptisms of his children and grandchildren at the church. He and his wife, Migdalia, renewed their marriage vows at its altar.

About fifteen years ago, the east wall started pulling away from the rest of the structure, so the church built three concrete buttresses, but the work was sloppily done by a contractor and never corrected. Meanwhile, a worrisome crack on the north wall grew larger, signaling the risk of collapse. His Eminence, Cardinal Edward M. Egan, visited the church to see it himself, and in June 2001, he ordered the church closed.

The pastor, the Reverend Michael Conway, began celebrating Mass in the parish school's cafeteria. He also established a restoration fund, appealing to parishioners and to others, especially Irish-Americans, who might appreciate the historical significance of St. Brigid's. But he did so without the approval of the archdiocese, according to its spokesman, Joseph Zwilling.

Still, every week the parish bulletin published the amount raised. Little by little, the number grew.

Mr. Torres continued as Mr. Everything—soliciting bids for the restoration work, for example—because he believed the church's reopening was a matter of when, not if. His faith was misplaced.

In September 2003, the archdiocese quietly filed an application with the city to convert St. Brigid's into apartments. Mr. Zwilling said that despite what the application indicates, the archdiocese never planned a conversion, but instead was protecting its options in the event that people—wounded parishioners, say—blocked the more-favored option: demolition. "By this stage," he said, "there was general consensus within the archdiocese that St. Brigid's would not reopen as a church, and would probably be demolished."

The two hundred or so parishioners of St. Brigid's did not know this. Every third week they continued to put money in envelopes labeled "My Donation to Rebuild St. Brigid." They eventually raised more than $100,000.

The archdiocese closed just one parish in 2004: St. Brigid's. Given that, Cardinal Egan could have made the announcement himself to Mr. Torres and the other parishioners. He could have explained the prohibitive cost of repairs and the risk of collapse. He could have answered questions, offered counseling, been a shepherd to his flock.

Instead, Bishop Robert Brucato, vicar general for the archdiocese, came to a Sunday Mass in the school cafeteria last August. He told the people of St. Brigid's that in two weeks there would be no St. Brigid's. They cried; they had questions. But the bishop left quickly, Mr. Torres recalls. "He was obviously in a rush to get out."

Father Conway left soon afterward, but not before entrusting some parish records to Mr. Torres—including a copy of the year-old application to convert St. Brigid's to apartments. Seeing that document for the first time, he recalled, "really crushed me."

After four years of neglect, St. Brigid's Church has so deteriorated that the archdiocese says that full restoration would cost at least $6.9 million. As for the $100,000 raised through that "unauthorized" fund, it says that it would refund the money to those who provide proof of their donations.

If you are so inclined, pray for these parishioners without a parish. They have formed the Committee to Save St. Brigid's Church. They have solicited bids that they say suggest the wall could be repaired for less than $500,000. They have filed suit against the archdiocese and obtained a court order blocking it from demolishing the church, for now at least.

Pray too for this tone-deaf archdiocese, as its agents remove the valuables from an empty, echoing church. The organ. The crucifix. The statues. And all those sculptured faces of proud Irish shipwrights.

MAY 28, 2005

A Tower Packed with Dentists, and They All Have to Come Out

Dentists, dentists, dentists. Orthodontists, periodontists, and those conversant in lower porcelain laminates. Lerner, Greenberg, Klemons, and Teplitsky. Donato, Eisenberger, Franzetti, and Klein. Dentists.

For decades now, the sight of the Williamsburgh Savings Bank building rising from the Brooklyn flatness has reminded people to open savings accounts, invest wisely, and brush their teeth twice a day. That is because within its light-brick facade, high above the bank vault, there lurk dentists drilling, filling, and speaking of gingivitis.

It is not entirely clear how the tallest building in Brooklyn, a bank building at that, came to be a castle of dental care. Could have been the cheap rent during the Depression. Could have been the lure of the Atlantic Terminal transportation hub across the street. Or maybe one dentist told another dentist, and, well, there went the neighborhood.

Before long, dozens of dentists were distracting their benumbed patients by pointing out the windows to a breathtaking panorama of Brooklyn and beyond. It was a jaw-dropping view, which helped with the business at hand.

"Beeueefoo!" the patients exclaimed.

Well more than one hundred dentists had offices in the building—which is actually in Fort Greene, not Williamsburg—along with lab technicians, dental-supply businesses, and the august Second District Dental Society. How many children studied the tiny tiles in the lobby's ceiling and imagined them to be the extracted teeth of other kids? How many people gazed at the building jutting from the horizon and thought of the single tooth in the maw of that hapless cartoon character, the Brooklyn Dodgers bum?

"This building has a long history with dentistry," lamented Dr. Ian Lerner, a dentist on the twenty-ninth floor. He might as well have used the past tense.

The building has only forty dentists now; new ones have not come along to replace the old ones. More devastating, though, was the thirty-five-story building's sale last week to Canyon-Johnson Urban Funds and the Dermot Company, which plan to transform it into a luxury condominium complex. The current tenants—doctors, non-profit groups, and so many dentists—have been told it's time to go. Time to pack up those pamphlets on periodontal disease.

This means Dr. Gilbert Kringstein in Suite 2301, a tenant since the mid-1960s, who remembers the convenience of practicing in a dental colony. "I'll bet you I had—on the sixteenth floor?—maybe eight referring doctors," he said. It means Dr. Gary Klemons in Suite 708, whose father, Jerry, retired in December after working in the building for fifty years. "Dad was a dental technician," he said. "He made the dentures. Actually fabricated the teeth."

And it means Dr. Lerner, who jokes that his occupancy of the highest office makes him "Brooklyn's top dentist—in a geographic sense." Devoted to his profession, he is vice president of the Second District Dental Society and even displays a "History of Dentistry" poster in the office bathroom. ("249 A.D. Apollonia, the patron saint of dentists, is burned after having her teeth knocked out. Depictions of her are usually shown with forceps.")

He is also devoted to this building, so much so that his business card depicts its famous dome and clock face. His deep understanding of its place in dental history includes this little nugget: "I think the office I have now used to be an oral surgeon's office that treated some of the Brooklyn Dodgers."

When it became clear that the luxurious renovation would not have room for dentists, Dr. Lerner became Dr. Braveheart, rallying a small band of fellow tenants to stand up for dentistry. This week, he presented the owners with a proposal to reserve some space for dental and medical suites. At the very least, he argued, tenants need more time to find or build new offices.

Andrew MacArthur, one of the principal owners, knew of Dr. Lerner's proposal, but said, "That's not in our plans." He said that some dentists in the building were close to finding office space elsewhere and that he would try to accommodate those who needed more time. But he emphasized that the owners wanted to move forward with their "major gut rehab"—a total extraction, if you will.

Suspended between its past and its future, the tallest building in Brooklyn has a spooky air these days. HSBC Bank, which sold the building, has moved out of most of the offices it occupied. Other former tenants are remembered only in the gold lettering on the frosted panes of their old offices. Abandoned sets of letters—D.D.S. and D.M.D.—are everywhere.

The other day, a dentist, surgical mask dangling from his neck, walked down the nearly empty sixteenth floor. He was whistling— maybe in sadness, or maybe in gleeful contemplation of affluent condo owners with aching teeth, and no good dentist nearby.

Shown a Door They Know So Well

These days the doormen of the Plaza stand warily at the threshold of the misty past, as though fearing a tree-clinging Central Park fog that might drift over and swallow them whole. They continue to perform their graceful ballet of at-your-service in front of the city's most storied hotel, but when they summon a taxi, the darting white of their gloves could also be signaling distress.

For nearly a century now, they and their predecessors have stood before the Plaza with a formal yet friendly bearing, reflecting an establishment that is both luxury hotel and public space—a place where a room with a king-sized bed cost $369 last night, and where restrooms are available to anyone with a modicum of Midtown savvy (down the stairs and across from the gift shop).

But the door is closing. Elad Properties, which bought the 805-room hotel for $675 million last year, plans to convert the building into condominiums, stores, and a 150-room hotel whose entrance will face a shadowed side street. All this has rattled many lives, including those of the dozen men of the palace guard, whose golden coat buttons bear the Plaza crest, and whose greeting to the world is, "Welcome to the Plaza."

Come April 30, they will say goodbye to the Plaza. Then they and some nine hundred other hotel workers—bellmen and busboys, waitresses and maids—will disappear into the blur of New York's great revolving door, not knowing whether the old place will have use for them when it reopens many months, if not years, from now.

Tony Guerrero, a Plaza doorman for sixteen years, worked the grand entrance on a recent night with an easy grace and his usual, fine view of Central Park to the left and Fifth Avenue ahead. He called, "Good evening, young ladies," to ladies of a certain age, looped Plaza tags to luggage, and tucked suitcases, men's shoes, and even a child into the back of a luxurious black S.U.V.

Standing on the hotel's steps in his gray hat and gray overcoat, he seemed rooted in the Plaza infrastructure, like some supporting concrete pillar. But the stress of an uncertain future—of how to support his family in Washington Heights—seems to have created stomach problems so severe that he is seeing a doctor on Monday.

"I've got to get the Plaza out of my system," Mr. Guerrero said. "I'll take a couple of months off, clear my mind, then try to find a job at another hotel—not that anything would be like the Plaza."

Beyond the pain of uncertainty, Mr. Guerrero and his colleagues are also suffering the pain of breakup. Like veteran police officers and old ballplayers and aging journalists, they bonded their identity to an institution and became not just doormen, but Plaza doormen. Now their hearts ache beneath those gray overcoats, because they are learning what they always knew: We are all expendable.

Who, really, holds the door for the doorman?

A couple of them will retire. But the rest of the men, many in their forties and fifties, will have to find jobs at other hotels, where their status as former Plaza doormen will mean nothing. They will be starting all over.

Miki Naftali, the president of Elad Properties, has said that his minibar hotel would retain as many as 150 unionized workers— down from the 900 working today. Yesterday, through a spokesman, he said that he would offer jobs to many, though not all, of the Plaza doormen.

But Neil Johnson, a Plaza doorman who has been active with his union, the New York Hotel and Motel Trades Council, said that information about the owner's Plaza plans have been so vague and contradictory over the past few months that "I don't trust one thing that man says."

Mr. Johnson started a recent evening shift by reminiscing with Mr. Guerrero about the lavish leftovers of divine banquets once dined upon in the employees' cafeteria downstairs, and about the oversized lockers they need to store the three different uniforms of a Plaza doorman.

"And every day we have kids tugging on our coats and asking, 'Where's Eloise?' " said Mr. Johnson, the father of a nine-year-old girl.

Out came another doorman, James O'Connell, with sixteen years invested in the Plaza and three young children who, he says, "are always anxious to tell people that my dad works at the Plaza."

Inside, past the massive chandelier that glittered like a thousand dangling diamonds, the harpist in the Palm Court played an elegant version of "Send in the Clowns." And outside, the doormen of the Plaza waited to be of service.

JUNE 26, 2004

Last in Flophouse, Alone with Bowery Ghosts

Being the last man living in one of the last flophouses on the Bowery has its benefits. No wait for a shower or a toilet. No sounds of casual sex coming from the other side of the wall. No need to keep an eye out anymore for Juliano, that big bully in stall Number 36.

Juliano died a year ago, bequeathing to George, a man of seventy-four, the odd mantle of sole inhabitant, Stevenson Hotel, 106 Bowery.

Each night George shuffles past the deserted clerk's office, where the men used to slide dollar bills through a slot under a cagelike grill. Now a folded newspaper rests on the clerk's counter, its 1990 headline of a "Missing Girl Found Slain" muffled by time and dust. On the wall is a notice bearing the names of people to contact in case of emergency: Lawrence and Juliano. Gone, and gone.

George walks along the shadowy rows of green-painted cubicles that once rented for less than five dollars a night to tenants he barely knew: the Indian man who was robbed of two hundred dollars; an Italian man named John; an old man called "the Professor." Each cubicle has a number on its door. Each cubicle has a ceiling of chicken wire. Each cubicle is unoccupied, except for Number 40. This is George's address.

Cubicle Number 40 is four feet by eight feet, maybe, and is so cramped by clothing and the mattress that the door opens only a crack. To get in, George removes his jacket and slides his old body through. He loops heavy wire around a hook on the inside of the door; this helps him feel safer.

Here, among flophouse ghosts, is where George sleeps, to the concern of many people trying to help him and to the consternation of a landlord who has other plans for the $1.2 million building. George, you see, refuses to leave.

George prefers that his Greek surname not appear in print; it might not put him in the best light among people he knows. He has no teeth, one eye that is sightless and another not much better, and long fingernails that jut like blades from his dirty hands. He also has diabetes, and lives on about $660 a month in disability, much of which is spent on cheap Chinese buffets and subway trips to Astoria, where he buys Greek newspapers and small cubes of feta cheese.

Once, he was a published poet. But fortune has been a stranger since he came to the United States in the mid-1960s, what with the loss of a restaurant job, the eviction from an apartment, the mental and physical problems. In 1980 he took one bed among the dozens at the Stevenson, one of the many flophouses that defined the Bowery.

The Four Roses whiff to the Bowery gradually evaporated as real estate values rose. Speculators bought the flophouses and tried to push out the struggling and broken men, sometimes with cash, sometimes with violence. The new owner of the Stevenson, Chun Kien Realty, paid many tenants to move to another flophouse nearby, but some refused, including George.

Things got tense. In 1989, George charged that his belongings—including a manuscript of poetry—had been stolen, and that one of the owners had broken into his cubicle, injuring him. But George was in the hospital the day of the trial, and his charges went nowhere.

The landlord tried, but failed, to evict George after he stopped paying his five dollars or so a day in rent. Then came settlement talks that ended when the landlord decided that George was asking too much money for the gift of his departure.

"He's very traumatized by the assault that took place and the attempts to get him out," said Marilyn Nieves, a caseworker with the Institute for the Puerto Rican/Hispanic Elderly. "He's also very stubborn."

So is Chun Kien Realty, which cannot redevelop the building until George is gone. Laurence Olive, the lawyer for the landlord, said that he had no answer for why the owner never resolved the matter of George; perhaps, he said, it was merely a case of "mutual accommodation."

George's advocates, though, say the landlord's strategy has been simple. Someday, George will die.

Years passed. One by one, other men died. One day a foul smell led to the discovery of the body of Juliano in cubicle Number 36. George eulogizes the man this way: "Too many times, he hit me."

George was alone. Negotiations began again, with the landlord offering first $50,000 and then $75,000 for George to leave. George responded by raising his demand, with $130,000 growing to $200,000.

George explains his reasoning this way: He needs $30,000 for dental implants and $40,000 for eye surgery, which almost eats up the landlord's best offer. He also needs money for rent and for furniture, he says—although his fixation on that assault allegation many years ago suggests a desire for some payback. He also does not like change.

Thinking that a judge might resolve the matter, Ms. Nieves persuaded George to file a complaint in Housing Court about sealed-up windows, falling plaster, and other code violations. This led to an impromptu visit to the Stevenson Hotel by Judge Kevin McClanahan, along with an entourage of lawyers, court officers—and George.

At a court hearing a few days later, Judge McClanahan said that George's living quarters—a flophouse in suspended animation—appalled him, and he wondered aloud whether the landlord had decided "to wait everybody out."

The judge then tried to reason with George, his coaxing words translated into Greek by an interpreter. It would be in your best interests to move out, he told George. The landlord is offering a reasonable settlement, and what you ask is excessive.

George's body language said that he would not lower his $200,000 demand, so the judge asked that he at least consider moving into the flophouse's old day room, near the clerk's counter. This way, the judge said, he would have light, ventilation, and space, including room enough for at least a hot plate.

Again came averted eyes and slumped shoulders that said no. George says that he is safer in his fetid cubicle.

Judge McClanahan told George that he was engaging in a fruitless waiting game with the landlord. "And who do you think will last the longest?" he asked the hunched man.

The frustrated judge advised Mr. Olive to have his client address the outstanding violations, scheduled another hearing for mid-August, and moved on to the next difficult case.

Afterward, Mr. Olive said that he doubted the landlord would raise its "substantial" offer, and wondered whether George was in his right mind. Mary Rosado, a lawyer appointed by the court to represent George's best interests, said that she would continue to seek a settlement but was worried about how the case would play out for her client.

"He doesn't realize that he's hurting himself," she said.

George left the court building, on Centre Street, and worked his way through Lower Manhattan to a place once called Skid Row. He muttered along the way about that assault back in 1989, about the high cost of Greek newspapers, about his lost poetry.

A few steps up the Bowery, he stopped in front of the old flophouse, key in trembling hand.

APRIL 23, 2005

At Howard Johnson's, a Final Few Scoops of Pistachio

The longtime manager of the last Howard Johnson's in the city had only a moment to spare. He seemed distracted, even harried, as though he sensed a clamor for menus from all those empty orange-and-brown booths surrounding him.

First, he wanted to know something: What is this about?

When posed inside the time warp that is the Howard Johnson's, this question takes on greater weight somehow; it is mystically dipped in a metaphysical Frialator before being presented with garnish on a chipped ceramic plate. What is this about?

One answer came from the aquarium-like view of Times Square that his restaurant's large windows offered. There, on the other side of the glass, the Broadway parade flowed past, its participants oblivious to the massive HOWARD JOHNSON's sign above, blinking in neon orange and blue and featuring that familiar trio: Simple Simon, the Pieman, and a salivating dog.

People did not stop to read the sun-faded advertisements whose words strive to be Rat Pack cool yet ache with Perry Como earnestness. It's Happy Hour from four to seven, with all drinks just $3.75—"except for premium brands." May we suggest a decanter of manhattans, or martinis, or daiquiris? Your Host of Broadway Welcomes You.

Around the corner, on West Forty-sixth Street, another ad promotes the seafood at Howard Johnson's—"A Wish for Fish!"—with an artist's rendition of a clam strip platter that even Simple Simon's slobbering dog would pass up. Oh, and free hors d'oeuvres served from four to nine.

What is this about?

For nearly a half century, this Howard Johnson's has been an orange-and-blue stitch in the crazed Times Square quilt, dispensing clam strips and milkshakes to the wide-eyed masses.

In many ways it has served as a mooring for visitors adrift in the asphalt Midtown sea.

Here was a Howard Johnson's, nearly identical in ambience and cuisine to the hundreds of others scattered like rainbow sprinkles along the highways of America. Daddy, can we stop? The answer was sometimes yes and sometimes no, but you had to ask. After all, they had twenty-eight flavors of ice cream.

Today, only a dozen or so of the restaurants remain. And soon that will be minus the one with the best location of them all, the Howard Johnson's in Times Square.

The owners, the Rubinstein family, have signed a contract to sell the four-story, mid-nineteenth-century building to a Jeff Sutton, who has no interest in muscling scoops of ice cream from ice-flecked tubs. "It's unlikely it would be developed as anything but a great retail box," said Mr. Sutton's broker, C. Bradley Mendelson. "And there will be a great signage component."

Human nature almost demands that you weep for Howard Johnson's, as it prepares to take its place beside other sentimental Times Square discards: the Horn & Hardart Automat, Hubert's Museum, on and on.

But if you were honest, you would admit to liking the thought of Howard Johnson's more than the reality of it.

If you went there at all, it was either to affect ironic hipness or to imagine your parents there, in their happy times before you, sipping ice cream sodas after a show.

In the encroaching shadows of a late afternoon, Times Square continued its brassy and boisterous assault upon the senses. Over here, teenage girls screamed for a television camera; over there, two men handed out fliers, one for Falun Gong, the other for a strip club.

But inside the all-too-quiet Howard Johnson's, Happy Hour ticked away without chuckle or grin. No one sat at the bar in the back nursing a Rob Roy, or a Rusty Nail, or an Apricot Sour. No one set aside dignity to ask for something called the California: amaretto, peach schnapps, coconut, and pineapple.

A man walked in and asked the waitress point-blank, "They're closing this place, right?" Stunned by his forwardness, she could only say, "Yeah."

The waiter at the ice cream counter seconded his colleague. "I think it's going to be at the end of the summer," he said, looking through the window at all the people not coming in for a scoop of butter pecan.

Happy Hour crept along. A middle-aged woman sat in one booth, alone, eating French fries and staring down West Forty-sixth Street. In another booth, the tortilla-shell remnants of a long-gone someone's lunch sat untouched for more than an hour. The restaurant's manager appeared, disappeared, reappeared, then asked: What is this about?

The imminent closing of this Howard Johnson's, of course.

"We know nothing as of now," he said, then hurried off to tend to phantom customers. And you wished him twenty-eight flavors of happiness.

Rents Soar. Stores Close. Life Goes On, a Little Poorer.

The father and son keep the letter in a lockbox behind the counter of their hardware store on the Upper East Side, out of sight but never out of mind.

"Gentlemen," it begins. "As of May 1, your rent for the narrow storefront at 1396 Madison Avenue will double to $6,600 a month. Should you not acknowledge your acceptance of the above, we will assume that you will be vacating the premises by and not later than April 29, 2005.

"Very truly yours," it ends. David Harounian, landlord, 261 Fifth Avenue.

The father and son did not write back. How could any letter convey the despair caused by a nonnegotiable doubling of the rent? How could it capture the decades of sweat equity invested by the father, a Holocaust survivor, or the pride that a son took in carrying on the family business, M and E Madison Hardware?

How could they write "Dear" in front of their landlord's name?

"I'm a capitalist too," the son says. "But how much money is enough?"

Businesses come and go in this city. Neighborhoods change, owners die, partners quarrel, rents go up. Call it commerce; call it life.

But as Manhattan gradually morphs into a precious outdoor mall for the affluent, let us remember what it loses in the process: character; neighborhood distinctions; places like this hardware store, where one hundred credit accounts are kept for good customers, and the kids all call the father Pops.

That father sits at his counter, eating a cheese sandwich from home. His name is Manny Schwarz; the *t* in the family name got misplaced somehow when he arrived here by boat in 1950. He is small, unshaven, nearly eighty, and he doesn't want to talk about it, but he will.

He was born in Poland, in a small town called Koropiec that is now part of Ukraine. His father, Elie, died in a Nazi work camp. His mother, Golda, died in what he calls "one of the actions." Their son was lucky, if you can call it that. He escaped from a work camp and cowered for more than two years in a shallow, hay-covered cellar that a friendly farmer built in his stable.

As he talks of those days of terror, a customer walks in and asks for a specific kind of appliance bulb.

"Sure," Mr. Schwarz says. "Do you remember if it was clear or frosted?"

With the customer satisfied, he returns reluctantly to his story. He survived the war, met his future wife, Genia, in an Austrian refugee camp, and came to the United States. "By the way," he says, "what does this have to do with the store?"

"Manny, that's what's called background," his son, Eric, says.

In 1953, or maybe 1954, Mr. Schwarz opened a five and dime in this cramped space, replacing a Chinese hand laundry. The landlord, a Mr. Bunwin, charged him $125 a month, but gave him six months' free rent.

"He wanted me to succeed," Mr. Schwarz says. "He was an immigrant, too."

He says he did all right for a while, selling "bobby pins and whatnot, thread and needles." Then a huge five and dime opened up a few blocks away, forcing him to change his product line to housewares.

He worked six days a week in close quarters, sharing a bathroom with the dry cleaners on one side and inhaling the greasy exhaust of the diner from the other side. And on the seventh day, he drove to his wholesalers to buy merchandise.

Mr. Schwarz worked alone for twenty-five years, and then, gradually, his son began helping out. After Eric Schwarz graduated from college, he worked full time in the store and nudged his father into changing the product line again—to hardware. Their world became one of flathead screws and saws, caulking guns and hammers.

The father and son became partners, and best friends. The son says that his father taught him how to cultivate loyalty. Fix the baby carriages without charge. Wave off the carpenter's dollar when all he wants is a couple of screws. Be a good neighbor.

Commuting from their homes in Queens, they developed their own idiosyncratic routine. For example, every hour an egg timer on the shelf rings, and Eric Schwarz grabs some quarters from the cash register and runs to fill two parking meters.

The routine was disrupted last year when Rafael Sassouni, the building's managing agent, warned Eric that the $3,300-a-month rent would be going up—many times more than the usual 5 percent annual increase.

Eric Schwarz, forty-five, became so depressed that he stayed home for a month. After that, he imagined for a while that the landlord was bluffing or would change his mind—until the arrival of that letter, now in the lockbox. Including real estate taxes, the Schwarzes would have to pay more than seven thousand dollars a month—for about 360 square feet of grimy space in a century-old building.

Neither Mr. Harounian nor Mr. Sassouni—whose wife, Bita, is listed in city records as part-owner—returned telephone calls. Mr. Harounian's letter, though, refers to "the need to charge you the market rate."

To which Eric Schwarz mutters, "These guys make up the market rate every six months."

He looks out onto Madison Avenue, past window signs announcing the store's imminent closing—"This neighborhood has been like our home and you have been like family to us," the signs say—and talks about all the other small stores that will surely be displaying similar signs. In the background, his father is getting angry again. "I live here," Manny Schwarz says. "I come here and my life starts again."

Another customer stops by. "I'm sorry you're leaving," she says. "We'll miss you."

"We'll miss you too," Eric Schwarz says.

Then the egg timer went off. And an old man watched from his little store as his son went out to feed the meters.

A Gas Station Filled Up with Regulars

The owner of Monetti's Shell station in Howard Beach is talking about neighborhood when the pay phone rings in his scuffed little office. A short man with a silvery cane appears from nowhere to answer it.

"Excuse me, Joe," he says to the owner. "A Mrs. Goldstein on the line."

Joe Monetti handles the call with the reassuring calm one seeks from car mechanics and doctors. Then he returns to discussing how the imminent closing of his full-service gas station after forty-three years will affect so many people, and not just the older folks who have never pumped their own gas.

Mr. Monetti, an oversize shock absorber of a man, explains that he will be moving his garage to Ozone Park, two miles away. Two miles is a walk in the park for some in Queens, and for others, a journey to the moon. "They're in a panic," he says of some customers. "They think they won't be able to find it."

Again the telephone rings, and again that short man materializes to answer it. "Excuse me, Joe," he says.

He vanishes as quickly as he appeared, and Mr. Monetti is asked if the man works for him. "Nah," he says, smiling. "He just hangs out here."

The man, a Con Edison retiree named Joel, lost his mother nearly two years ago. Now he spends his time not at the water's edge in the Rockaways but at this Shell station on Cross Bay Boulevard. "He's here before I am in the morning," Mr. Monetti says. "And if he isn't, you start to get nervous."

Joel is one of several regulars, you might call them, who linger at the Shell. There's Tony Tools, who parks his truck on the side. And Gagoots, the fruit-and-vegetable salesman. And Carmine, a baggage handler at Kennedy International Airport who gets teased because he used to work for long-gone Pan Am. "He put them out of business," Mr. Monetti jokes. "Probably stealing all their nuts."

And here comes Maurice, who bakes cakes when he's not fueling airplanes at Kennedy. The other day he presented the gas station gang with a farewell butter-pecan beauty. "I like baking cakes; I just don't eat 'em," Maurice says to a stranger. "I'll make you one, too. How long you be here for?"

A Nissan Pathfinder eases into the station. "Here's another one, this guy with the oxygen tank," Mr. Monetti says, referring to Bob, a retired bank analyst. "He's coming just to sit here, too. That's why we have so many stools."

On some afternoons, so many regulars congregate in the office that customers can barely reach the counter. The men settle onto stools whose cushions are adorned with an oil-filter company's yellow logo, and they talk, talk, talk, while the cars pull in and out and the air guns in the bay loosen and tighten lug nuts, *vvvit, vvvit, vvvit.*

Mr. Monetti looks past the American flag decals affixed to his office's gritty window, out onto the hypnotizing flow of Cross Bay Boulevard.

His father, Louie, opened this station in 1962, when fruit trees used to grow next door, where the florist shop is now, and clam shacks and boatyards lined the boulevard. See that nail salon across the street? Used to be a fish store with a smokehouse out back. Many a lunch of smoked eels came out of that place, right to this counter.

Louie died years ago, and Joey became Joe the Boss, den mother to the regulars. But on April Fool's Day, he was informed that Shell was not going to renew the lease for the lot, and that a Hess station would be opening soon—self-serve, no doubt. So, at fifty-two, he has to start over in some industrial park in Ozone Park.

"How are things, Mr. Boss?" asks Carmine, the baggage handler, though he knows the answer. "You don't find men like Mr. Monetti. He comes far and in between, Joe the Boss."

Joel, the man with the cane, agrees. He points to a 1989 Toyota Camry in near mint condition that he bought a couple of years ago. "Would you believe me if I tell you that it sat in a garage for fourteen and a half years? Guess how many miles."

He barely waits for a guess. "Three thousand eighty-three," he says. "Three. Oh. Eighty. Three. Go ahead, open it up. Sit in it."

And how did Joel find such a car? Joe the Boss, of course.

But when this Shell morphs into a Hess, a seismic moment that will slow the boulevard flow for not one second, will Joel drive his Camry the two extra miles to Ozone Park?

"Sure," he says. "If they'll have me."

MARCH 29, 2006

Wriggling Through the Cracks in the Urban Facade

Holes dapple this great city. Some are imagined, allowing us to slip into private catacombs of the mind. Some are real, allowing us to take the A train. And some are surreal, hidden portals to the past, known to a curious few.

Steve Duncan taps some loose tobacco into paper and lights it, perhaps because this is what an urban explorer is supposed to do. He conducts a quick inventory of the equipment in his backpack: headlamps, rock-climbing ropes, gloves, nylon ladder, and a hand-size meter that measures oxygen levels in the air and can detect your most common poisonous gases.

Check, check, check, check, and check. Now to find that secret hole, a hole that reveals a part of who we were, and how we came to be who we are. He crosses when the light turns green, and continues through the sun-brightened valley of brick known as Northern Manhattan.

Down and around he goes, this way and that, with exact coordinates

left vague for legal reasons; namely, that this might not be exactly legal. Finally he finds the underground gateway he seeks. He looks up
to make sure no one is watching, clears away some bramble and debris, and slips like a startled rabbit into the earth.

Mr. Duncan, twenty-seven, is not a son of this city, though he
might as well be. Raised in Maryland, he graduated from Columbia
University with a bachelor's degree in urban studies, with an emphasis, it seems, on the subterranean. He now describes himself as a
"guerrilla historian in Gotham," disappearing through the cracks in
the urban facade in search of the abandoned, the forgotten, the invisible. He climbs, crawls, and shimmies into the deserted crevices of a
crowded city, returning to the living with evocative stories and photographs: a closed subway station adorned with eighties-era graffiti; a
ghostly, scuttled tugboat on Staten Island; an abandoned mausoleum
with human bones exposed.

"The city has layers," he says later. "We normally operate on one
layer. I like to go below that to another layer, or above, to another layer.
That's when I feel like I've gone somewhere."

In quest of that other layer, Mr. Duncan wriggles his wiry frame
through a two-foot-wide metal grill and into a long, round tunnel
about three feet wide. Up ahead cool darkness awaits, disturbed only by
the jittery shaft of light from his headlamp. Flecks of tunnel rust pepper
his hair. Clouds form with his every breath. His voice ec-ec-echoes.

The tunnel, which he describes as a massive overflow valve, briefly
gives way to a large square hole that leads ten feet down to what looks
like mucky, yucky nothingness. There it is, he says, with unabashed
reverence: the Old Croton Aqueduct.

Peering into the hole, a visitor might think—in fact, does think:
I crawled thirty feet underground, like some six-foot *Rattus norvegicus,*
for this? A wall of brick and some watery stuff on the ground that
I don't want to think about?

Headlamp shining, Mr. Duncan explains.

By the 1830s, the growing city of New York had an inadequate,
polluted water supply that contributed a lot to the outbreak of disease
and little to the fighting of fires. So, with the help of thousands of laborers, most of them Irish immigrants, the city built a forty-one-mile
conduit from the Croton Dam in Westchester to a reservoir in what is
now the Great Lawn in Central Park.

Among the most spectacular elements of this ambitious public works project was the construction of the High Bridge across the Harlem River to carry the aqueduct to Manhattan from the Bronx. Pointing into the darkness, Mr. Duncan explains that if you were to walk way, way down this leg of the aqueduct and turn right, you'd be inside the bridge.

The city welcomed the fresh, revivifying water in 1842 with a thirty-eight-gun salute, a parade, and a seven-verse song, sung by a choir of two hundred at City Hall. It began:

> *Gushing from this living fountain,*
> *Music pours a falling strain,*
> *As the Goddess of the Mountain*
> *Comes with all her sparkling train.*

Within a few decades, another, much larger aqueduct was built to address the city's ever-growing thirst, and by the second half of the twentieth century, the "Old" Croton Aqueduct was dry and largely forgotten. Now, Mr. Duncan stands in its hollowness and marvels, calling it "the lifeblood that saved the city."

More than eight feet high and more than seven feet wide, it is a thing of beauty: glazed brick, held together by hydraulic cement, curving seamlessly and endlessly into the darkness. Imagine the engineers, conceiving, calculating, designing. Imagine the laborers, digging the dirt, laying the brick, clearing the way.

Imagine the first roaring gush through this very spot, on its way to bless Manhattan.

Here, in this hole, Mr. Duncan lets that wave wash over him.

A Thousand Words? This Stash Is Worth a Trillion

It began with Moe. Just Moe.

He spent his days clipping photographs and drawings of everything and anything, using scissors large enough to pass as shears. He smoked cigarettes, played the ponies, used a pay phone for all business, and heated his coffee with a device that dangled from the ceiling light. He had his own way, Moe did.

Long ago, before the Internet, Moe ran a company called Reference Pictures. Say you were an illustrator trying to conjure a unicorn, or an art director trying to envision the Grand Canyon for some advertising pitch. You'd call up Moe, and soon a messenger would appear with an envelope of inspiration: images of unicorns, images of canyons, culled from assorted periodicals by Moe and his mighty shears.

Moe died in the early 1980s, leaving to posterity his many pictures, his rotary pay phone, and a long wooden table bearing telltale signs of a life of distraction, the burn marks of forgotten cigarettes.

Imagine the poor executor of Moe's estate. Who in the world would want so many boxes of pictures, all categorized according to a system known only to a dead man?

Arnold Blumberg, it turned out. One of Moe's old clients, he saw an auction notice and could not abide the thought of all those images lost to the ages. He bid and won the treasure trove of Moe.

"He had it in his mind that he had to have all these pictures," said Mr. Blumberg's wife, Doris. "It was completely emotional."

By this point in their long married life, the Blumbergs of Queens had enough distraction.

Arnold was an artist and an art director for a large advertising firm. Doris was a jewelry designer and a saleswoman. Their children, Hilary and Denise, were studying to become doctors, which meant endless tuition bills.

But Mr. Blumberg had bid with his heart, and now the Blumbergs owned whatever was behind a certain door in the Flatiron district.

"Dust," he recalled.

And beneath that dust, boxes and boxes and boxes of photographs, spilling from above, overflowing from below.

"Doris," Mr. Blumberg said, "it's yours."

Mrs. Blumberg spent a few months trying to break the Moe code of what was where and why; she found herself thinking, "Now, where would he put this?" She bought new boxes, began replenishing the files with images that she cut from periodicals herself, and focused on developing a Doris system.

For example, she said, Moe kept one box called, simply, Dogs. If a client called for images of a dachshund, he would flip through dog pictures with a wet thumb until he found dachshunds. Now, under the Doris system, which includes eighteen boxes of dog files, you look up dachshunds—and they're right there.

Soon Reference Pictures was again serving the needs of artists, designers, fashion directors, and anyone else who wanted visual kickstarts to enhance their ideas. Its files grew in number and in girth, as the Blumbergs and some employees snipped and filed pictures of everything.

"You could never tell what somebody would ask for," Mrs. Blumberg said, recalling the time someone requested an image of an elephant on water skis.

The Reference Pictures office has six rooms of shelves and file cabinets, all groaning under the weight of photographs—and each one, it seems, holding a special place in Mrs. Blumberg's heart.

"There's just everything," she said, sitting in front of boxes labeled Circus (Clowns: B&W, Bozo the Clown, Full and Half-Fig Clowns, Hobo Clown—Emmett Kelly) and Auto (Parts: Freshener,

Fuel Injector, Gas Caps, Gas Cans, Hood Ornaments, Horns). "This place is filled with ideas."

Dare to try and stump Mrs. Blumberg, and you lose. Ask for photos of Tarzan, and you have your choice of Elmo Lincoln, Johnny Weissmuller, Buster Crabbe, Lex Barker, and anyone else who ever donned the loincloth. Ask for Veronica Lake, and there she is, peeking from behind those golden bangs. Ask for 1950s automobiles, and you're told to be more specific. The Nash? The Willys station wagon? The Thunderbird? Which year?

"If you look at the Internet, you don't see this," Mr. Blumberg said, rubbing a photograph of a 1957 Oldsmobile Golden Rocket 88 Holiday Coupe. "You don't hold it in your hand."

The Internet, he said, has changed how we experience the visual. Where art directors once lingered at Reference Pictures, studying the elongated body of a dachshund, they now sit at their desks and simply Google a dachshund. But would the Internet, say, show a dachshund from the front, back, sideways, trotting in a park—and encased in a hot dog bun?

That is but one example of why the Blumbergs see their collection as an invaluable reference library: millions of tactile images, all cataloged, giving specific detail to the past and offering creative energy for the future.

But the couple say that it is time to try something else: retirement, for example. Who, then, will buy and preserve the millions of images assembled by Doris, Arnold, and long-gone Moe?

"We can't keep being altruistic," Mr. Blumberg said.

"It's for younger people," Mrs. Blumberg started.

"To take it to the next step," Mr. Blumberg finished.

The Blumbergs fell silent for a moment in the midst of their collection, one that includes six files for Radio (Announcers, Transmitters, Walkie-Talkies . . .), three for Lamps (Assorted, Aladdin, Candles . . .), and nine for intangible Love.

In This Mess, Memory Lane Is a Foot Wide

From somewhere deep in the canyons of memorabilia there comes a faint crash, and what has fallen this time is anyone's guess. It could be that an avalanche of dead-celebrity accessories has sent Vincent Price's top hat toppling. Or maybe a spill of publicity stills has oiled the floor with forced grins.

No one panics, though. Landslides of ephemera are commonplace in the Times Square office of Joe Franklin, city institution. So common, in fact, that picking up what has fallen is one of the assigned duties of his faithful office manager, Jose Lara.

"I'll pick that up," Mr. Lara says. "Not a problem."

Reporting that Joe Franklin is a New York character is like reporting that the Empire State Building is tall. Many know that in a half-century career as a television and radio talk-show host, he has interviewed tens of thousands of would-bes and never-weres, and that he has amassed enough valuable and worthless relics to clutter two New York apartments, one Florida home, and this office.

"I just want to know it's here," explains Mr. Franklin.

"He doesn't want to let go," adds Mr. Lara.

As the two men reflect on Mr. Franklin's quirky habit, they are dwarfed by mounds of memorabilia so high that only a rock climber would dream of reaching certain corners of the office. That is, if footholds could be found in the newspapers reporting Allied advances, or in the old 78's, including Billy Murray's Prohibition-era lament "How Are You Goin' to Wet Your Whistle?"

This Collyer Brothers–like collection grows by the day, as people hungering for recognition drop off their demos, as retirees moving to Florida find items in the attic that should be entrusted to Joe. Things accumulate so rapidly that every now and then Mr. Franklin pays a man one hundred dollars to clear a footwide path through the office.

But here is the news: The stuff is beginning to get on Mr. Franklin's nerves, ever so slightly. So he is planning to put it all—even that cracked Jimmy Dorsey record—into storage. "It's gotten out of control," he says. "I'm a little bit overwhelmed."

His collection follows him wherever he goes, like some material manifestation of all he has seen and done in his seventy-four years. Detritus engulfs him as he hunches in his chair, answering the hundreds of calls that jangle his two Princess phones every day ("Breakfast? Don't forget me." Click).

He is proud of all that he has saved, and brags that he and Mr. Lara have a better than even chance of locating what he needs. "I say, 'Get me half a dozen Fred Allen radio scripts for the radio nostalgia convention,'" Mr. Franklin says. "And he knows where to look." He goes through fifteen bags until he finds them.

But his acquisitions can tease as well as please. Lost somewhere in these piles is the monogrammed wristwatch that Veronica Lake once gave him. Lost too is Al Jolson's razor. "I know it's in there," Mr. Franklin says. "I saw it five, six years ago."

Auctioning a few items hardly made a dent, and Mr. Franklin refuses to have his stuff archived or organized. "No, no, no, no," Mr. Lara says. "If I clean up, he won't find anything, and I'll get fired."

Mr. Franklin says he has no choice but to put everything in cardboard boxes and have them carted away to a storage facility, beginning next month. "The only things in here in about six weeks will be me and Jose," Mr. Franklin calls out from somewhere.

Mr. Lara, forty-three, who has worked for Mr. Franklin for seven years, says that he has grown accustomed to his unique workplace. Stepping carefully along the cleared path, he leads an expedition that includes stops before an old tuxedo hanging from a pipe and a wall of

unalphabetized CDs. "This section here is the seventies and sixties,"
he says. "This here, the forties up to the nineties."

He points to a room that has been inaccessible for years, and then
to a ten-foot column of record albums. "Last time I searched up there
was three or four years ago," he says. "And I haven't been up there
again." An errant touch of a hand, and artifacts leak onto the floor,
including a Nat King Cole album and an old Zachary Scott movie
poster. "It'll go in, it'll go in," Mr. Lara says as he shoves the material
back into the fresh crevice.

Mr. Franklin joins in the expedition. "Those are the hats of Edward G. Robinson, Al Jolson, Eddie Cantor, Rudy Vale, Kate Smith,"
he says, nodding toward the sky. "I'm a fanatic on hats."

Something somewhere falls to the ground.

"Try not to mess up the office, Jose," Mr. Franklin says. And both
men smile.

PART III

Suzanne DeChillo

Seizing the New York Day

Where Grace Knows No Age, and Stardust Is No Memory

They have the room for an hour. Marge slips into silvery pumps, while Donald shuffles in soft-shoe anticipation. She rises, ready. He presses "Play."

Sweet "Stardust" fills the air, courtesy of the late Artie Shaw and his orchestra. Marge and Donald begin to dance a dance of their own design, with spins, kicks, and glorious sweeps of graceful limbs.

No flubs, no grunts, no soft mutters of one-two-three, one-two-three. Only the pure, precise joy of two pros you might remember.

Marge is eighty-six. Donald is eighty-five, but brags that he'll be eighty-six in January. Twice a week, when schedules allow, these two friends rent a studio room in the theater district to dance on a shoe-scraped gray floor. The only ones in the audience are usually those reflected in the mirrored wall: a small woman with a coif of silver gray, and a tall man with hair gone thin and white.

They stride onto their private stage and begin their dance with finger turns that send Marge twirling like a music-box figurine beneath

Donald's outstretched arm, as the instrumental version of "Stardust" in the background summons to mind the unspoken lyrics: "Love is now the stardust of yesterday, the music of the years gone by."

Marge is Marge Champion. Nearly seventy years ago, animators for Walt Disney used her as the central live-action model in drawing *Snow White and the Seven Dwarfs.* When you see Snow White dancing, you are seeing young Marge dancing. When you see Snow White shooing Dopey and Doc, you are seeing young Marge shooing imaginary dwarfs.

The same with the Blue Fairy in *Pinocchio;* the same with the Hippopotamus Ballerina in *Fantasia.*

Nearly sixty years ago, she and her husband, Gower, became the dancing heirs to Fred Astaire and Ginger Rogers. They performed in nightclubs across the country, emerged as two of the earliest stars of television, and appeared in several movies for Metro-Goldwyn-Mayer, including *Show Boat* in 1951. Here is one measure of her fame back then: When she had an appendectomy in 1955, it made the news.

And Donald is Donald Saddler. He worked for MGM too, in the chorus, but you missed him if you blinked. There: the back of his head in *Rosalie,* 1937, with Nelson Eddy and Eleanor Powell. There: the side of his face in *You'll Never Get Rich,* 1941, with Astaire and Rita Hayworth.

But fame came soon enough. A successful dancer and founding member of what became American Ballet Theater, he was a featured performer in *High Button Shoes,* a Broadway hit in 1947, and emerged as one of entertainment's premier choreographers. He twice won Tonys for choreography: in 1953, for *Wonderful Town*—in which he helped Rosalind Russell to summon her comedic grace—and in 1971, for *No, No, Nanette.* He knew all the stars of Broadway; he called Bernstein Lenny.

Marge and Donald glide across the gray as though on air. Their elegant dance includes a series of moves and steps that are complicated but second nature by now. Here, in a tiny, third-floor room on West Forty-seventh Street, two people celebrate ballroom and ballet; Vernon and Irene Castle; Fred and Ginger; nightclubs; MGM; Broadway.

Marge smiles as she dances. Gower Champion, her ex-husband but so much more, died in 1980, a few hours before another show he had directed, *42nd Street,* was to open. Several months later, her husband,

Boris Sagal, a film director, died in a helicopter accident. A few years later, her younger son, Blake, died in a car crash, at twenty-five.

She kicks her leg high.

Donald smiles too, though his is smaller, as if in gentleman's deference to hers. Many of his close friends have died over the years, and, out of love and a sense of propriety, he has arranged memorial services befitting their stature. Jerome Robbins, the choreographer. Alexandra Danilova, the ballerina. So many gone.

He cradles his pirouetting partner in his arms.

A few years ago, Marge asked Donald if he would dance with her at a tribute to MGM musicals, at Carnegie Hall. He said he would be delighted. In a room filled with the stars from another Hollywood, the real Hollywood, Marge and Donald stopped the show.

They danced together again, in 2001, in the Broadway revival of *Follies.* Since then they have made a few other public appearances, but mostly now, they dance for themselves.

She exercises and practices yoga. He does Pilates. And before each dancing session in this small room, they play the blood-pumping theme to *Chariots of Fire* while they do fifteen minutes of squats and stretches, as much to focus the mind as to prepare the body. Then comes "Stardust."

The man who helped Rosalind Russell spins and catches the woman who was Snow White. She bows to the mirror. They walk off together.

FEBRUARY 7, 2004

Miss a Catch? Life Goes On, Ordinarily

The word wafted across the stillness of the night as though it had broken loose from someone else's dream. In the early-hour quiet of Midwood, Brooklyn, it seemed so completely out of context, this word that few want to hear and no one ever wants to say.

Help!

It came from the lips of a young woman in pajamas, perched on the front-porch roof of a house set supernaturally aglow by the fresh fire consuming the place her family called home. In her arms she held her daughter, also in pajamas and just three.

Help! Help!

Suddenly, a stranger emerged from the Brooklyn Avenue freeze-frame. He called up: Throw the baby! I will catch her! Hurry! Throw the baby.

The woman, Nicole Walkes, hesitated. She was nineteen years old, and new to adulthood. Behind her, a fire that would kill her own mother; before her, a stranger urging her to part with her baby, her Tiara. She kept hesitating, and he kept calling up.

I promise! I will catch the baby!

On the words of a stranger, the young mother tossed her toddler into the cold night air.

The stranger's name is Alberto Wickehem, and he says that he has "excellent" hands. He played a lot of football in his day, first at Midwood High School and then for a couple of semiprofessional teams. "I had my game on," the former halfback says.

It has been more than a decade now since he last played, but no matter: He still has that solid build, and he still has the hands. What's more, this stretch of Brooklyn is home field to him. He has lived in Midwood for most of the last twenty-nine years, ever since he moved here from Costa Rica at the age of ten.

"They know me," he says of his neighborhood.

One evening last week, he left Midwood to work his usual shift as a maintenance worker in a fifty-story office building in Lower Manhattan. As the lawyers and stockbrokers leave the building, he comes in—to strip and wax their floors, shampoo their carpets, clean their restrooms, take out their garbage.

He punched out at 12:21 A.M. and caught a ride with his friend, Horacio, back to a street corner in Midwood. He walked through the sleep of Brooklyn Avenue to the second-floor apartment he shares with his brother Eduardo. He showered, grabbed a roast beef hero, and plopped down to watch his favorite sports program.

"That's my thing," he says.

When he heard words that were not emanating from his television, he figured that neighbors were quarreling. He heard the words again—Help! Help!—and looked out his front window to see flames roiling in the house across the street. He hustled outside in his shorts, slippers, and a long-sleeve T-shirt.

Seeing the woman and child on the roof, he ran to the foot of the burning house: close enough to feel the heat pressing against his body, to smell things melting, to worry about his own safety. He thought of his children—Alicia, ten, and Alberto Jr., eight—who are living with his ex-wife in Trenton, and he stretched out his hands.

"Listen," he told the crying young mother. "The fire's on the second floor now. Throw the baby to me."

The clock was winding down. The game was almost over. The play had to be made.

Because of the bushes along the house, Ms. Walkes could not just drop Tiara; she would have to toss her several feet out and a dozen feet down. But Mr. Wickehem felt the brashness known to good athletes.

"I had confidence that I would catch the baby," he says.

In the minutes, hours, and days to come, so much would happen.

Firefighters, as many as 175, would spend four hours reining in the four-alarm blaze. Investigators would determine that an overloaded electrical cord had caused the fire. A demolition team would raze the damaged house, leaving a dirt lot dotted with charred wood.

And young Tiara would be in attendance at Calvary and St. Cyprian's Episcopal Church for the funeral of her grandmother, Beverley Joseph Walkes, a native of Barbados who had spent her last moments rousing others to safety.

But none of this was known yet to the mother on the roof or to the man on the ground. The child sailed through the Midwood air and landed safely in the arms of an old football player, who would say later that he cradled his catch as though she were his own.

May the Floor Rise Up to Meet You

Your man carried his black bag of magic into the evening quiet of a Sunnyside bar.

He scuttled past the bottles and taps to enter a dry back room where the finish had long since been scuffed from the center of the wood floor. Home for the night.

Out of the bag came a portable compact disc player. Out too came a stack of index cards covered with block-letter notations, and a dozen CDs, from *Heather Breeze* to *Dance Music of Ireland, Volume 13*.

"This is more social than anything," explained the man, Denis Keane, a protagonist in a familiar New York story: came from County Kerry in 1956, served in the Army, joined the carpenters' union, raised a family, opened a couple of restaurants. Now seventy, he lives in Bayside and, with his lady friend, Eileen Cotter, teaches his passion, Irish set dancing.

Students trickled in. Here was Billy Haugh, over from Clare since 1962, and his wife, Kathleen, from Roscommon. Here were the McGrory sisters from Donegal—Philomena, Maggie, and Anne—all married and living in Whitestone. "Pat there, he's from Kilkenny," Mr. Keane said. "And Mona. Mona, you're Galway, right?"

The women slipped into hard-heeled dancing shoes and the men shook free of sweaters; things can heat up. They divided into two groups of four couples each, and waited. Then, with the simple push of a button, Mr. Keane unleashed a fury of music.

With a whoosh, sixteen pairs of shoes began sliding across the worn floor, sounding like a platoon of brooms in full sweep, all to the fiddle skat and accordion sigh, as Mr. Keane called out instructions for the Kilfenora Set. "Cross over!" he cried. "Cross over!"

Outside on Queens Boulevard, the marquees of immigrants sang out in neon harmony, of Turkish cuisine, Romanian food, and Spanish baked delights. But the background music to it all, at least this night, came from the back room of the Breffni Bar, where Irish men and women performed an old dance, weaving and turning and stomping for joy.

These set dances, rooted in the French quadrille but long ago transformed into something entirely Irish, used to break out in Irish farmhouses, at country crossroads, even in New York dance halls. They faded from popularity for many years, but came back strong a couple of decades ago, so now here were the gone-away children of Ireland, retracing the dance steps of forebears in a place called Sunnyside.

Their dancing had nothing to do with St. Patrick's Day, for they dance every Monday, and other days as well. They did not talk about who should be able to march in the Fifth Avenue parade, or about the current travails of Sinn Fein. They just danced for the dance of it, pausing only for sips of soda, a bit of a chat, and maybe a taste of that Irish sherry trifle, made by the teacher himself.

"If you have any mental problems—within reason—you come here and they go right out of your head," explained Mr. Keane, as he slid another CD into its laser-beam cradle and grabbed the index card bearing instructions for the next set.

"Up, everybody, up!" he called. "The Caledonian Set."

The dancers reached for hands and formed two circles of eight. In and out, back and forth, paired with one and then another, they wove intricate patterns of elation upon the floorboards. By now Mr. Keane's reddened face burned beneath his white hair, but still he called out: "Dance it home! Dance it home!"

The twirling dancers surrendered to the music. Their minds wandered, even cleared, but not so much that they did not heed Mr. Keane's calls.

Mr. Haugh thought of the benefits of exercise, and of his farmer father, who died when his Billy was four, but who was said by all to have been a great set dancer. Mona Boyle, of Galway, thought of her

mother, who loved to dance, of the music always playing in the house
she left in 1957, at eighteen, and how music remains her tonic.

Pat Whelan, of Kilkenny, thought of his wife, Maureen, a lovely girl
from Cork, who struggled with multiple sclerosis for nearly twenty years,
the last five in bed, before dying. He was in a fog for years after that,
until his daughter—and the three McGrory women of Whitestone—
insisted he take up the dance.

"She would have loved this," he said, perspiring from the last set.
"She was a terrific dancer."

And what does the instructor, Mr. Keane, think about? One of
the fundamental rules of set dancing, he said: Keep your feet close to
the ground.

JULY 12, 2003

With the Fish, and Feeling Quite Herself

At first the lookdown fish, those silvery dinner plates of the
sea, wanted nothing to do with her. The moment she dipped her tail fin
into the water, they darted off to the coral-reef corners of the aquarium, as if to shun another creature that would dare to be as exotic.

But Julie Atlas Muz was intent on using what she calls her "huge
water karma." Sometimes it seems as though all of Manhattan is one
large conch shell pressed to her ear; she hears the ocean beckoning,
feels her inner mermaid stirring. Besides, she needed the gig.

Night after night she pedaled her secondhand bicycle through the
Chelsea streets, toting bags jammed with towels, goggles, a nose clip—
and three homemade tail fins that tuck right up to her pierced belly-
button. Night after night she climbed twelve feet up a hidden ladder
at the back of the Coral Room, a new club that recently replaced a
wholesale fruit business on West Twenty-ninth Street.

There, perched above the nine-thousand-gallon saltwater tank
that looms behind the club's bar, Ms. Muz strapped on a bikini top,

shimmied into a tail fin, and eased fin-first into the drink. She knew that she could win over the lookdown fish—so called because it appears to look down its nose as it swims—given that she had been dealing with its human counterparts her entire adult life.

Now, a few months later, the fish serve as her shimmering aquatic chorus as she flips and glides through the warm waters they share.

There is something serenely seductive about being a mermaid who frolics in a tank to amuse the addled hip, at least judging by the number of women who inquire daily about job openings. Paul Devitt, one of the Coral Room's owners, said he kept four mermaids on staff, although the club has had some turnover since opening in the spring.

"It's harder than it looks," he said. "And Julie was the first to grasp that it isn't just swimming around; it's performing."

Since there is no traditional career path for becoming a professional mermaid, Ms. Muz's might as well be the template. She is thirty, a native of Detroit whose parents and only sibling are doctors. She is a college graduate who attempted a desk job upon graduation, but it didn't take. Now she is a performance artist whose repertoire includes a dark-humored burlesque act that ends with her dead— "like on-the-ground-with-a-twitch dead," she says.

A few months ago the Coral Room put out its "Wanted: Mermaids" pleas, and Ms. Muz went down to test the waters. As she grew accustomed to the tank, she sensed the job's "burlesque-esque" possibilities. It was then that she heard an inner voice telling her what generations of fledgling artists who come to make it in New York have heard:

"This is something I can do."

The other night, a towel over her shoulders, Ms. Muz sat naked on one of the wooden planks that rim the top of the tank, discussing mermaid techniques. This space is her pool deck—her sanctuary— between her five-minute performances every half hour. Above her dangled the wet tail fins of previous acts; beside her was the paperback novel by Colette that she is reading when on break.

So far she has learned that her long blond hair can be used to mask the goggles and nose clip. That exhaling before submersion reduces buoyancy. That depending on how she focuses her eyes, she can study her own reflection or see the faces and shadows of the people staring at her from the other side.

"I gauge the duration of the swim by the reactions of the people in the bar," she said. "They'll be talking, and then—'Ooh, a mermaid!' They stop and stare, but after a while they start talking again, and I know it's time to get out."

Ms. Muz has learned, too, that it is hard to be upset underwater. Even mermaids have problems when they come up for air, and she is no different: a father deep into Alzheimer's dementia; an older brother unhappy with his sister's choices in life. But the water swallows her up, blocks out noise, transports her.

"It's like, 'Where am I?'" she said. "'Oh, I'm here. Oh, look: fish.' Instead of thinking so hard, I'm on another plateau. I've become comfortable as a mermaid."

In a few hours, sometime around four A.M., Ms. Muz would cycle home to rinse out her tail fins and hang them to dry on the shower stall. She would read for a bit, and then go to bed. But right now it was only midnight, and she was still a mermaid.

She thought for a moment, and then decided to go with the pink mermaid's tail next. Yes, definitely pink.

JULY 20, 2005

A City Too Hot to Bother with a Hero

In the shorthand language of the police, a 10-54 took place Sunday evening on the shores of Coney Island. A thirty-three-year-old male, beginning to drown, was rescued from the water, and a 911 call was placed. The police and Emergency Medical Service personnel responded. Said male was taken to Coney Island Hospital, where he was listed in poor condition.

As for the person largely responsible for the salvation in this 10-54, or medical emergency, the incident report says that witnesses identified a man named Gary Heath as "the civilian who rescued the aided from the water."

Sunday melted into Monday, and Monday into Tuesday, in a city too large, hot, and bothered to reflect on every act of valor to occur within its expansive limits. It has no time to pause and thank Mr. Heath for what he did, which he intimates is just as well. He just happened to be in the right place at the right time, he says, summoning the grand cliché that comes so readily to the lips of the heroic.

Mr. Heath, forty-three, is six foot two and 210 pounds but more teddy bear than Olympic swimmer in physique. Originally from Chicago, he moved to New York eight years ago for the opportunity, the buzz. He lives in a high-rise apartment building on the West Side, and works at Weber Shandwick, the public relations agency, as a "human resources information systems manager."

Late Sunday afternoon, Mr. Heath decided to escape the pizza oven that is Manhattan in July. He threw a towel and a bathing suit in a vinyl bag and took the Q train to Coney Island. By the time he reached the beach, the sky was brooding, rain was falling, and the lifeguards had called it a day.

"But I just wanted to go in for a quick dip," he says. He changed into his bathing suit, waded out a few feet, and plunged into the undulating Coney Island relief.

After a few minutes of bobbing and bouncing in water at his neck, he noticed a man about ten feet farther out who seemed to be struggling. Mr. Heath kept the man in the back of his mind as he plunged again, came up, and checked the shoreline to make sure that his bag was still on the beach. When he turned toward the Atlantic horizon, he saw that the other swimmer was now doing the dead man's float—facedown, still.

Mr. Heath, who describes himself as a decent swimmer, someone who remembers his YMCA lessons back in Niles, Illinois, swam out, lifted the stranger's face from the dark water, and began pulling him to shore. The man was overweight and dead weight, his wet skin slippery to the touch. But the human resources information systems manager clutching him pressed on, his mind blank save for his goal: the shore.

"When it became shallow, that's when he really became dead weight," Mr. Heath says. "Then a couple of people came out and helped me drag him onto the beach."

People assumed roles. Mr. Heath grabbed a cell phone and dialed 911 to report a man pulled from the water, unconscious and not breathing. A woman began to administer CPR. Another volunteer provided mouth-to-mouth resuscitation. The man gurgled up some water, but his eyes remained closed.

Police officers arrived, followed by EMS technicians on a dune buggy. The victim received more CPR, was loaded onto a stretcher, and rushed to an ambulance. The police jotted down the names and addresses of the people involved in just one incident in a city of incidents, and said goodbye.

It was over, sort of. Mr. Heath and the other rescuers comforted one another, exchanged hugs, and went their separate ways. He remembers that the woman's name was Betsy, and that she lived in Astoria.

He cannot recall any other name, other than that of the victim: Reuben Delgado Garcia of Elmhurst, Queens. (He was discharged from the hospital yesterday.)

With Coney Island now as dark as the water, Mr. Heath changed into street clothes and shoved his wet bathing suit into his bag. He stopped at Nathan's and ate a fish sandwich. He thought about the victim. Couldn't believe the man was still alive after taking in so much water. Hoped that he would be all right.

He caught the subway, found a seat, and gazed out upon the Brooklyn blur of this large, oblivious city. His city now.

While rocking to the Q train rhythm, he called his mother at her home beside a lake in northern Illinois. He told her what had happened.

And she told him how proud she was of her Gary.

DECEMBER 10, 2005

On This Team, Good Hands Are a Given

In a high school gymnasium where youthful exuberance is more felt than heard, the visiting team gathers at one end of the basketball court to stretch before the game. "One, two, three, four, five, six, seven, eight, nine, ten," they chant, then clap, clap, clap. One, two, three, clap, clap, clap.

At the other end the home team, the American Sign Language and English Secondary School, warms up in silence. Only the basketball talks, pinging off the floor, slapping against the backboard, making that whisper-grunt sound, whup, when meeting a bed of soft hands.

With tip-off approaching, the visitors from Seward Park High surround their coach as he exhorts them to play a zone defense. The home team Tigers do the same with their coach, Bruce Rogers, their eyes finding a pep talk in his moving lips and signing hands: Remember what we've practiced; look to teammates; relax.

The Tigers reach in to form a hand pile of solidarity, then emit a guttural shout that sounds like "Go!" With that, the starting five walk out to face undefeated Seward Park, a school on the Lower East Side.

The twelve boys playing for American Sign Language, a school on East Twenty-third Street, are pretty much the twelve boys who tried out. They are 0–3, their first game a 130–30 loss to a school whose coach may still be grappling with the concept of sportsmanship.

The loss reflects the growing pains of an old school with new ambitions. The principal, Martin Florsheim, decided a couple of years ago to shed its special education status as a number of hearing students, often the children or siblings of deaf people, were enrolling to learn American Sign Language. The hearing and the deaf can learn in the same educational environment, he reasoned; they can learn from one another.

Now here are five Tigers, eyes on the jump ball in midair. Seward Park takes possession. In an old city gym, under dull lights, another basketball ballet begins.

Mr. Rogers, the Tigers coach, paces the sidelines, sometimes waving a white jersey to attract his team's attention. A product of the raucous asphalt courts of Queens, he occasionally struggles with the challenge of quiet in a game of shouts.

"It's very difficult to coach during the game," he says before tip-off. "If they're looking at me for a sign, they're not watching the game." Still, he says, his players "are very in tune" with one another.

Jonathan Fabian, the team's stocky captain, agrees. Through an interpreter named Rachel Nekoukar, he explains how a wink, a subtle hand gesture—a furtive glance—can convey an on-the-spot basketball strategy. The blink of an eye and the slight nod of the head might mean: I need someone to block my defender; I need a pick.

A player who gets double-teamed can call for help with facial gestures. "Depending on how you change the face, that signals urgency," Jonathan says. "When my eyebrows go up like that, it's more urgent."

The eyes are "superimportant," emphasizes his lanky teammate, Jherry Alexis. "We're more attuned to our visual sense than a hearing person is."

The game moves fast, as Seward Park's point guard shouts, "motion, motion." Meanwhile, Narinderpal Singh, the point guard for the Tigers, conveys with nods, gestures, looks.

"See the play where they went to the same guy three times?" asks a frustrated Mr. Rogers as boys run back and forth before him. "That's what they don't pick up. And I can't tell them."

Until the next timeout, when he does. He also tells Narinderpal that defenders are reading his eyes, helping them to anticipate where he plans to throw the ball. Calm down, the coach says, through gesturing hands faced palm down. Relax.

At halftime, Seward Park leads 40–23. But the Tigers refuse to give up. Jose Santiago, the center, fights for every ball. Narinderpal calls a give-and-go play that ends with a nice short jumper. Jonathan makes his layups and hits his jump shots.

After every score, they find approbation from fans and teammates who wave arms, raise voices, and stomp feet. Sometimes all this sends vibrations of praise through the floor, Jonathan says. "I can feel it."

With the scoring gap widening, Mr. Rogers calls another timeout to urge his players not to give up. "You're playing a good game," he says. "A nice game." He pats several of the boys on the back, giving that universal sign of encouragement.

At this point the game is all but over. Still, Jonathan emerges from the huddle and draws imaginary whiskers across his face. The gesture says: *Let's go, Tigers.*

Keeping His Hands on Wheel . . . and on Bow, and Strings

It being Wednesday, Hugh McDonald parked on the West Side and reached for the large black case that contains his obsession. He tugged on the bill of his baseball cap and started walking east, toward Carnegie Hall.

You might guess his profession just by looking at his clothes: gray pants, blue sweater, white shirt bearing the company name, and blue tie with the pattern of small buses. Mr. McDonald is a bus driver, at least by day.

He is fifty-four, unassuming and agreeable, the kind of man who says, "Yes, uh-huh" a lot. But once he makes a decision, he can be as rigid as a bus schedule. He now eats salad every day for lunch, because no way is Hugh McDonald going to be another overweight bus driver.

He and his wife, Beverly, live with their four dogs in Berlin, New Jersey, near Philadelphia. She runs a pet-grooming business out of the house, and he steers a forty-five-foot, fifty-seven-passenger commuter bus for Academy bus lines.

At five-thirty every weekday morning, he drives thirty miles to the bus depot in Westhampton, climbs aboard his assigned bus, and drives twenty-five miles to East Windsor, then Monroe, then James-burg, and finally to the park-and-ride lot at Exit 8-A of the New Jersey Turnpike. Next stop, Manhattan. He lingers a few hours, collects his passengers, and returns to deep New Jersey, though he does not reach his own home until eight or nine at night. His long bus drives have no music to help pass the time, only a two-way radio offering dispatcher chatter.

One afternoon about three years ago, while killing time until rush hour, Mr. McDonald came upon a man playing Bach on a cello in the Times Square subway station. The sweet song of this cello, the first one he had ever heard, soared above the train rattle and jangle.

"The sound, the feeling, the intensity, the emotion of it," he re-called. "It was like a wave that came over me. I had never felt that before."

Suddenly he wanted to play the cello.

When he was a child in a Bronx housing project, he had wanted to learn a musical instrument. But the bleats of a trumpeter-in-training would have been too disruptive for the neighbors, his parents had said, so that was that. Later, as a young man, he often listened to classical music on a transistor radio in his bedroom, recognizing some of the pieces as ones that he had heard in church.

But this cello music.

For nearly a year that subway cellist's music lingered in Mr. Mc-Donald's mind—as he drove, as he ate his salad, as he drove some more. Finally, his passion to learn overcame his fears of being too old. Between one day's rush hours, he went to the New York Public Library and picked a school at random out of the telephone book: The French-American Conservatory of Music at Carnegie Hall.

"They said, 'We'll teach you cello,'" he recalled. "I said, 'I can't play a note, can't read a note.' They told me, 'No problem.'"

Cellos cost several thousand dollars, so Mr. McDonald began rent-ing one for forty-nine dollars a month, which was on top of the forty-five dollars he paid for his weekly hour of instruction. But cost did not matter, he said. "I wanted to play the notes the way I heard them coming off that train."

He spent nearly four months trying to get the sound of bow upon string to evoke sounds that were pleasing to the ear. And when that moment came, when the stroke of his bow summoned sweetness, he thought, wow, this is Hugh McDonald making that sound.

"It was like, 'Oh, I've reached it,'" he recalled. "At least I can make it sound good."

Now, some eighteen months later, he can coax recognizable music from the cello, thanks to his commitment to practice. On most days, during his break between rush hours, he parks in a Hoboken bus lot and heads with that black case to the back of his empty bus. He has discovered that if he sets the cello in the aisle, lays out his music on a seat, and lifts a couple of arm rests, he has just enough room to play.

On Wednesdays, though, he does not drive to Hoboken. He parks instead on West Fifty-fourth Street in Midtown and carries his obsession to Carnegie Hall for his weekly session with Biana Cvetkovic, cello instructor.

Ms. Cvetkovic, imbued with the patience of a natural teacher, continues to drill the basics into Mr. McDonald. Keep the back nice and tall, the legs spread apart, the feet flat. Keep the thumbs soft and the fingers nice and round. Relax the right elbow. Keep the bow stroking the cello's powerful place—the highway. Now listen to the tempo. Tap, tap, tap.

Last Wednesday, Mr. McDonald took his seat in Ms. Cvetkovic's studio and began to summon music from his rented cello. He played haltingly. But the afternoon rush was hours away, and he had the time.

JULY 6, 2005

Lifting a Saint, and the Heart of a Father

Joey understood. Other children might have ignored the Giglio Feast, or dismissed it as an anachronistic passion of their elders. Not Joey; he understood.

"He loved it," says Joseph Dente Sr. as Virginia, his wife, looks away. "Everything was the feast—the *giglio.*"

Joey was a few months short of eleven when he died of an immune deficiency. Twelve years have passed, and while his parents can smile and joke and engage themselves in everyday life, they quietly convey the ache of acute loss, of struggling for breath after a blow to the chest.

But they have each other, they have their daughter, Maria, and they have the Giglio Feast in a small Italian neighborhood in Williamsburg, Brooklyn. Now, more than ever, the feast reminds them of a little boy who gloried in what is called, simply, the *giglio* (pronounced JEE-lee-o).

The Italian word means lily, but in Williamsburg it refers to the elaborately decorated seventy-foot tower—topped by a statue of St. Paulinus—that is carried along Havemeyer Street by some 120 men every July to celebrate the sacred narrative of the saint's freedom from captivity. The men twist, turn, and even cha-cha, while a brass band carried on the same platform plays joyous music, and the saint above sways and bobs in liberty.

The ritual and intrigue behind the celebration, which is generations old, are complex enough to cross a statue's eyes, beginning with its caste system. Many of the men who carry the *giglio*, called lifters, aspire to elevated ranks—to lieutenant, to apprentice, to capo, and then, maybe one day, to Number 1 capo: the man ultimately responsible for the start-and-stop procession of the tower.

To be Number 1 capo during the Feast of Our Lady of Mount Carmel in July-baked Williamsburg is to be bigger than the mayor. He has his own color, his own theme song. And this year he is Joseph Dente.

As Mr. Dente, forty-eight, worked his way up from mechanic to administrator at Consolidated Edison, so, too, did he ascend within the closed world of Brooklyn steeples and lilies. The son of Italian immigrants, he grew up on Withers Street, where his heart ached for the raising of the *giglio*. It meant smiling priests and dancing in the street.

At eight he became a rope boy, keeping lines taut to control the crush of crowds. At fourteen, he began supervising the rope boys. At eighteen, he became a lifter, and at twenty-one, a lieutenant in charge of a crew. At thirty-five, he became an apprentice, which meant that he could direct the movement of the *giglio* for a few yards, all to his own theme song, "Finiculi, Finicula."

Back at the Dente home on Long Island, his son, Joey, was all but sleeping in his *giglio* T-shirts. Among the cartoon characters and Mets tributes in his sketchbook, he also drew *giglios* he'd like to see, with trumpeting angels and the likeness of St. Anthony of Padua—"his patron saint," his mother says. He even built miniature *giglios* and staged feasts for neighborhood children in his backyard.

Mr. Dente smiles at the memory of Joey working on the towers alongside the men of the feast in the basement of the Shrine Church of Our Lady of Mount Carmel. "He'd come down and paint," he says. "He learned a few choice words."

The face of the *giglios,* made mostly of papier-mâché, paint, and polyurethane, are ephemeral by nature, and the lifters had been complaining that the one they've carried for the last decade was pretty heavy. A few months ago, men began gathering in the church basement to build a new one. Among them were Joe and Peter Peluso, Joe Rubino, Mr. Dente. There, too, was that sketchbook of Joey's, with its carefully drawn *giglios* soaring from a child's imagination.

The finished product now stands near the front of the church, as if in impatient wait for the feast that begins with a Mass tomorrow evening. Several tiers high, it includes depictions of several angels and cherubs, Our Lady of Mount Carmel, the Sacred Heart, St. Joseph, and St. Anthony, patron of Joey.

On Sunday afternoon, after Mass and coffee, the Number 1 capo will lead a cheering throng to the base of the *giglio,* where the lifters will be waiting for their signal.

"*Musica!*" Mr. Dente will shout. And the band will strike up "*O' Giglio è Paradiso.*"

Taking their cue from a moment in that song, the lifters will raise the *giglio,* the crowd will roar, the confetti will fly. And Joe and Virginia Dente will know that one cherub near the top of the *giglio* bears the name Joey.

MAY 22, 2004

In the Bronx, a Graduation with Honor

Kathleen Mercadante took her place in the second pew of the main chapel at Manhattan College, joining the cap-and-gown sea of men and women about to receive a diploma. Cameras whirred and clicked in the back of the room, while outside, rain clouds parted for the sun to bless a graduation day in the Bronx.

On one side of the center aisle sat dozens of young adults waiting to receive master's degrees in education and engineering. And on the other side, people in their thirties, forties, and fifties, a few with gray hair beneath their caps, and old enough to be the parents of those in gowns to their right.

These older graduates had finished Manhattan's Adult Degree Completion Program, which is intended for people who once began but never finished their college careers, because of children or hardship or just life. According to its director, Jeff Katz, the program helps people to "complete what has been unfinished."

Ms. Mercadante sat among these older graduates about to receive a bachelor's degree. She did not fidget; she did not share whispers. She sat with back erect and eyes trained on a podium arrayed with academics in gowns. Her mortarboard cap fit snug on her auburn hair.

In a way, she could not believe where she was. She is thirty-seven, with a husband and two children, including a daughter just three years from being of college age. Then again, she thought, this is where I belong. This is exactly where I belong.

Less than an hour before, Ms. Mercadante and her two older brothers, Daniel and Thomas—steamfitters both—had discussed among themselves who would sit where. Who would wear the cap and gown?

"Honestly, we all wanted to go up there and get it," she said later. "Then my brother Danny, the oldest, turned to me and said, 'I think that you should go up and receive it.' And you know what? I was so hoping that that was the way it was going to happen."

Then there she was, among the first row of graduates being beckoned to stand to the side of the chapel. Brother Thomas J. Scanlan, the college president, stood ready to present diplomas, shake hands, and wish all the best in the future.

Mr. Katz began to call out the names from the lectern, and one by one, in alphabetical order, working men and women stepped forward to grasp what they had finally earned. And when Ms. Mercadante appeared at the front of the line, Mr. Katz called out the name:

"Colleen Carey."

Ms. Mercadante remained still, her face set in an expression that said I will not cry, as Mr. Katz explained that Colleen Carey had died—and that Kathleen Mercadante would be accepting the diploma for her older sister, Colleen, college graduate.

Colleen Carey died last June, suddenly, of diabetes; she was forty-two. She loved to cycle and to golf and to tell jokes. She loved taking her nieces and nephew to concerts and plays. She loved helping her neighbors, so it was only natural that when one of them became ill, she treated him to takeout and cared for his cats. Oh, and she loved cats.

Colleen especially loved education, no matter how life often side-tracked her pursuit of a college degree. Little by little, though, she collected credits at local colleges, and when she learned that Manhattan's adult program was being made available to employees at the Entergy Corporation, where she worked as a manager, she seized the opportunity.

"She always wanted to better herself," her sister said. "She wanted more. And I guess she knew that without her bachelor's degree, it wasn't going to happen."

Colleen constantly emphasized the importance of an education to her family, and supported her younger sister's decision to pursue an associate's degree. But Ms. Mercadante had to drop out.

"There were just a few too many things going on," she said. "I finally had to say, which ball am I running with today? School will have to wait. But I'll pick it up again when the time is right."

When finally Ms. Mercadante stepped forward to accept her sister's degree, she felt gratitude to Manhattan College for making the moment possible. She felt admiration for all the people around her who had worked so hard. She felt pride in her sister's accomplishment, and a little angry. More than anything, she wanted to be in the gallery, snapping photographs of Colleen in cap and gown.

After a moment that seemed like a lifetime, Kathleen Mercadante stepped forward, collected a handshake, good wishes, and a diploma, and returned to her seat.

"When I sat back down," she said, "I was trembling."

NOVEMBER 2, 2005

Button Up Your Overcoat

These days have been uncommonly mild for autumn, but Derek Ivery insists on wearing a sweater and jacket over his tall and very thin frame. He cannot get sick. He has things to do.

Mr. Ivery is an office worker in a city of office workers. He works Mondays through Fridays, nine to five, in the biology department at Queens College. He answers the telephone, registers students for classes, and makes sure that professors get their mail. Then he walks to the home he shares with his mother in Flushing.

An average man, living an average life. But he is only twenty-six, with plans to go to graduate school. He has things to do.

Growing up, he did not stand out among the thirty-three hundred students at John Bowne High School, save for a brief speaking role in the school's production of *Les Misérables*. And he didn't stray far when he enrolled at Queens College, down the street, to become one student among some seventeen thousand.

His only extracurricular activity was with the college's peer advisement program, which trains students to assist others in making the sometimes difficult adjustment to college life. Soon, he was helping to recruit other students for the program.

One day in 2002, he met another one among the seventeen thousand: Nidha Mubdi, a young student who wanted to become a peer adviser. The daughter of Bangladeshi immigrants living in Briarwood, Queens, she had a riveting smile and an upbeat demeanor that belied the life story she shared with him.

In August 1998, when she was eighteen, Ms. Mubdi was told she had leukemia. When she was nineteen, she underwent a bone marrow transplant. When she was twenty, her kidneys failed—the payment due from all that chemotherapy and medication—and she began dialysis treatment.

Through bad movies and graduation parties and gentle teasing, a platonic friendship developed between this Muslim woman and this Methodist man. Mr. Ivery became accustomed to her dialysis routine. Three mornings a week, she sat for three hours in a medical office in Jackson Heights, hooked up to a machine that did the work her kidneys could not. After that, several hours of sleep. This was her life, at twenty-one, twenty-two, twenty-three, twenty-four, twenty-five.

A year ago, Mr. Ivery had an idea, but set it aside. No, he decided. No.

Then, a few months ago, Ms. Mubdi e-mailed to her friends the address for her Web site, which included a section called "My Story—Looking For a Miracle." It began: "Could you be a person of selfless sacrifice & godly humanity able to donate their spare kidney?"

That idea returned to Mr. Ivery. Without telling his friend, he had his blood type checked and learned that it matched hers. Then he sent her an e-mail message that opened with a couple of goofy jokes and ended with the words: "But if you want a kidney you can have mine."

Ms. Mubdi did not answer right away, and has trouble articulating why. In the past, others had expressed interest in donating a kidney, but for this reason and that reason those plans fell through. "I was taken aback," she says.

A week later, the two friends went to a fast-food place on Union Turnpike. He had a vanilla milkshake, she had some strawberry-ice concoction, and they talked about it. She was surprised that he didn't have any questions about the process. He was surprised that she was so quiet—brought to wordlessness, it seemed, by the enormousness of what was being offered.

That evening, the Methodist gently patted the hand of the Muslim. "To let her know it's all right," Mr. Ivery says.

The two friends underwent testing to confirm the compatibility between his kidney and her body. He had to meet with his "transplant team." He had to have a CT scan. He had to be examined by a psychologist, to make sure he knew what he was doing.

Through it all, Ms. Mubdi has assured Mr. Ivery that he can still change his mind—it would be all right. Mr. Ivery has assured her that this is what he wants to do. They both worry about complications, including the possibility of rejection.

Now the time is upon them. Ms. Mubdi and Mr. Ivery are scheduled to report early Friday morning to New York–Presbyterian/Columbia hospital in Upper Manhattan. But they have been warned that the transplant will be postponed if either one of them gets sick.

That is why Mr. Ivery bundles up during these uncommonly mild autumn days.

NOVEMBER 26, 2005

A Friendship Sealed by the Scalpel

Nidha Mubdi needed a kidney and Derek Ivery had one to spare. It was that simple, that complex. Now they lay in adjacent operating rooms, being prepped for a transcendent transfer of ownership.

The two met three years ago at Queens College, and a platonic friendship developed. Mr. Ivery learned that Ms. Mubdi had prevailed in a battle with leukemia, but only after a bone marrow transplant and at the cost of her kidneys. Three times a week she endured a taxing dialysis treatment that would be part of her life for the rest of her life, unless she found a kidney donor.

One day Mr. Ivery sent an e-mail message to Ms. Mubdi that began with a joke and ended with the serious offer of one of his kidneys. She accepted after overcoming her shock, but repeatedly assured him that it would be OK if he had a change of heart.

He never did. He submitted to every test required of him, including one to determine whether he was of sound mind. It is no small thing to offer up a vital organ.

Here they were, then, three weeks ago: two people in their mid-twenties, wearing thin hospital gowns in cold rooms on the third floor of New York–Presbyterian/Columbia hospital in Upper Manhattan. Mr. Ivery shivered so much that nurses draped a warmed blanket over his long, thin body.

Someone placed a mask over his mouth, told him to take deep breaths—and he was gone. Minutes later, in the adjacent room, Ms. Mubdi joined him in that cottony, anesthetized world of life suspended.

A surgeon, Dr. Marc Bessler, performed a minimally invasive procedure called a laparoscopy that removed a fist-size kidney from Mr. Ivery, but left only three small scars near his navel. The kidney was washed of blood and immediately cooled with an icy solution to slow its metabolism. It became pale.

The kidney was placed in a small bassinet filled with slushy ice. Dr. Mark Hardy, the transplant surgeon, carried the organ into the room where Ms. Mubdi lay. He had already made an incision in her lower abdomen to expose the blood vessels to which the new kidney would be attached.

Dr. Hardy, who is sixty-seven years old and has performed two thousand kidney transplants in his career, reconstructed the blood vessels, attached the kidney, and released the clamp. The organ that was pale received the flow of blood, and turned reddish maroon with life.

A few minutes later he began the delicate procedure of attaching the donated kidney's ureter—a duct that conveys urine—to the bladder. Once that was done, Ms. Mubdi's new kidney, enjoying its good blood supply, began to produce urine that flowed through the ureter, into her bladder, and out to a catheter that would be removed in a couple of days.

What did this mean? Dr. Hardy answered in practical rather than metaphysical terms. "She is not beholden to the dialysis machine," he said this week. "As she gains strength, her time really becomes her own."

The operation lasted about four and a half hours.

Sometime the next day, Mr. Ivery took his IV pole for a walk around the hospital floor, and stopped to chat with Ms. Mubdi, who now possessed a part of him. "I told her I was happy to see her," he recalled. "And she wanted to know if I was OK."

Two days after the transplant, the doctors sent Mr. Ivery home. Three days after the transplant, they released Ms. Mubdi, whose body seemed to be adjusting quickly to the new kidney. The two friends, who live about three miles apart in Queens, fell into a routine of resting all day and talking by telephone at night.

They finally saw each other late last week, when Ms. Mubdi's father, Shelley, drove them both to doctors' appointments at the hospital. "Just chitchat," Mr. Ivery said, though he recalled that his usually upbeat friend seemed discouraged by some complications.

On Monday, a tired Mr. Ivery returned to his office job in the biology department at Queens College. Three weeks ago, he donated a kidney. Now he picks up the ringing telephone and says, "Biology."

That same day, Ms. Mubdi was admitted to the hospital because of debilitating complications that included high blood pressure, mouth sores, and gastrointestinal distress. Her doctors say that the bone-marrow transplant in her past may be slowing her recovery, and they are tinkering with her medication to find the proper balance.

For her Thanksgiving dinner in the hospital, Nidha Mubdi had mashed potatoes, which is how miracles unfold sometimes.

JANUARY 21, 2006

At Age Twenty-six, Finding Words to Live By

Ana Arias bathed her two girls, wrestled them into their pajamas, and left them in the care of her mother. She fixed her dark hair just so, slipped on that sharp pink jacket she had just had dry-cleaned, and said goodbye to the overcrowded house in the Bronx she hoped to leave for good someday. But first things first.

Up the concrete hill of 167th Street she walked, a thing of pink bobbing toward the black-coated men rooted in the pavement outside bodegas. Hanging out did not interest her. She kept climbing toward the Grand Concourse, where she would board a D train bound for Manhattan. She had an appointment to keep.

At twenty-six, Ms. Arias is wise enough to recognize that too much has happened to her, and not enough. She grew up in a Washington Heights apartment where the father disappeared and the stepfather should have, which meant that as the oldest of three children, she became more the protector and mediator, and less a child.

As she remembers it, when the stepfather threw the pot of dinner across the room on the grounds that the spaghetti was too salty, she spoke up. When the telephone bill needed to be paid, she spoke up. When eligibility for food stamps lapsed, she spoke up.

All the while, Spanish-language television programs babbled in the background. No one read books; there weren't any.

She went to George Washington High School, where her quick mouth sometimes got her out of potentially embarrassing situations. If a teacher called on her to read, she would answer with some half-serious, half-kidding sass: C'mon, I read yesterday. You're just picking on me. But her glib ways could not help her during written tests, when "Time's up" would come before she had deciphered the exam's wording.

Her teenage years passed too quickly; there was no *Wuthering Heights* to slow the time, no *Go Ask Alice* to spur reflection. She got into a fight with another girl and won a suspension from high school. She worked at Burger King and CompUSA. She made big plans with a boyfriend, but her pregnancy altered those plans and prompted him to split. Suddenly she was twenty, with a blessed baby named Anastasia and little else.

She thought of returning to high school, but returned to CompUSA instead. A move to Florida changed nothing, so she moved back to Washington Heights, and then to the Bronx. She became pregnant again and gave birth to Lihana. She was a waitress day and night, a mom in between, and tired all the time.

At this point you could almost predict her future—one of tossed pots, blaring televisions, and untapped promise. Except there is something different about Ms. Arias: a refusal to accept her circumstances.

After getting another job, as a receptionist, she resolved to earn a high school equivalency diploma. She took a pre-test for the coursework at a community college, but when administrators asked her to come to the office for a chat, she did not need to ask why.

"I already knew," Ms. Arias said. "I felt like crying. But I felt great relief."

What she knew, what she had taken great lengths to hide for so many years, was that she could barely read.

There was no turning back. Ms. Arias wanted to improve her life. She wanted to move out of her troubled corner of the Bronx, where some people stand still. Most of all, she wanted to read to Anastasia and Lihana at night, to correct their homework—to inject the written word into the family conversation.

The D train pulled into the West Fifty-ninth Street station, and Ms. Arias stepped out. She walked down a dusky Eighth Avenue, past the restaurant where she used to wait on tables, and into an office building's cafeteria. There sat six dozen other Ana Ariases—men and women, young and old—listening to tutors, scribbling on paper, studying chalkboards, learning to read.

Ms. Arias joined these classes, which are run by a nonprofit organization called Literacy Partners, last September, and quickly impressed her advisers with her dedication. She began at a second-grade reading level and is now reading at a fifth-grade level. Soon she will be ready for the next stage, which will prepare her for earning her high school equivalency diploma.

Before, there were no books at the Arias home. Now there are many, including a Reader's Digest condensation of mysteries that she keeps by her bedside.

Before, she could read little more than the horoscopes in the newspaper. Now she can read stories, including this one: about a young woman who is worth every word.

JUNE 25, 2003

Sing Out! To the Spirit from the Soul

In the beauty of the lilies . . ." sang the choir.

Again.

"In the beauty of the lilies, Christ was born across the sea."

No. I need four distinct parts: alto, tenor, soprano, and bass. Again.

Outside, a rare June sun graced the evening. But inside Calvary

Baptist Church of Jamaica, three dozen choir members were spending another weeknight practicing, practicing, raising their voices toward the wooden cross behind the vacant pulpit.

"In the beauty . . ."

Again, said the church's music director, M. Roger Holland II. "Y'all are faking it, but I ain't buying it."

Rehearsal for the Sanctuary Choir had begun on a high note. Its members had asked God to hear the songs they were compelled to sing. They had ooohhed and aaaahhed through vocal exercises. They had captured that wondrous blend of pain and release in "I'm Free": "My soul is resting, it's just a blessing. Praise the Lord, hallelujah, I'm free."

But their struggles with the last verse of "The Battle Hymn of the Republic"—the one that marches into the final round of "Glory! Glory! Hallelujah!"—yielded a look from Mr. Holland that said we're a long way from glory, my friends. A long way from pleasing the pastor, who had requested this demanding hymn for his Fourth of July weekend service.

"Again," the choirmaster said. "This section needs to be the gem at the center of the necklace."

The choir members fidgeted in the pews, and who could blame them. Many had worked all day; many had families awaiting them. By now a magnificent dusk had descended upon all of Queens, and here they were, missing the beauty while stuck on "In the beauty . . ."

But choir practice is about sacrifice, and prayer—and community. The black Baptist service all but requires the enveloping swell of many voices raised as one, testifying to spiritual triumph over trial and doubt. It lifts you up; you cannot fake it. And this church already knows what happens when harmony is not in the house.

Calvary, which set roots in Jamaica in 1929, once had an acclaimed choir that specialized in what is known in black Baptist congregations as "high church" music. Its members took special pride in performing the classical European music of Bach and Brahms and Mendelssohn. But that was yesterday.

Today, many black congregations demand more from their choirs. The gospel blues of Thomas Dorsey was powerful in its day, but give us Kirk Franklin, the superstar who infuses gospel with hip-hop. Give us both, and more. Give us—us.

A few years ago the tension between old and new split the music program at Calvary Baptist. The Reverend Victor T. Hall Sr., the church's pastor, recalled those discordant times as he sat in his office, the strains of the choir's battles with "Battle Hymn" emanating from beyond his door. The schism brought revelation, he said. "To do ministry in these times, you just can't sing the old hymns like you used to."

The church endured bad music and no music for several years, Mr. Hall said, while he searched for a music director "who could allow us to stay in touch with the past while reaching for the future." Finally, three years ago, he found Mr. Holland, a classically trained musician and former member of the Boys Choir of Harlem—a man comfortable, Mr. Hall said, "with the Bach and the rock."

But if more contemporary music is the way of the future, the reverend was asked, why then had he requested "The Battle Hymn of the Republic"?

Mr. Hall smiled and said, "Just love that piece."

Acutely aware of the pastor's request, Mr. Holland was pushing his choir to excel. He is thirty-eight and barrel-chested, with a voice that needs no microphone and a manner that shies from no challenge. "I'm going to stop you right now," he told his bass soloist, a lanky computer technician named Robert Canton. "Use all of the body, not parts of the body! You've got to be a 290-pound preacher!"

Nighttime in Queens, and Mr. Holland's hands were still darting and diving, coaxing and pleading. No, he said. Again. Almost. Everybody stand! Again.

Three dozen people rose to their feet. This afternoon they were nurses and counselors, educators and technicians; tonight they were the Sanctuary Choir. They began with "In the beauty of the lilies," soared through "His truth is marching on," and did not stop until they had reached a transporting, raise-the-roof "Amen" that filled the empty pews.

Better, said Mr. Holland.

JANUARY 14, 2006

A Final Call on Track 15, Clearly Heard

He woke up, or came to, in that cardboard cubbyhole he and other homeless men shared beneath the platform of Track 15 at Penn Station. And for some reason, he just knew it: He was done.

Looking back over a hard life of nearly sixty years, some blocks of time seemed as blurry as a bar counter seen through the bottom of a bottle. Other periods, though, were as sharp as broken glass.

His middle-class parents back in Michigan had done their best. But he was a wild teenager, and he doesn't blame his father for pushing him into the Navy. When his three-year hitch was done in 1966, he found himself in New York, with no plans and an unquenchable thirst.

He drank away his dockworker's pay with a purposeless sense of purpose. Swept along by the times, he joined a commune in San Francisco, used drugs, sold drugs, saw the light, sobered up, joined a Christian sect, got a bank job, wore wingtip shoes, and rarely had a drink for a dozen years—until one day when he had many.

Back to New York for more fits and starts. A longtime girlfriend dumped him because he could not commit—"I should have taken that step," he says now—so he went on a binge.

He sobered up and worked on a tuna boat for two years before taking a building superintendent's job on Fifth Avenue. Then one bad day at work triggered a two-year swirl of booze and crack that in 1996 cost him his job and his home.

One night he wrapped himself up in a bolt of cloth he had found

in a Macy's Dumpster, chose a doorway, and quietly joined the ranks
of this city's homeless.

Slowly, he learned. Hide belongings in the eaves of the PATH station in Herald Square. Grab a second sandwich at the early-morning
breadline outside St. Francis of Assisi Roman Catholic Church because you'll need it later. Wait until after the city's lunch hour to collect cans. Scout out restaurants with locking bathrooms suitable for
"bird baths."

All the while, he tried to control his craving for alcohol by trying
to summon the willpower. I will not drink, I will not drink. "I'd
make it to three o'clock and then I couldn't go any further," he says.

After two years of sleeping in the PATH station, he and a couple
of buddies moved to that spot at the end of Track 15 in Penn Station,
past the storage room for the Long Island Rail Road's bar cart. They
kept things clean and dry, which thwarted the rats. They caused no
trouble for the police. They even left written messages for one another in the gray lockers at the end of the platform—"Our in-and-
out box," he calls it.

When he drank, he would down two forty-ounce bottles of St.
Ides malt liquor, then start a twenty-two-ouncer. Sometimes he
would black out, wander, and come to in Harlem or Bedford-
Stuyvesant or some hospital with "my wrists strapped and tubes going
in me."

Other times, in Penn Station, he'd hear the constant track calls—
"The 2:19 to Port Washington"—and not know whether it was 2:19
A.M. or 2:19 P.M.

He was in his late fifties, and he could feel himself calcifying, dying.

Still, certain words and images seeped through. A Penn Station
panhandler he knew told him she had given up crack, just like that;
after a while, so did he. Then a SWAT team of burly men burst out of
a van one night, only to tell him they were outreach workers who, by
the way, had once been where he was.

He was sober for eleven months, then relapsed for another nine.
Until that moment in July 2003 when he came to in his cubbyhole
and felt something come over him: spirit, resolve, call it what you will.
All he knew was, it was over. He approached some Amtrak outreach
workers and said he was ready.

After detox and rehabilitation came the gradual, awkward immersion into life above the Track 15 platform. He lived in shelters, took classes, attended Alcoholics Anonymous meetings, and found support with the Street to Home Initiative of Common Ground, an agency that seeks solutions to homelessness. He now lives with other veterans in transitional housing in Brooklyn.

Ron Blackburn is sixty-one years old and eighteen months sober. He goes to Penn Station to do his banking and to develop film at Kmart. And when he hears the track calls, he knows the difference between night and day.

MAY 20, 2006

A Wandering Lamb Finds a Sheepskin

His long forefinger traced the journey of his lost childhood, across a map of East Africa that detailed the rivers and mountains, but not the lions and hyenas, the gunfire and death. "My home is supposed to be here," the young man said, allowing his fingertip to linger on a spot where the Sudanese village of Wangulei would be.

The atlas lay open like a prayer book on a polished table in the hushed library. With the semester over, the chairs sat empty. A clerk pushed a rattling book cart. A vacuum moaned. And Joseph Malual Thuc, a name not quite his own, used his finger to draw the path from there to here, the pastoral campus of Wagner College on Staten Island.

Six foot four, usually dressed in blazer and tie, so thin his pants can bunch up in his belt's cinch, this black man called Joseph has glided across Wagner's leafy whiteness with regal bearing for the last four years. He stood out so much that every semester, several students approached him to say they had chosen him as a class project.

They had questions. Where is Sudan? What is a Lost Boy?

Out of a duty to bear witness, out of a sense that stories like his have immediacy—think Darfur—the man called Joseph carefully answered their questions. "Basic stuff," he said. "But not everything."

In 1983 civil war broke out in Sudan between the Muslim military regime in the north and Christians and animists in the south. The violence eventually consumed Wangulei, in southern Sudan, where there lived a young boy of the Dinka tribe named Malual Manyok Deng Duot. His baptismal name was Joseph.

His father was killed, his mother was wounded, and he and his siblings were scattered like leaves from a shaken tree. He became one of the so-called Lost Boys of Sudan: thousands of orphaned or disconnected boys who wandered the African plains in an almost biblical search for refuge.

Joseph estimated that he was eight when he left home. Maybe nine; no more than ten.

"I remember a lot of traditional stuff," he said, recalling Wangulei at that time. "In wintertime we would come together and celebrate the end of one year and the beginning of the new year. We would slaughter a lot of cows. Everybody get to be happy, dance and play. Peaceful. No violence."

Then war. His finger moved along the page, reflecting the circuitous path of boys moving eastward toward Ethiopia, where safe haven proved fleeting. They were forced back to Sudan in a flight that included crossing the Gilo River, where some drowned or were dragged under by crocodiles. Two relatives helped carry young Joseph across.

"I rotated around," he said, his finger stopping on places he had been: Bor, Mallek, Mongalla, Torit, others. Military attacks took their toll, as did starvation and thirst. Joseph saw boys stop walking, heard them say, "I can't go." He heard the muffled cries of boys set upon by lions and hyenas. He saw boys die, friends.

"Wandering, walking all over, not knowing where to go," he said. "But keep going. Don't give up."

Finally, Joseph's band of boys reached Lokichokio, in northern Kenya. "From here, we didn't walk anymore," he said.

Joseph spent nine years in the Kakuma refugee camp in Kenya, where he learned to read, write, and speak English. At some point an official rechristened him Joseph Malual Thuc. When he began to argue that Thuc was not his last name, the official told him to shut up or he'd never leave Africa. Like all the other boys, he was given a birth date of January 1.

Through a special program established by the United Nations High Commissioner for Refugees and the Immigration and Naturalization Service, thousands of Lost Boys came to the United States. Joseph arrived in Philadelphia in December 2000, shivering in a white T-shirt and a white baseball cap. He had never seen snow before.

He and another Lost Boy moved in with Louise Shoemaker, a retired dean of the University of Pennsylvania School of Social Work, who is associated with Lutheran World Relief. Of Joseph, she recalled: "The first three months he was afraid every day that I would say, 'You can't stay here anymore.'"

Such words never came to Ms. Shoemaker's lips. Joseph graduated from a local high school in 2002, then chose to attend Wagner College because of the financial aid it offered, its quiet setting, and its location within the great city of New York. He wanted to study international affairs.

In some ways, Joseph was like any other college student. He got involved in campus politics, ran up big telephone bills calling siblings and friends around the world, and even wore a basketball jersey on Halloween to tease all those who made assumptions based on his height and skin color.

In other ways, though, he remained a Lost Boy—for reasons beyond the bus accident in 2004 that killed his mother, whom he had not seen since he was very young.

Joseph did not go out too often, in part because he was often sending money to siblings in Africa. He did not gorge on the cafeteria's cornucopia of food because he knew so many without. And when he rode the Staten Island Ferry, he thought of what a wonderful graduation present a ferry would make—for use on the Nile River back home.

During Wagner College's graduation ceremony yesterday morning, 462 men and women received their bachelor's degrees, including a very tall and very thin black man who strode to the podium with aristocratic grace.

The name on the diploma was his own: Malual Manyok Duot. Lost boy found.

At Age Thirty-one, Hanging on to the Ball

Derek Wooten has the basketball. He is standing on a Brooklyn park's asphalt court, known to him since he was seven. Behind him, the elevated D train, squealing. To his right, the Marlboro Houses, looming. And before him, a netless hoop, seducing from twenty feet away.

They get some good games going on this court in Bensonhurst, with players coming from the Marlboro projects and from Coney Island who twirl and dunk with the same effort it takes to breathe. But there is no five-on-five this morning, only Mr. Wooten and another man, shooting jump shots with a wet basketball, while the wind snaps the city flag against a nearby pole, and the smell of fried dough wafts from a Dunkin' Donuts.

At thirty-one, he has played hundreds, no, thousands of games here, shooting from downtown one possession and then driving hard the next, and so what if he's five foot nine. He knows every ping in the metal backboard, every bump in the pavement—even the owner of those abandoned sneakers over there.

And he knows that he has more behind him than just the D train.

People who watch him play often ask, where did he play in college? Man, what are you doing here? they say, you ought to be in the NBA with Stephon—as in Marbury, as in that kid from Coney Island he used to play ball with.

"And that hurts," he says. "Time's going by too fast."

In this corner of the city, basketball can be the great false god.

Prowess on the court is worshiped over prowess in the classroom, and then school's out: game over. But at a time when many of his hoop peers are working menial jobs or just hanging around, Mr. Wooten clings to the belief that he has a shot at the pros. He wakes up thinking about it.

"Age don't make no difference," he says, sounding as though he's trying to convince himself as much as his listener. "I'm healthy. I can run through guys, put the ball in the hole, get the team involved. And I'm gifted. Why not?"

Fifteen years ago, Derek Wooten terrorized opponents; he was that good, and that tough. He and his twin brother, Dexter, used to run the courts, and woe to anyone who complained about a bloodless foul. Dexter played at Lafayette High School—though he missed some games after being shot in a schoolyard fight—while Derek played the point at Lincoln High School.

But Derek Wooten dropped out of Lincoln just as Stephon Marbury was coming in. Then the years sneaked past in the Marlboro projects.

One minute he was seventeen and dreaming of playing in the NBA; the next he's thirty-one, with a couple of kids, but still dreaming of playing in the NBA—in part because Mr. Marbury made it, and he knows that man's game.

Mr. Wooten says he spent a lot of time—a lot of time—over the years trying to find a college that suited him best. He says he worked at a McDonald's; as a messenger; as a maintenance worker; as a porter at an Edward's supermarket; as an escort for mentally retarded children. He leaves out the eighteen months he served in prison for attempted burglary.

"I wasted a lot of time," he says.

Now, though, he has a plan. For the last three years he has been taking classes at a local branch of Touro College, he says, and is one semester away from earning an associate's degree in human services. After that, he hopes to go to a Division III college where he can earn a bachelor's degree and play basketball.

"I know somebody's going to pick me up," he says. "That's a guarantee."

So he does push-ups and squat thrusts in the bathroom of the apartment he shares with his mother and brother, and joins the basketball

games down at Seth Low Junior High School—when he doesn't have
class—and comes to this park, alone, to pirouette past phantom defenders.

All the while, he keeps in the back of his mind his encounter with
Mr. Marbury at some function in a Coney Island playground last
summer. The two men hugged, he says, and Mr. Marbury whispered
these words: Keep the ball. Don't lose it. Because you never know.

If Mr. Wooten understands how slim his chances are of leaving the
projects by way of the NBA, he does not let on. As the wind whips
and another D train grinds past, he launches the ball into the air.

It sails through the hoop, in Marlboro affirmation.

JULY 30, 2003

Mexican, But the Dream Is American

With the weight of a day's labor in their step, they
trudged along the baked Bronx pavement, through the evening heat.
They turned down a concrete alley at one of those apartment buildings that loom over the Grand Concourse like man-eating Gargantuas
and followed its path to the dank coolness of the utility room, where
the meeting was to be held.

Water pipes and utility meters decorated their makeshift conference room, and the furniture was more discarded than distressed. But
the setting did not matter as much as the agenda, which was:

We have been residents of New York City for many years, yet we
are outsiders. We are skilled laborers, yet we have little to show for our
toil. We are proud men, yet our employers take advantage.

We are Mexican. What now?

It is the defining question of the immigrant, one that echoes
through the memory of this city. We are Irish; we are Italian; we are Polish; we are Puerto Rican; we are Korean; we are Jamaican. We are New
Yorkers. What now?

As it did for others before them, the intimation of an answer is revealing itself to some Mexican immigrants in the borough's Bedford Park section. The answer may be in the chrysalis stage, but the men seem to sense the unfolding of wings. Something about banding together, pooling resources, working by—and for—themselves. Something like that.

People who come without governmental blessing to this city from Puebla, or Guerrero, or Veracruz, often expect to return to Mexico after a few years. But Brother Joel Magallan, the director of an outreach program for Mexicans in New York, Asociación Tepeyac, said that the rub of reality gradually erases those dreams, until all that remains is the naked question: "What am I going to do in Mexico?"

For a couple of years, the companion question—what now?—has vexed a few dozen Mexican men who belong to Our Lady of Mercy parish. Recently they began to meet outside the church to share desires that were like those of most other people: better lives for their children.

They realized that their days of sweating in garment district factories were behind them. Most of them were working in construction, with expertise in certain jobs. The resulting thought was, "We could build or fix up a house," one, Pedro Galaviz, explained. "I work inside. He works outside."

A few weeks ago, three dozen men agreed to start a construction business. Although they have not named the corporation or filed incorporation papers with the state, they have appointed corporate officers.

German Flores, the president, carries a piece of paper with the names and telephone numbers of his many partners. That they elected officers is a telling step, he said. "It means that we have gained enough trust among ourselves."

Trust is the glue. As treasurer, Maximo Mendoza has been charged with collecting twenty-five dollars each week from the members; he records payments in a spiral-bound book. He is also researching which bank is worthy of receiving the group's deposits, a decision that hinges in part on the conditions of loans that the men expect to take out once they have credit.

Mr. Mendoza had worked all day for a New Jersey construction company whose owner he has never met. Now he was talking enthusiastically about the future while sitting behind a discarded desk in a Bronx utility room, as a fan propped on a bucket stirred the tight air and two boys slurped juice boxes through straws. The boys, the sons of the group's vice president, Rodolfo Baez, listened in silence as adults around them gave voice to dreams.

"We have already had three meetings," said Mr. Mendoza, thirty, who has lived in this city thirteen years.

"I need something better for my family," said Jesus Valbuena, twenty-five, who has nine years in this city.

"Now we're starting to work for ourselves: Mexicans!" said Mr. Galaviz, thirty-four, who has eight years in this city.

It is possible that reality will rub away their enthusiasm. Robert C. Smith, a professor of sociology at Barnard College and an expert on the Mexican experience in New York, said that their venture requires *confianza*: deep trust.

"There's a lot of things that could go wrong," he said. "What if the guy who's supposed to do the plumbing doesn't come through? You really have to trust each other."

So far, *confianza* remains intact in this corporation with no name. While two boys watched, each man reached into his pocket and pulled out twenty-five dollars.

JUNE 28, 2003

First Summer of the Rest of Her Life

Learning the correct time can be a challenge at Public School 29, thanks to its collection of free-spirited wall clocks. It might be 8:45 at one end of the hall, 11:04 at the other end, and 6:35 in the classroom. At any given moment a student might want to eat breakfast, finish that quiz, or just call it a day.

But wall clocks are not the only measure of our minutes and hours. When this Brooklyn school called it a day on Thursday, ending the academic year, the students and teachers walked into the naked noon sun with a fuller appreciation for time's passage. Nothing, they had learned, is timeless, not even life within a school's protective brick.

Last September might as well have been last week, so fresh was it in the mind. In Room 305, Elizabeth Holden was beginning her first year as a teacher, while in Room 425, Penny Pritchard was embarking on her last. The eight hundred students were everywhere, and so was the new principal, Melanie Raneri Woods, an ever-spinning top of an educator with many, many plans.

Then June came, in about the time it takes to sharpen a pencil. So much had happened in those nine months at the eighty-two-year-old school in Cobble Hill; so much.

The potluck dinners. The monthly writing celebrations. The sudden death of a six-year-old boy in kindergarten—"the saddest day of my professional career," Mrs. Woods said. Jazz Night. The spring concert. The last day of school.

Mrs. Woods spent Thursday morning spinning with grace: saying goodbye to parents, preparing for the delivery of new furniture, warning students to be careful on the stairs. Meanwhile, in the classrooms, the hot breath of summer wafted through the open windows, conjuring thoughts of watermelon seeds to spit, of wet footprints to form at poolside.

Lily Frost was thinking about baking a cake of celebration, while her second-grade classmate, Lily Bondy, thought about bottom front teeth already growing in. Annie Hutchinson looked forward to visiting art museums, but Misha Macnie's hopes extended no further than getting some water balloons and going to the park.

Third-graders harbored similar plans. Madeleyn Valenzuela will be frolicking beside her father, who has a job working at a beach house. Sofia Johnson has some grandparents to visit, in Wisconsin and Mississippi. Jun Huron has an appointment with a dance camp, and Benjamin McKenna has one with a Fudge Kitchen in Cape May, New Jersey.

As these students planned their immediate future, Penny Pritchard considered her immediate past: thirty-five years of working in the city's school system, including the last fourteen right here, in Room 425.

Sitting in the swelter of her classroom, out of her students' earshot, Mrs. Pritchard talked of what she would not miss. All those fitful Sunday nights spent planning the week's lessons. All those mornings of rising at 4:15, in hopes of finding a parking spot and getting some work done before the students arrived.

In truth, there was little she would not miss. But she turns fifty-five in September, and something was telling her to retire before burnout sets in. "I like teaching," she said. "And I want to go out liking teaching."

Somewhere in P.S. 29, at least one clock was correctly reflecting the imminence of noon, her students' long-awaited moment of release. She had to gather them about her one last time.

"Everybody to the rug," she announced.

Twenty-one boys and girls took their places on the rug at the back of the classroom, and looked up to study this woman whose neck glistened from the heat, this woman who had been so important in their young lives.

"As you know, I'm retiring," Mrs. Pritchard said. "And I wanted to tell you that I am so happy that I got to spend my last year with you."

She told them to write to her. She told them she loved them. And she told them she expected goodbye hugs in the playground.

Mrs. Pritchard would linger into late afternoon, cleaning up Room 425 and distributing the equipment she no longer needed—the overhead projector, the materials for arts and crafts—to teachers returning in the fall. And then she would be gone.

If her future includes a visit to Fudge Kitchen, she did not say. She intends to travel with her husband for a year, she said, and after that, "I'm going to have to find a new life."

But as time goes by, she will have this: On her last day of school, twenty-one third graders waited in the playground heat to hug and kiss her before dashing off to the rest of their lives.

MAY 6, 2006

A Gambler Sees Beyond the Jackpot

Victor Ramdin considered the cards dealt to him.

Around him stood hundreds of people watching this hand of the Foxwoods Poker Classic. Across from him sat a Yale student so gifted he could teach a doctoral program in Texas Hold 'Em. And now, in his hands, promising everything and nothing, the jack of spades and the ace of fast-beating hearts.

Mr. Ramdin, thirty-eight, whose pleasant smile masks a killer's instinct, considered the odds, among them: the chances that as a hard-working Guyanese immigrant from the Bronx, he would take up poker and within three years be vying for a $1.3 million jackpot in a casino in eastern Connecticut. Ten to one? Million to one?

The Yale man, Alex Jacob, signaled all in, which meant that he was dedicating all his chips to this hand of Texas Hold 'Em. Mr. Ramdin called, which meant that they would dispense with bluffing and expose their cards.

Mr. Jacob revealed the king of diamonds and the jack of clubs. Mr. Ramdin showed his ace and his jack.

The dealer placed three cards—community cards, to be used by both players—faceup on the table: the three of spades, the queen of hearts, and the seven of hearts. Nothing favoring either player, really. Two more cards to go before a winner could be determined.

Seventeen years ago, Mr. Ramdin entered this country illegally and worked, and worked. He became a guard at the city morgue, but was so spooked that he quit after his first day, never to return for his

check. Then he got a job packing and delivering fish all day, after
which, he recalled, he would board the subway "and nobody would
stick around."

He managed his mother's grocery store in the Bronx. He saved up
and started a 99-cent store. He helped family members with other
businesses, and started investing in real estate. Along the way he got his
green card, and became an American citizen.

He began to play poker with friends. It appealed to his compulsive
nature, which was already manifesting itself in the way he drank, shot
pool, played darts. Most of all, he liked how success equaled cash.

Poker became everything. He entered qualifying rounds for tour-
naments to try to win, of course, but also to learn from veteran players. He made mental notes of what card combinations they favored,
of when they called and when they bluffed. He learned to detect the
"tell" of other players—the scratch of the nose, the dart of the eyes—
that betrayed their feelings about the cards in their hands.

The dealer presented the next card, the eight of spades. Mr.
Ramdin's ace gave him the best hand. The only way he could lose was
if the seventh and last card—"the river," they call it—was a king that
would give Mr. Jacob a winning pair.

Earlier in the week, while he was checking into the casino's hotel,
Mr. Ramdin overheard a distraught woman telling the clerk that her
bus had left without her and that she needed a room. But the clerk
told her that the hotel was booked solid.

Seeing no other play, Mr. Ramdin arranged to have the woman
stay in the room reserved for him, while he doubled up with a poker-
playing friend. The next day, at a point in the tournament when he
was down to three thousand dollars, the grateful woman appeared as
if from a dream. I'm praying for you, she told him. You will win.

He took heart in her words; he had plans for some of the winnings.

Finally, the river. The dealer turned over the last card of the last
hand in the four-day tournament: the jack of hearts—not a king!—
which meant that Victor Ramdin, Guyanese immigrant from the
Bronx, held the winning hand of a pair of jacks with an ace kicker.
With the flick of one card, he was $1.3 million richer.

"I jumped straight over the table," he recalled.

But the story does not end with Mr. Ramdin on that table four
weeks ago in Connecticut. In addition to being a poker player, in

addition to owning a 99-cent store, he is a philanthropist, having worked closely with Guyana Watch, a nonprofit organization that tries to meet the medical needs of poor children in Guyana.

After winning the Foxwoods tournament, he put to work that estimable mind of his, the one forever whirring with calculations. He determined that with $200,000 of his prize money, he could pay for heart surgery for ten children from his native country.

With one call, ten new hands were dealt. All hearts.

AUGUST 3, 2005

Keeping Unjaded Eye on the Ball

Like most of us, Joe Burke worked on Monday. He drove his five-year-old Honda out of Brooklyn and over the Verrazano-Narrows Bridge to Staten Island, where he is employed as a baseball catcher. He earns twelve hundred dollars a month, plus expenses.

Earlier in the day came word that Major League Baseball had suspended one of its multimillion-dollar stars, Rafael Palmeiro of the Baltimore Orioles, for testing positive for steroids—a development that seemed to belie his congressional testimony five months ago that he never used steroids, never, ever.

But this was not Mr. Burke's concern. His team, the Staten Island Yankees, was about to play the Auburn Doubledays, a rival in the New York–Penn League. And though he knew that he would not be playing this night, he had to prepare, for baseball is his job.

Mr. Burke, twenty-one, looks eighteen. Five years ago, he was just another baseball-obsessed kid from Marine Park; two months ago, he was playing for St. John's University. Now he wears Number 26, carries a black catcher's glove along with a weak .207 batting average, and draws strength from his previous two games.

"Last night I went one for four with a single," he said. "And the night before I went two for four with a stolen base and an RBI."

The challenge in watching a ballgame these days is to block out the ubiquitous, syrupy voice of television sports that equates baseball with life, courage, and fealty to country. Once that voice is silenced, a ballgame can be seen for what it is: a joyful distraction, a grassy pursuit—and, as on this Staten Island night, a social communion be-. tween those who play and those who wish they could.

Before the game, the team's owners, Stanley Getzler, seventy-six, and his son, Josh, thirty-six, sat just outside the Richmond County Bank Ballpark, dispensing tickets and charming customers. The elder Mr. Getzler left the New York Stock Exchange several years ago because he wanted a change, and now he works beside cowlike mascots named Scooter, Huck, and Red.

The team has yet to woo crowds from Manhattan, though a benefit to this is that the Getzlers now know just about everybody, from the man who complains about the lack of nonalcoholic beer ("Because we used to have one case that would last the entire season," Josh Getzler confided) to the local potentates. When someone whispered "Guy Molinari's coming," its gravity suggested the imminent arrival of the pontiff, and not a former borough president.

Young Joe Burke emerged from the dugout with his pinstriped teammates for the Pledge of Allegiance. A schoolgirl with a ponytail belted out a version of "The Star-Spangled Banner" that was three times her size. Then: Play ball.

From the edge of the dugout, Mr. Burke watched as his teammate and fellow catcher P. J. Pillitere crouched low to catch the first pitch of the game. A strike. Mr. Burke turned and, with a studied nonchalance, glanced up into the stands.

Somewhere up there, among the forty-seven hundred, were his parents, Edward and Karen; he works as a sergeant for the postal police, she works as a legal secretary, and now they have a professional ballplayer living in their house.

Up there too: a regular patron with a taste for nonalcoholic beer, a former borough president, and a couple from London, Paul Eversfield and Bobbie Brown, attending their first baseball game and struggling to appreciate its rules and beauty.

"Are you not allowed to run if he catches it?" asked Mr. Eversfield, a cricket player.

It's complicated, he was told. Very complicated.

By the fourth inning, and with dusk settling, the Yankees had pulled ahead in a game they would eventually win, 9-3. Young men from Chandler, Arizona, and Rock Island, Illinois, from Venezuela and the Dominican Republic, performed their baseball ballet, swinging, throwing, pirouetting. Maybe you'll know their names someday; maybe not.

Just beyond this dirt-and-grass stage, past the outfield wall and hard against New York Harbor, the metropolis preened—as if daring any other city to match its majesty. The Staten Island ferries glided back and forth, each one a glowing, floating stadium. The Brooklyn Bridge twinkled its lights. And the August haze played such tricks with the eye that the Statue of Liberty might have been doing the wave.

For a moment, steroids did not matter. For a moment, the recent bombs in that visiting couple's London were set aside, as was the threat of terrorism here. Young Joe Burke, professional baseball player from Brooklyn, was batting .207, a wonderful, glorious .207.

DECEMBER 20, 2003

Private Lessons in the Halls of Old Masters

In that hushed hour before the doors open to Fifth Avenue, a young man named Fabian Berenbaum enjoys private consultations with Rembrandt and Rubens, El Greco and van Dyck. They whisper across the centuries. Notice, they say. Learn.

On some mornings the great masters demonstrate the varied uses of light and shadow. Other mornings they suggest ways to convey emotion through the smallest details: purity of soul in a child's eye, perhaps, or world-weariness in the arch of an old man's brow. Their ability to grant a kind of everlasting life to those long dead—with paint, brush, and canvas—can leave Mr. Berenbaum breathless.

These lessons end when the wooden floor says so. It creaks faintly under the weight of the day's first visitors to the European Paintings galleries. They have made their way up the grand staircase to the second floor, and now the sighing of wood—along with the murmurs of anticipation and the jingles of pocketed keys—announces their arrival.

Having lost their bearings in the midst of so many masterpieces crying out for attention, some visitors seek help from the people wearing the blue blazers and gold lapel pins that identify them as security guards. Can you tell me where the El Greco exhibition is? Can you tell me how to get to the gift shop? Can you tell me where the bathrooms are?

Certainly, answers a smiling Mr. Berenbaum. Go to the end of this hall and . . .

In his day's brief intervals of quiet—between all those earnest questions so politely answered—the young man hears other voices. Hey, Berenbaum, Rembrandt whispers. Check out what I did with this portrait.

The Metropolitan Museum of Art employs hundreds of guards and supervisors to provide assistance to visitors and to protect its priceless collections. You may take photographs, but please, no flash. You may bring your face within inches of a Manet, but do not touch, do not brandish a pen, and please—please!—never use your umbrella as a pointer while making some profound observation about artistic technique.

If you do, you may hear from Fabian Berenbaum. He tends to be protective.

Mr. Berenbaum, twenty-nine, has worked as a guard at the museum for four years, and has stood in silence, eyes wide, in just about every section of the building: the American wing, the Asian galleries, the Islamic, Egyptian, and Modern. But years ago he requested that his primary assignment be in European Paintings, among the work of artists born before 1865. "Basically, I wanted to be closer to the old masters," he said.

He had his reasons. He is also an artist, with a master's degree in fine arts.

In the hour before the museum opens, he chooses two or three paintings in his section to be alone with. On Sunday, for example, he took another close look at a self-portrait of Rembrandt's from about

1660, a study in aging, and noticed again "how he was able to capture feeling through the eyes and the brow."

And on Wednesday morning, he spent time before *Venus and Adonis,* the Rubens masterpiece from the mid-1630s. He admired how the artist achieved the desired flesh tone through layering; how he achieved a sense of dimension by casting Venus's left leg against a dark cape.

"This morning I also looked at this Brouwer, another great little painting," he said while retracing his steps that afternoon. He gazed again at *The Smokers,* a lively tavern scene from about 1636 by Adriaen Brouwer, and muttered, "The brush strokes are so gestural."

Two women with a map approached Mr. Berenbaum. "Hi," one said. "Can you show us where we are?"

As he spends his workdays among some of civilization's greatest artwork, Mr. Berenbaum rarely feels the crushing despair of why bother. Instead, he said: "It helps with my work ethic. You see the production, and you get a sense of the work that goes into being a great painter."

If, in his own painting, he wants to capture gold, he can seek inspiration from the chain that glitters in Rembrandt's *Aristotle with a Bust of Homer.* If he is trying to get a hand gesture just right, he might drink in *Merrymakers at Shrovetide* by Frans Hals.

"But you can't try to imitate," he said. "You have to be inspired to do your own thing."

When his shift ends, Mr. Berenbaum boards the 4 train to the 7, and gets out in Sunnyside, Queens. He walks up two flights to his small apartment, where he has converted his bedroom into a studio that is furnished with two easels. This is where he paints, often until well past midnight.

He does not listen to music. He has no television. There are just those whispers.

JUNE 11, 2005

Into Character As George, and into a Fix

She eased herself into the monkey suit. We all have to start somewhere.

An eager and earnest performance artist—a dancer, actually—she tried to summon her inner monkey, but she wasn't supposed to be just any monkey. She was supposed to be the most famous monkey in literature. She dug deeper, deeper, until she found her inner Curious George. There.

So what if it was at a book exposition at some Off Off Off Off Broadway outpost called the Jacob K. Javits Convention Center. So what if technical difficulties would soon leave her shrink-wrapped. So what if she had to ape about in anonymity. It was the New York debut of Kat Arbuckle, twenty-two, three weeks fresh from Pittsburgh.

"Just trying to make it," she says.

Every day, maybe every hour, people arrive from somewhere else to make it here, with "It" the stand-in for stardom, wealth, or some other imperfect measure of success in life. They come to this city prepared to don monkey suits, literally or figuratively, to prove that they have what "It" takes.

Ms. Arbuckle has the smile, the chops, the ambition. She graduated from Point Park University in Pittsburgh with a bachelor's degree in the performing arts on April 30. Two weeks later she put her dance shoes in a carry-on bag and flew to New York, a place so foreign to her that she hesitates before saying the name of the airport: "La Guardia?"

She knew four people among this city's eight million, all of whom happened to have Point Park ties. She describes three of them—Allison, Holly, and Kelsey—the same way: "dancer, singer, actress."

She unpacked at Allison's apartment on the Upper West Side and went on a couple of auditions, including an instructive one for the Rockettes. "The girls they kept were mainly five foot nine and up, very thin, very tall," says Ms. Arbuckle, five foot seven.

At the moment she is auditioning to be a waitress at Isabella's, an Upper West Side restaurant. She has shadowed waitresses, spent time in the kitchen, and taken the required wine classes. "We learned about unoaked and oaked chardonnay," she says.

A couple of weeks ago, the fourth person she knows in New York called. His name is Ryan Stana, and he runs an entertainment company. He knew that Ms. Arbuckle could use a paycheck, and he had a "character costume" job he needed to fill at an event called Book-Expo America. A two-day job, four hours a day, twenty-five dollars an hour.

"I'll do it," Ms. Arbuckle said.

The furry brown outfit, folded neatly in a trunk, included a red shirt with "Curious George" written across the front. It had a zip-up head, two vents, and a battery-operated contraption that blew air to flesh out the costume and cool the person inside. She wriggled into it, zipped up, and peered through the dark-mesh mouth at her reflection in a mirror.

"I just thought about a monkey, and what a monkey would do," she says. "I was so Curious George."

Curious George does not speak. So Ms. Arbuckle tapped into her talent for pantomime, monkeying around in the Curious George area of the Houghton Mifflin publishing company's booth. Nearby, an actor played the man with the yellow hat, the Ed McMahon to Curious George's Carson, always there to take George by the hand whenever he gets in trouble.

Of course, it's the least he could do. According to H. A. Rey's first entry in the Curious George canon, the man with the yellow hat abducted the mischievous monkey in Africa and, after some misadventures, placed him in a city zoo. "What a nice place for George to live!" the book concludes.

The gig went well at first, with people posing for photographs with Curious George and talking about his impact on their child-hood. Then, just like that, the costume's fan shut down—and Curious George deflated.

"It was as if cellophane came down and molded against my body," she says, laughing. "It got really hot, really quickly. And the head kind of collapsed. I had no vision."

The man with the yellow hat became concerned and began ask-ing: "George! George! Are you OK?"

Determined to stay true to her mute character, Ms. Arbuckle just raised her arms and shrugged. Her life was not in jeopardy; the Jaws of Life were not required. Still, she needed help.

The man with the yellow hat took one arm, a Houghton Mifflin publicist took the other, and together they led a temporarily blind Ms. Arbuckle away from the booth and toward a back room. It was a long, long walk, she remembers, with passersby asking: "George! George! What's wrong? You drunk?"

In the back room, they peeled her out of the costume, gave her some water, and told her to take a fifteen-minute break while a new battery was installed. Then she climbed back in to become Curious George, because sometimes that's what you have to do to make it.

PART IV

Librado Romero

Leaving New York

OCTOBER 1, 2003

Puppet in Lap, and Audience in His Palm

Stan Burns, Magical Ventriloquist, Versatile Ventrilo-Wit, and historian of the art of throwing one's voice, died five years ago. He was seventy-nine. He left behind his wife, Sylvia, a trove of memorabilia, and six dummies: Bruce, Cecil, Susie, Lulu, Uncle Sam, and Dr. Litchi, as in the nut.

It is fitting that Stan used an unconventional spelling of litchi, given that he dedicated his life to the whimsical violation of rules—particularly the one holding that inanimate objects cannot talk. He was a boy with a stutter when he saw his first "vent" act, at a Harlem dime museum back in the 1920s. And when he tried the illusion himself, words poured forth uninterrupted, as if by magic.

His first professional dummy was a smart-alecky boy named Willie. But Willie was stolen from a car's backseat one night, an abduction that taught Stan to keep his puppets always in sight. But for years afterward, Sylvia said, "Stan kept looking for him."

Although he was no Edgar Bergen, Stan's ability in extracting vaudevillian banter from dressed-up pieces of wood served him well.

There was the occasional bit on television or in a movie, but most of the time he lugged his suitcases around the world, going from Catskill resort to Caribbean cruise to children's birthday party, drinking water or smoking a cigarette while the dummy on his lap cracked wise or cute.

Those cruise gigs were a grind. On Saturday mornings, the ship would dock on the West Side, Sylvia would hand Stan his mail, they'd have a quick cup of coffee, and then he'd be gone for another week. He diligently sent letters from his various ports of call, but he never signed his own name; it was always Bruce, or Cecil, or "the Kids."

Sylvia could never forget Stan in his absence, even if she wanted to. Their Manhattan apartment was a veritable vent exhibit, with Charlie McCarthy memorabilia on display, rare ventriloquism books on the shelves, and movie and vaudeville posters adorning the walls: all material for the exhaustive history of ventriloquism that he would someday write.

For thirty years Stan talked about his book project, so much so that others in the vent fold thought that one of his strings had snapped. "It almost became a joke," recalled Todd Stockman, a former professional ventriloquist who was a friend of Stan's. " 'Oh, Stan Burns—still work-ing on that book?' "

He finished his manuscript, called *Other Voices: Ventriloquism from B.C. to TV,* in 1996, but publishers said it wasn't for them. Then, when his health began to fail, Sylvia took charge. By the time she got fifteen hundred copies of the handsome coffee-table book published, at a personal cost of fifty thousand dollars, Stan was four months dead.

Still, what a tribute. Vents everywhere—from Paul Winchell and his dummy, Jerry Mahoney, to Jimmy Nelson and his puppet dog, Farfel—applauded Stan and Sylvia.

With Stan dead, Sylvia was alone in an apartment awash in vent ephemera. This was Stan's stuff, after all; she had been a nurse.

When no museum could promise a permanent exhibit, she slowly began to sell the items. Most of the wall art, from a movie poster for *Charlie McCarthy, Detective* to that advertisement for a long-gone French ventriloquist ("*L'homme qui parle du ventre*"), sold at auction. But there was still the matter of the Kids.

Bruce, the redhead, and Cecil, his small sidekick, went to relatives of Stan's. Dr. Lichi, who moved by remote control, and sexy Lulu— "she had a lot of husbands, none of whom were her own," Sylvia said, repeating Stan's old line—were sold to a collector in the Midwest.

Uncle Sam, though, sits in a chair in the living room. And stored in the cluttered hall closet, next to cardboard boxes marked "vent stuff" and "various vent heads," is Susie, tucked safe in her case.

"She's got dimples and blue eyes," Sylvia explained, and suddenly Stan's old Susie routine came to life, from the water that Susie used to pour into Stan's ear to the flowers that would sprout if the children said the magic word.

"What's the magic word?" he'd ask. "Abracadabra," they'd shout.

"No, that was last week's word," he'd say, and the kids would laugh and laugh.

Sylvia plans to keep a few things, of course. How could she not? They were introduced many years ago at a dinner party given by mutual friends. One guest that night was a funny storyteller, and Stan and Sylvia laughed so hard that they grasped each other's hands under the table. After that, Sylvia became his living doll.

"Stan was a good vent," said the ventriloquist's wife.

DECEMBER 7, 2005

For Police Officer and City, a Wound to the Heart

Bunting the color of a bad bruise draped the Tropical Paradise Restaurant in East Flatbush yesterday. It was hung in memory of Police Officer Dillon Stewart, who used to eat breakfast there, but now lay dead in a coffin in the church across the street.

The black-and-purple fabric that rippled in the chilly Brooklyn air also reflected the smallness of this vast, 322-square-mile city. Here, eight million people ache when a police officer or firefighter unknown to them dies in the line of duty. Here, the paths of strangers cross; fates intertwine.

One night six months ago, in this restaurant, a group called the New Release Band had a neighborhood crowd swaying, and the owner, David Gayle, smiling. He had opened the place in 2001 after retiring as a city correction officer, and his combination of Caribbean food and music seemed to click.

A local man wandered in, smoking a cigarette. When a waitress informed him there was a ban on smoking, the owner recalled yesterday, the man blew smoke in her face and bumped her. She told her boss, who walked over to the man and asked him to leave.

After muttering a challenging "What are you gonna do?" Mr. Gayle recalled, the man sort of backpedaled out of the restaurant— only to pull a gun from nowhere once he stepped outside the door. "Within a second, he started shooting toward me and the windows of the establishment," the owner said.

The gunman's back was to the church across the street, the New Life Tabernacle Church, as he fired again and again, the owner said. The bullets pierced the door, smashed through the plate-glass windows facing Avenue D, and exited through the windows facing Utica Avenue. Mr. Gayle never fired his own gun, so busy was he trying to duck the bullets and glass.

The next day, he said, neighbors identified the gunman as Damian Henry, who lived around the corner; he was soon arrested and charged with attempted murder, though no gun was recovered. And Mr. Gayle was soon serving Caribbean food again to his regular customers, including a friendly, diligent officer named Dillon Stewart.

Last week, a little more than a mile from the Tropical Paradise, Officer Stewart was shot and killed while chasing a driver who had run a red light. He was thirty-five. The police now say the bullet that evaded his protective vest and pierced his heart was fired by the very same 9-millimeter Glock that was used to shoot up the Tropical Paradise six months earlier. Same neighborhood. Same block. Same gun.

Now, outside the repaired windows of a place promising paradise, there unfolded a sad pageantry born of a Glock that had been sold to a Florida gun dealer in 1994 and reported stolen in Florida in 1999.

A widow who would not celebrate her tenth wedding anniversary. Two young daughters, one just five months old. A mayor. A police commissioner. And twenty thousand police officers, almost all of them in dress blues, almost all of them standing in the cold, facing the church within which their fallen brother lay, the gold detective's shield he earned in death pinned to his uniform.

As the morning memorial service unfolded inside, loudspeakers mounted on top of a police van at the corner of Avenue D and East Forty-ninth Street broadcast the prayers and songs and tributes—words that at first seemed not to sink in, but only to float above a swath of blue: "I am the resurrection and the life. The God of Jacob is our fortress. The city of the Lord stands firm and tall. We will not rest until his killer is prosecuted and punished to the fullest extent of the law."

The words echoed off brick and pavement, as police officers from New Jersey, from Suffolk and Nassau and Westchester Counties—but mostly from this city—chatted, smoked cigarettes, and drank the free coffee being dispensed from police union trucks.

But as the service drew closer to its end, the chitchat about pensions and "the job" gave way to quiet. Thousands and thousands of officers lined up on the south side of Avenue D, faced north, and listened, as Officer Stewart's closest friends and colleagues remembered him. When they choked up, their words broke in the street.

Inside, the church's pastor, Bishop Micheal Mitchell, delivered a long eulogy of Pentecostal passion—"the demons tremble at the name of Jesus"—while outside, the police of this city, with names like Gomez and Andino, Walsh and Mey, stared into the December horizon. They listened to the final prayer and the benediction.

An idling hearse awaited its burden. But before it departed, there fell upon this crowded corner of loud, crazed, anonymous New York City a long, long stretch of small-town stillness.

JULY 26, 2006

Man Who Told Many Secrets Kept His Own

Some forty years ago, a young man who called himself by the distinctive name of William M. V. Kingsland appeared on the Upper East Side scene. Intelligent and engaging, with a fondness for sly puns, he became a regular among a subset of rarefied New York.

He possessed a thorough knowledge of art and books, but his particular expertise centered on the stories of the buildings around him—stories of the privileged and rich as well as of the brick and mortar. Blessed with an astonishing memory, he knew pedigrees better than the pedigreed.

Fond of leading friends on informal tours through the streets of the East Side, he would point out a building's new metal railing—a clear landmark violation!—then share with glee the generations-old melodrama that once played out behind the repointed brick. "Who had run off with the nanny, who had shot his mother-in-law—all their foibles," Elizabeth Ashby, cochairwoman of the Defenders of the Historic Upper East Side, said. "If you walked around with him, there was always something that sprang to his mind."

Looking back, his friends now smile at the thought: William seemed to know everyone's past—but no one knew his. It was as though he had simply appeared one day, fully formed, with that mustache.

The spare details he shared painted an intriguing background. East Side, it seemed. Groton and Harvard, it seemed. Of rich parents who had lived in Switzerland and died in Florida. Divorced long ago from a French woman of royalty. Wealthy enough to work when the mood struck him, mostly by dealing in and writing about art.

Where he lived was even vague. He said that he lived on Fifth Avenue, but stored his artwork in a one-bedroom apartment on East Seventy-second Street that very few remember entering. As for M. V., it stood for Milliken Vanderbilt, he confided, but let's keep that to ourselves, shall we?

Sure, he rarely answered his telephone, had no answering machine, and preferred to be contacted by mail; but then you would bump into him in the park, and hours would pass in conversation. Sure, his shabby-prep style of dress announced his frugality; but then birthday presents for your child would arrive in the mail, courtesy of William M. V. Kingsland.

He was a passionate preservationist, whose frequent notes to the Landmarks Preservation Commission—"metal railing installed above 4th floor level"; "stone ornament (previously unpainted) painted white"—earned him distinction as a one-man violations bureau. He was a gifted genealogist who volunteered his services to, among others, the New York Marble Cemetery. Prickly, evasive, witty, kind: a New York character, a friend.

Mr. Kingsland died, suddenly and alone, in his East Seventy-second Street apartment in early spring; he was either fifty-eight or sixty-two. All around him were stacks of books and pieces of art, including two of particular interest: a bust that appears to be by Alberto Giacometti, and a small painting by Giorgio Morandi. It could be that his estate is worth as much as $2 million, but no will has been found. His death prompted a frantic search for relatives and for other assets, but the exercise has been like chasing shadows. No Kingsland knew of William M. V. Kingsland. No Fifth Avenue apartment could be found.

"Here he was, an expert on other people's families, and we know nothing about his," Anne Brown, the president of the New York Marble Cemetery, said. "Many of us are convinced he's up there, holding his sides, laughing at us."

If he is laughing, or even just smiling, it might be because William Milliken Vanderbilt Kingsland was born Melvyn Kohn. In March 1960, when he was either twelve or sixteen, his name was changed to one that evoked Old New York—although his parents, Robert and Loretta, remained the Kohns.

The reasons why a boy would take such Gatsbyesque steps are unknown. It could be that he simply chose to avail himself of that familiar gift of vast New York: the opportunity for redefinition.

Some friends say they suspected it all along, but add that his embellishments were harmless. "There were things that didn't add up," said Spencer Compton, a close friend. "But the man was so intelligent and charming and full of goodness that one enjoyed him far too much to worry about the accuracy of his pedigree."

And many say it doesn't matter. "We were fond of William the person, not William the name," Ms. Ashby said.

Friends arranged for a funeral in mid-April. William M. V. Kingsland was buried at the New York City Marble Cemetery; heirs of Melvyn Kohn have been contacted.

An Old Hand, Betrayed by His Belt

Joe Gillum of Harlem fell from the sky last week. He plummeted silently through the air of a Silk Stocking neighborhood and broke upon impact, as did that extra appendage of his, a squeegee.

He washed windows for a living, often working so high above the ground that, just thinking of it, your hands perspire. At sixty-eight, he was still strapping on his trusty old belt—too old, it turned out, and not so trusty—and suspending himself in the air, his back to the world, his silhouette reflected in the soot-caked windows of others.

Until last Thursday, that is, when he dropped nine stories in about the time it takes to soak a rag in a pail of soapy water. Up above, the two canvas straps that he had secured to the sides of the window could do nothing now but wave goodbye in the breeze.

The initial police report on his accidental death attached his middle initial of L to the end of his given name, and so in most of the brief news accounts he was rechristened Joel Gillum. "It was Joe," said his wife, Ollie. "It was Joe."

Mrs. Gillum, sixty-seven, small-boned and white-haired, sat deep in a couch's hug in the worn apartment on Adam Clayton Powell Jr. Boulevard that she had shared with her husband for more than thirty years. She seemed composed, but this was Monday morning, within the exhausting awkwardness that comes after the death and before the wake.

The telephone beside her rang again, but her sister-in-law, Marie Colbert, in from Oklahoma for the funeral, was fielding calls and jotting messages in a spiral-bound notebook. "Thank you for calling," Mrs. Colbert said again into the receiver.

Some of the callers were friends and relatives. Others were wondering where their window washer was. "His clients don't know," Mrs. Gillum said. "They're expecting him today."

Joe Gillum, of Georgia, and Ollie Colbert, of Oklahoma, met nearly forty-nine years ago in a Harlem nightclub on Eighth Avenue. He was working in a hospital morgue then, and she was setting fake gems in costume jewelry at some factory. They talked about where they came from, how they had wound up in New York City—jobs, basically—and what they liked and disliked. At some point she revealed her love for apricots. Next day, here comes Joe Gillum, bearing apricots.

They married in 1957, and shared more fruit, bitter and sweet. The first child, Joe, died in infancy. The second child, Sabrina, would give them three grandchildren. And one of those three would give them a great-grandson.

The years can blur into one long workday. But Mrs. Gillum said she is sure that her husband started his own window- and floor-cleaning business in the mid-sixties, because it was after President Kennedy's assassination and before Martin Luther King Jr.'s.

After thirty years of wrestling electric sanders over parquet floors—those machines have minds of their own—his back hurt so much that he decided a decade ago to concentrate on windows. By then he had built up a good clientele, which meant that every spring he was out, and up.

"He never was afraid of heights," said Mrs. Gillum, her eyes looking for distraction from a muttering television.

"That was his life," said her brother, Nemiah Colbert. "That's what he did for a living."

The telephone rang again. "They're calling for him to come to work today," Mrs. Gillum said to the television.

Last Thursday morning, the Gillums made plans to go food shopping that evening. Mrs. Gillum told her husband that she might be a little late from her job minding an apartment on the Upper West Side. "His last words, and it was so soft," she said, "was, 'I'll be right here waiting for you.'"

Then Mr. Gillum headed for a job at a nice brick apartment building at 430 East Fifty-seventh Street, carrying, his wife recalled, "his belt, his pail, and his squeegee." When asked whether her husband ever updated his equipment, Mrs. Gillum slowly shook her head and said, "Uh-uh."

By eleven, he was dead. By noon, his blood had been scrubbed and sprayed from the sidewalk by one of the building's employees. And by the afternoon, a neighbor of the Gillums who had spoken to detectives had taped a note to their door, saying, "Please see me, it's an emergency."

A funeral service was held at Canaan Baptist Church in Harlem yesterday morning, followed by the long ride out to Calverton National Cemetery on Long Island for the burial of a fallen window washer.

For the record, his name was Joe Gillum. Joe L. Gillum.

JULY 19, 2003

He Conned the Society Crowd but Died Alone

David Hampton's pursuit of a fabulous Manhattan life ended last month in the early-morning hush of a downtown hospital. No celebrities keened by his bedside, no theatrics unfolded in the hall; there was no last touch of the fabulous. Just the clinical cluck that follows the death of a man who dies alone at thirty-nine.

His name may not resonate, but his story will. David Hampton was the black teenager who conned members of the city's white elite twenty years ago with an outsized charm. He duped them into believing that he was a classmate of their children, the son of Sidney Poitier, and a victim of muggers who had just stolen his money and Harvard term paper—a term paper titled "Injustices in the Criminal Justice System."

The scam yielded a modest payoff: temporary shelter, a little cash, and the satisfaction of having mocked what he saw as the hypocritical world of limousine liberalism. He also briefly experienced the glamorous Manhattan life that had first seduced him from his upper-middle-class home in Buffalo, a city that he once said lacked anyone "who was glamorous or fabulous or outrageously talented."

"New York was the place for him," Susan V. Tipograph, a lawyer and close friend, said. "In his mind, the fabulous people lived in New York City."

But Mr. Hampton paid long-term costs for his New York conceit and deceit. For beguiling the affluent under false pretenses—the formal charge was attempted burglary—he received twenty-one months in prison. And for being such a distinctive character, he received eternal notoriety as the inspiration for *Six Degrees of Separation,* a 1990 play by John Guare that became a hit and then a movie.

The play indeed centers on a young black man who poses as Sidney Poitier's son, and uses many details from the case. For example, it includes the singular moment when Osborn Elliott, a former editor of *Newsweek,* and his wife, Inger, evicted Mr. Hampton after finding their charming houseguest in bed with a man he had smuggled into their apartment. But Mr. Guare created many other details in writing a play that is a meditation on race relations, art, and self-delusion.

Still, the thought that others were profiting from his hoax—his performance art, really—galled Mr. Hampton; in a way, he was the mark. He sued Mr. Guare and others for $100 million, and lost. He was tried on charges of harassing Mr. Guare, but was never convicted. He took a shot at acting, but his artistry clearly resided in the con.

Mr. Hampton continued duping others for money, for attention, and for entrée into what he saw as the VIP room of New York life. He would meet men in bars, dazzle them with his good looks and intellect, drop celebrity tidbits gleaned from prior scams—and then fleece them. Sometimes he was Patrick Owens; sometimes Antonio Jones; sometimes, just David.

But his name appeared more often in crime reports than in the society pages, usually for matters that fell far short of being fabulous: fare beating, credit-card theft, threats of violence. He once told a judge that he had missed a court date because of a car accident; the ambulance report that he produced to back up his claim was, of course, a fake.

"He would often call me for advice," said Ronald L. Kuby, a

friend and well-known lawyer who had represented him in the harassment case. "All I could tell him was to stop doing these things." .

Something about David Hampton, it seems, prevented him from the enjoyment of simply being David Hampton. Although he felt used by the Guare play, he was using people well before and well after the *Six Degrees of Separation* phenomenon. What's more, he could be a real snob in determining one's fabulousness.

"There were times when I was socializing with people who wouldn't even dare have an Elliott, much less a Guare, at their dinner table," he told *New York* magazine in 1991. "But yet I had been at their dinner table. Legitimately, too."

Ms. Tipograph, who cleaned out his small room at an AIDS residence after he died at Beth Israel Medical Center, said that in the end, Mr. Hampton had a difficult life.

She said that she chooses to remember the warmth of a con artist who was also a friend. "I'm a fifty-two-year-old overweight lawyer with bad knees; clubbing is not my thing," she said. "But we had a very regular friendship. We had lunch together. We had a very unfabulous relationship."

Mr. Hampton, she said, "gave enjoyment, even when he did bad."

One of his last victims, at least as far as law-enforcement officials know, was Peter Bedevian, who went out on a date in late October 2001 with the man he knew as David Hampton-Montilio.

Before heading for a restaurant, Mr. Hampton said that he wanted to take Mr. Bedevian to a 9/11 celebrity benefit, but that he needed to be fronted a thousand dollars for the two tickets. Mr. Bedevian withdrew the money from an ATM, Mr. Hampton dashed into a downtown hotel to buy the tickets—from "friends from L.A. who were in town," as Mr. Bedevian recalled—and then the two sat down to eat.

They lived it up. They ate and drank, and talked about everything from the need to break out of their post-9/11 funk to the extraordinary talents of Billie Holiday. "He was able to pick out a little information, extrapolate, and use it to make me feel even more comfortable," Mr. Bedevian remembered. He added, "He knew how to tease you with 'Oh, we're going to go to this benefit, and so-and-so's going to be there.'"

Mr. Hampton ordered a couple of twenty-three-dollar shots of fine Scotch as after-dinner drinks, Mr. Bedevian recalled. But it seemed the right thing to do; both men were living for the day.

Later would come the pain of having been suckered. Of Mr. Hampton excusing himself to use the bathroom, never to return; of getting stuck with the $423 dinner bill; of pressing criminal charges to get back his thousand dollars; of identifying his charming dinner date through the glass of a police station's one-way mirror.

But Mr. Bedevian also had this to say about his night with the notorious David Hampton, seeker of the fabulous. "Honestly?" he said. "It was one of the best dates that I ever went on."

SEPTEMBER 17, 2005

A Face Seen and Unseen on the Subway

You might look past him as you sat across from him on the subway. If you briefly paused to study his face, you might wonder about his life's story—What have those eyes seen?—before turning to search the car for someone more interesting. Then, when you returned your gaze to his seat, he would be gone, assumed into the human blur of New York City.

That's the kind of man Jack Reimer was, from all accounts. Unassuming, unremarkable, among us.

Like many of us, he was an immigrant. Born in Ukraine in 1918, he arrived at the Port of New York in 1952 and settled on West 136th Street. He moved to Brooklyn and became a United States citizen in 1959.

Like many of us, he worked his way up. He landed his first job with one of the Schrafft's Restaurants that once were sprinkles on the New York sundae. He cleaned the kitchen and eventually was promoted to bartender. By the mid-1960s, he was managing a Schrafft's in Manhattan; you may have even eaten there. After that, he operated a Wise potato chip franchise that served Lower Manhattan.

He had a wife, two children, and some grandchildren. He often read the Bible. He liked to dance. And in 1992, when he was retired and living in Putnam County, agents of his adopted country called to say that they wanted to talk to him about his years as a Nazi.

Mr. Reimer, then seventy-three, took the subway to meet with Justice Department lawyers in Lower Manhattan, his old potato chip territory. He described himself as a kind of accidental Nazi: a soldier in the Russian Army who was taken prisoner by the Germans in 1941, then transferred to the notorious Trawniki training camp in Poland.

He was assigned to the Wachmannschaften, or "guard forces." Wearing uniforms and often carrying guns, these men helped to liquidate Jewish ghettos and to guard extermination and labor camps. Mr. Reimer, who rose quickly in the ranks, said that while he occasionally trained the guards, he worked mostly as an office clerk.

The five-hour interview eventually turned to a morning in either 1941 or 1942, when several dozen Jews were shot dead in a pit near Trawniki. Mr. Reimer claimed that he arrived late to the massacre because he had overslept. But after some prodding, he recalled that one man, lying among the dead, pointed to his own head—a soundless request to be put out of his misery.

Fearing the wrath of German soldiers, Mr. Reimer said, he shot once at the man, but waffled on whether he had killed him. "But after you shot he was no longer pointing to his head, was he?" he was asked. His answer: "No."

Eli M. Rosenbaum, now the director of the Justice Department's Office of Special Investigations, helped to question Mr. Reimer that day in May 1992. "I recall thinking how bizarre that this man came by subway, and was probably seen by any number of Holocaust survivors and children of Holocaust survivors," he said. "None of them could have imagined whom they shared their subway car with."

Mr. Rosenbaum immediately filed a lawsuit to strip Mr. Reimer of his citizenship, the first step toward his deportation, on the grounds that he had provided "assistance in persecution." Mr. Reimer countered by retaining Ramsey Clark, the attorney general during the Johnson administration.

A thirteen-year legal battle ensued. Mr. Clark maintained that his client had persecuted no one, and was himself a victim of World War II. Mr. Rosenbaum countered that such a position was an affront to the war's true victims; that Mr. Reimer provided support to the Nazi SS, participated in the liquidation of the Jewish ghettos in Warsaw and Czestochowa—and killed that man.

Meanwhile, Mr. Reimer told so many conflicting stories that he sometimes seemed to be wishing himself into another version of events. For example, he later denied shooting the man in the pit.

He never allowed his family to attend the court proceedings, where Holocaust survivors sometimes heckled him. He quoted the Ten Commandments a lot. And when Mr. Clark informed him in 2002 that his citizenship had been revoked, he said: "Oh, my."

Four months ago, Mr. Reimer exhausted his appeals, and the government began proceedings for his deportation. "We had reached an agreement in principle that he was going to give us the relief we sought," Mr. Rosenbaum said. "He was going back to Germany."

But the proceedings ended last month when word arrived that a man who had sat among us—potato chip salesman, grandfather, and old Nazi—had died. He was eighty-six.

MAY 25, 2005

On Henry Street, a Cold Trail for a Girl Lost

The century-old tenement is as it was, with paint chipped on the brick, garbage at the door, and a hint of sweatshop sighs escaping from its windows. The squat elementary school down the street hasn't changed either, save for classroom decorations by children who have little or no memory of 1997.

And the short distance separating these buildings on Henry Street, about four hundred paces, remains the yawning gulf of mystery that once swallowed a schoolgirl.

Eight years ago this month, Quin-Rong Wu, the daughter of a

noodle-factory worker and a seamstress, put on her red sneakers. She left her immigrant family's one-bedroom apartment in that tired tenement and began walking to that school, P.S. 2. She was eleven years old, she liked to play hide-and-seek, and she never made it to the door.

Two weeks later, a little girl's body was fished from the East River, near the Manhattan Bridge, which lords over this Lower East Side neighborhood. The police also found a single red sneaker. Manual strangulation, said the medical examiner.

Detectives, community leaders, and reporters crowded into the family's already crowded apartment, with the two beds that would be shared by four now, not five. The mother wailed in the universal language of grief and the father stared off with a glassy gaze.

We all followed our scripts. The detectives worked the streets, conducted dozens of interviews, and followed a tip that went nowhere, about a bearded man. The community leaders raised tens of thousands of dollars to help the shattered family. The reporters chronicled the sadness until the next big murder, just a few days later, that of Jonathan Levin, a schoolteacher and son of the chairman of Time Warner.

Time passed. The Wu family complained about being harassed by detectives, then returned to the anonymity that this city of millions so easily provides. The rumor mill that is Chinatown found other grist. The Police Department's "cold case" squad handed out more leaflets. Quin-Rong's fifth-grade class graduated to middle school, and then to high school.

One would think that the passage of eight years would bring justice, or clarity, or even a little peace. But the pall that enveloped the case of Quin-Rong Wu in 1997 has not lifted, and in some ways seems even thicker.

Sitting in his basement office in Chinatown, another cigarette on his lips, an advocate for immigrants named Steven Wong nodded in sad memory. After the discovery of Quin-Rong's body, he emerged as the Wu family's spokesman and champion, helping to raise donations that he remembers totaling $160,000.

"Money from New York Chinatown, Flushing, Sunset Park," he recalled. "All the way to Texas and California."

Mr. Wong, who says he has flashbacks of seeing police divers searching for the girl's body, said the money was supposed to pay for the funeral, ease the family's financial worries, increase the reward for the killer's capture—and, most of all, help to establish a foundation named after Quin-Rong Wu. It would be a children's protection foundation, he said, separate from the Fujian Children Protection Foundation, which he oversees.

No Quin-Rong Wu Foundation ever came to be, he said. "Besides the money that went to the funeral, I didn't see a return to the community."

The law firm that represented the Wu family split up so acrimoniously that the two lawyers in it no longer speak to each other. One of them, Chun Wong, who wound up with the pro bono case after the breakup, said that he knows nothing about plans for a foundation, and that as far as he remembers, all the donated money was placed in trust for the education of Quin-Rong's two siblings.

"The money's still there," he said. "I'm in the process of getting some of the money out for them."

He said that the Wu family moved years ago from that tenement on Henry Street, but he declined to say where they are. "In certain cases like this," he said, "I would rather let sleeping dogs lie."

The police would like to stir that dog, but they have little new to go on. "It's still open," said Sgt. Joe Gallagher. Then he gave the telephone number that somehow conveyed both hope and hopelessness: 1-800-577-TIPS.

Back on Henry Street, another day ends at P.S. 2. If a lost schoolgirl is remembered here at all, it is not with a plaque, but in neighborhood whispers that the school is bad luck. A couple of teachers have died, and there was that little girl from up the street. Quin-Rong Wu, wasn't it?

The Manhattan Bridge looms, the East River flows, and parents who know these things wait at the schoolhouse door.

Scraps of a Life, Amassed into Mountains

Friends used to tease William Buchanan Obermeyer about his hoarding habit, one worthy of Collyer brothers comparison. He bought several newspapers a day, but almost never threw them out, figuring that he would eventually get back to all those stories he had yet to read. So there went one room.

He also loved books; his best friends, he used to say. He stacked them several feet high around his four-room apartment, creating sky-scrapers of literature in a private city that he strode through like some well-read Kong. So there went the other rooms.

At the same time, he was famous on West Ninety-third Street for being exceedingly tidy. A tall and lanky man with a gray-white pony-tail, he picked up street litter, kicked cigarette butts into the sewer, and collected discarded clothes that he would wash and deliver to a local church.

Yes, Mr. Obermeyer had his ways. He often announced his re-fusal to become enslaved to the telephone that was often buried under newspapers. If you wanted to phone Bill, you had to call between six and seven in the evening, the one hour he might, or might not, pick up.

He also never cooked at home. Every morning at eight, he had breakfast at the Central Park Cafe, a couple of blocks north on Columbus Avenue. On the walk back, he bought a sandwich for lunch. He read until five, then ventured out again to eat dinner at the Pesce Pasta restaurant, a couple of blocks south.

On the first evening of June, he collapsed outside that favored restaurant of his. Bill Obermeyer, Navy veteran, retired nursing clinician, book lover, avid gardener, Philharmonic fan, city eccentric, dead at eighty-three.

Back on West Ninety-third Street, the telephone under newspapers rang for days. Sylvia Barker, a retired nursing administrator who once worked with Mr. Obermeyer at Mount Sinai Hospital, telephoned another close friend of his, Bonaventure Pierre, to ask whether he had heard from Bill recently. No.

They finally tracked down their friend's body at the city morgue. Mr. Pierre and Edward and Michelle van Vlaanderen, Mr. Obermeyer's longtime neighbors, identified him through a glass separating the living from the dead. "That's Bill, that's Bill," Mr. Pierre remembers saying, after which a city worker said, "OK, the five minutes are up."

Mr. Pierre filled out the necessary papers for his friend of forty years. Spouse: None. Children: None. Parents: Dead. Brothers-Sisters, Nephews-Nieces, Uncles-Aunts, First Cousins: No, No, No, and No.

But Mr. Obermeyer did leave behind Ms. Barker, with whom he enjoyed music and annual trips to Garden Week at the Mohonk Mountain House. He often laughed when she teased him about being the third Collyer brother, and dutifully reported to her whenever he disposed of a few newspapers. But in thirty-five years of friendship, she never entered his apartment, she says. "He never let me in."

He left behind Mr. Pierre, who cannot list his dead friend's many kindnesses without sobbing. He left behind the van Vlaanderens and other neighbors, who will remember him for nurturing the apartment building's garden, and for nursing them in times of sickness.

What he did not leave behind was a will, at least one that has been found. Without known kin or will, his became the 852nd estate for which the public administrator of Manhattan assumed responsibility this year.

The public administrator released the body for burial, in a plot that Mr. Pierre owns in Cypress Hills Cemetery in Brooklyn (where the Collyer brothers are also buried). Two investigators from the office then conducted an inventory of Mr. Obermeyer's apartment: a couple of dressers, some pots and pans, two bookshelves—and thousands of books, from textbooks on nursing to volumes of poetry.

Those books, 350 boxes' worth, now sit in a gunship-gray basement of a city building in Lower Manhattan. John J. Reddy Jr., a
lawyer for the public administrator, said that an appraiser would hunt
through the books for volumes of monetary value. Not long ago, another estate offered up a few first editions signed by Lewis Carroll.

Whatever is gleaned from that auction will be added to the Obermeyer estate, now estimated to be about $45,000. If no one ever steps
forward as a next of kin, the money that is left after funeral costs and
legal fees will vanish into the great general fund.

As for the old Obermeyer apartment on West Ninety-third Street,
it remains vacant, and seems to be missing more than just books.

DECEMBER 17, 2005

Her Name Was Erica; She Was Loved

Within five days last month, two young women from
Columbus, Ohio, were stabbed to death in this city. Both came from sta-
ble, supportive families, and both moved here in the belief that New
York air smacks of possibility.

You may already know about the murder of one of these women,
Catherine Woods. Many news reports essentially and unfortunately
summed up her death, and life, this way: wholesome stripper slain.

A daughter of the man who directs the Ohio State University
marching band, Ms. Woods harbored dreams of becoming a professional dancer. She trained, auditioned, and, to pay the rent for an Upper East Side apartment, occasionally danced at topless clubs. She was
twenty-one, and white. No one has been charged in her murder, but
the police are looking hard at an ex-boyfriend.

You probably do not know about the murder of the other woman,
Erica Robertson, whose death merited only a newspaper paragraph or
two, and usually with her surname misspelled as Robinson.

The daughter of an equipment operator and a hospital nurse, she worked as a guard at a homeless shelter to pay the rent for an apartment in the Concourse section of the Bronx. She was twenty-nine, and black. No one has been charged in her murder, but the police are looking hard at an ex-boyfriend.

The killing of Catherine Woods made the front page of at least one newspaper, lasted several news cycles, and became a topic of discussion on a few cable-news talk shows. Since the killing of Erica Robertson did not, here is her story, as conveyed by her older brother, Phillip, who spoke by telephone from the Ohio home of their brokenhearted parents.

Erica surprised her close family four years ago when she suddenly packed up her daughter, Brittany, and moved to the Bronx to be with a New York man she had met. "It didn't really sit well with anybody," Mr. Robertson recalled.

But time soothed the hurt, and before long Mr. Robertson, a truck driver, was driving 540 miles east every few weeks to sleep on a futon in his kid sister's apartment.

"At first I was worried about her being there," he said. "Once she showed me she knew what she was doing down there, I didn't worry too much."

Her relationship with the boyfriend gradually soured, amid accusations of domestic violence. She ended it four months ago, her brother said. "She would give a person chances, but when she was through, it was over." Still, she continued to raise one of his daughters, who, like Brittany, was twelve.

Erica saw a lot of her family. A few days before her murder, her older brother drove her to Columbus for their younger brother's wedding reception and drove her back to the Bronx, all in the same weekend. She talked a lot on the trip about the large Thanksgiving dinner she was preparing for her friends from work.

The day before Thanksgiving, authorities in the Bronx telephoned a home in Columbus. Erica's parents and two brothers settled into a Dodge Durango and drove through the night, through a snowstorm, and arrived in the Bronx at Thanksgiving dawn—only to get lost in the unfamiliar terrain.

"I couldn't think that night," Mr. Robertson said.

They identified her body. They collected her distraught daughter. They packed up some of the food she had prepared for that

Thanksgiving meal—the macaroni and cheese, the shrimp cocktail—and they drove back to Columbus, where they ate it in a shared state of shock.

Who killed Erica? All Mr. Robertson knows is that the ex-boyfriend had a key to the apartment that he refused to return to Erica. That the man's daughter, now in foster care, says she saw him in the apartment that night. That Erica's co-workers told her family he had been threatening her. And that the man, now living in Columbus, did not attend the funeral.

"He didn't call or give his condolences, nothing," Mr. Robertson said.

Last week Mr. Robertson and a friend drove back to the Bronx in a big white truck, while his mother and an uncle followed in a Chrysler. They spent five hours removing Erica's belongings from the apartment that she had once made so cozy. Her protective older brother choked up a bit as he threw that futon into the back of the truck.

"We came back right after that," he said.

And that is the New York story of Erica Robertson, the other woman from Columbus, Ohio.

DECEMBER 24, 2005

They Gather to Remember Mama

Grand Central Terminal. Christmas 1985.

Louis Napolitano remembers how it was. The restored terminal of today, all light and polish, bears little resemblance to its look and feel back then. With its large windows darkened and its glorious ceiling covered in soot, the building seemed cast in Dickensian dusk, while in nearly every nook and cranny, the homeless.

Back then Mr. Napolitano was a transit officer working the

overnight shift, the graveyard. He strolled the marble floors with his nightstick twirling, enforcing the terminal's homeless policy of "Get 'em up and keep 'em moving"—especially from one-thirty to five-thirty in the morning, when it was closed to the public.

His job was often wordless. A tap of his nightstick on a bench was enough to tell a drowsy loiterer to move on. Just the way he set his face could signal to a cluster of homeless people that they were OK there, he was just passing by—or that they had to scatter, another commuter had complained to the stationmaster.

Mr. Napolitano grew to appreciate the unspoken bond among the hidden, late-night people of Grand Central: the police officers, the floor cleaners, the restaurant workers, and, yes, the homeless. "The longer you're here, you see it's just people trying to survive," he said yesterday, sipping coffee in the terminal's lower level while a disheveled man browsed through a garbage can nearby.

He eventually established his own unofficial "no-fly zone" policy— "After closing, don't come out where people can see you"—and got to know many of the denizens. The young girls named April and Tina. The man called Camacho. And that hunched panhandler everyone called Mama.

Mama used to sit on a milk crate on what was called Kitty Kelly Ramp, leading into the terminal from Forty-second Street and Vanderbilt Avenue. She was short, stout, and bundled up in a housedress and pants. She spoke little English, so the bowl in her lap usually did her talking for her.

Tina Haluszka also remembers Mama, just as she remembers Grand Central.

Back then, Ms. Haluszka was a girl of sixteen who sensed that her mother would be better off with one less mouth to feed. She felt the pull of Grand Central, where she found the support she sought among the homeless and destitute. She begged for money, smoked dope, and slept near steam pipes beneath train platforms.

And Mama? Well, Mama watched out for young women living the street life. She handed out clean clothes from the Salvation Army and shared the rolls and doughnuts that a terminal bakery gave her every morning. In return, people like Haluszka gave her cigarettes and shared their food from Burger King.

"She always talked that we were her family," Ms. Haluszka recalled while sitting with Mr. Napolitano, as another unkempt man retrieved a half-empty cup of orange juice from the same garbage can.

Early Christmas Day in 1985, the temperature hovered in the twenties. The witching hour of one-thirty came, and Mama moved to an exposed edge of the terminal to rest on the concrete floor. When the doors to the terminal reopened, she lay down on one of the wooden benches in the main waiting room.

Christmas Day was usually the best day of the year for the panhandlers of Grand Central. But when Ms. Haluszka walked in early that afternoon, she noticed several paramedics, and soon learned that a regular had not responded to a nightstick's bang on a bench. Then she saw Mama, dead of pneumonia. "I seen her boots," she recalled. "Her old-lady boots."

But this Christmas story carries some cheer.

A man named George McDonald, who as a volunteer used to give Mama sandwiches, arranged to have her buried in a Queens cemetery, rather than in potter's field. Her death inspired him to create the Doe Fund, a homeless program that emphasizes self-sufficiency; it now has 350 employees and 800 participants in its Ready, Willing, and Able program.

And tomorrow morning at eleven, another Mama Doe candlelight vigil will be held at Grand Central Terminal, her last home. Mr. Napolitano, now the Doe Fund's director of security, will be there, as will Ms. Haluszka, now one of its dispatchers.

These two acquaintances of Mama finished reminiscing, and walked out of the building they know so well. The waiting room where Mama died is now an events hall, filled yesterday with holiday crafts. And in the spot where she used to sit with a bowl, a man with a white coat pulled over his head rocked and rocked.

NOVEMBER 30, 2005

A Sidewalk Where Looks Can Kill

Another makeshift memorial has materialized on a city sidewalk, this time in front of a bullet-pocked apartment building in Brooklyn. Come and pay respects.

Notice the care in its hasty construction. Cobbled together with plywood, plastic tarp, and a cardboard box that once contained bananas, it stands five feet high and stretches three feet deep. It protects from the elements a few remnants of a boy's abbreviated life, some offerings to heaven, and dozens of candles shimmering with teardrop flames.

See what sits on a shelf of cheap wood: a couple of melted-cheese sandwiches, cold to the touch; a few pieces of chocolate; a fallen stack of quarters; and a portrait of the boy they called Twitch, posing with the sullenness that boys often equate with manhood.

Other photographs draw the eye. Here is Twitch in the midst of other teenage boys; he's the one wearing glasses. Here he is at someone else's wedding. And here he is as a boy at a birthday party, no older than three. The glass of the picture frame catches the fiery dance of candles, lending the illusion of movement to the inanimate Twitch.

Twitch, whose real name was Ariel Paula, has been inanimate for three days now. To begin to understand why, walk over the waxy remains of burned-out candles that color the sidewalk red, white, and blue, and up the gray stoop to the door of the apartment building at 278 South Second Street, in Williamsburg.

See the crack in the glass? One bullet. See the dent in the frame? Another bullet. They tell the story of how Twitch went down, at seventeen.

Early Sunday morning, hours before dawn, some boys and girls were lingering here, on a block that seems to breed trouble from the pavement—the police call it a "hot spot"—and is within earshot of the Brooklyn-Queens Expressway's rumble and roar. Among them, a boy street-christened Twitch because he used to squint a lot before he got glasses.

Twitch had shown some talent as a boxer, but was now concentrating on college course work and his desire to become a veterinarian. But he hadn't given up the gloves entirely. He worked out at a boxing gym and, one friend said, didn't mind mixing it up at parties if the mood struck him.

All in all, though, a good kid. Everyone says that.

In the soft unnatural light of late night, where street lamps meet the midnight pitch, two figures appeared, at least one in a hooded sweatshirt, looking perhaps like a grim reaper in apprenticeship. Looks were exchanged, looks that could have said everything and nothing, but still just looks.

One of the figures apparently found something offensive in Twitch's imperfect eyes, witnesses say, and words may or may not have been exchanged. He pulled out a gun and fired at least five times at Twitch.

The two figures fled and have not been found. The boy called Twitch bled on this street of trouble, and died. And his friends did what children of this city do in fresh grief: They built a cheap memorial and festooned it with graffitilike farewells. Twitch Rest in Peace. My Dude, My Boo, My Twitch. Champ.

Now watch as two police officers pull up in their patrol car. They get out to examine the makeshift shrine.

"Yeah, I know him," one officer says, squinting at the photographs.

"I'm going to go to his funeral," the other officer says. "He wasn't a bad kid."

The two shake their heads at the thought of a boy losing his life because of a look, but they express no surprise. "You can't say nothing to them, you can't look at them, you can't step on their sneakers," one says. "Everything is a challenge to them."

"It's the machismo," says the other.

The officers get back in their car and drive away. The Tuesday morning sky darkens over Williamsburg, as if to remind everyone of the impermanence of plywood memorials.

Now, with respects paid, walk one block over, to South First Street, to an old four-story walk-up in sore need of a paint job. This is where the boy called Twitch lived with his mother, Maria Peralta, and two younger siblings. When she heard what had happened to her boy, her cries cut the night.

A more modest memorial has bloomed at the doorstep. A few candles, a yellow bouquet, a note saying the funeral will be Friday. Then the mother of Twitch appears at the door, with a look of her own. It cuts the day.

APRIL 13, 2005

The Boxer, the Beating, and the Widow

Many years ago, in another New York, a girl named Lucy fell for a boxer. Then he fell, and nothing could raise him: not the roar of the ring crowd, not her prayers from afar. When Benny (Kid) Paret fell that night at Madison Square Garden, he fell for good.

The Kid was known for being able to take a punch. But no one could have withstood those two dozen blows he took to the head, bam-bam-bam, his eyes closed, his body dangling from the rope in lazy crucifixion. They called Emile Griffith the victor, and rushed the unconscious Kid to the hospital.

He died a few days later, leaving a pregnant Lucy, a two-year-old son, and a new home in Miami. He was twenty-four, a kid.

Outrage briefly followed his death, as though the depravity of men pummeling each other for public delight had just been revealed. But writers continue to find life's meaning in the so-called sweet science, and fighters continue to die, including a female boxer less than two weeks ago.

And what of the Kid's widow? Still standing, alone.

With freshly done nails and an uncertainty of heart, Mrs. Paret arrived from Miami on Sunday for tonight's premiere of *Ring of Fire: The Emile Griffith Story,* a documentary by Dan Klores and Ron Berger that focuses in part on that 1962 fight, her husband's last. The movie makes her uneasy, the small woman confesses: "It brings back things I don't want to remember."

Benny Paret was an illiterate boxer from Cuba, destined to cut sugarcane like his parents if it weren't for those quick fists and that chin like iron. Lucy Hernandez was a teenage nightclub dancer born in Puerto Rico who grew up in New York. He spoke no English; she spoke little Spanish. He loved boxing; she detested it.

By sixteen, she had already weathered a few knocks. Her mother had died, her sister had committed suicide, her father had remarried, and her stepmother had wanted a clean slate—so Lucy was kicked out. She paid five dollars a week for a shared bedroom in an elderly woman's apartment and made money dancing at Latin clubs like the Tropicana.

One day the Tropicana enlisted some dancers in a Benny Paret fan club and sent them to cheer for the boxer as he dispatched yet another opponent at the old St. Nicholas Arena. After the fight Paret sent a thank-you bouquet to one dancer: Lucy.

"We were all there," she recalls. "But I got the flowers."

A bond formed between the boxer and the dancer, one that transcended language barriers. At seventeen she moved into his Bronx apartment, and at eighteen she gave birth to their son. A month later, in February 1960, the couple married.

Mrs. Paret, sixty-four, says she has forgotten so much from that time; the address of their apartment on Southern Boulevard, for example, and the names of the songs she once danced to. But she remembers other things. Benny smoked Camels, drank Hennessy with pineapple juice, did a mean mambo. And when he came home from a night's work, she gave him aspirin and an ice pack.

Sometimes his face would be so battered that he couldn't sleep on his side, she says. "The pillow would bother him."

Paret became a welterweight champion, which helped him buy a house for his family in Miami, where he hoped one day to become a butcher. He clearly needed a future beyond the ring.

In 1961, Paret lost in ten rounds to Gaspar Ortega in February, got knocked out by Emile Griffith in the thirteenth round in April, beat Griffith after fifteen rounds to regain his title in September—and then, less than three months later, got knocked out in the tenth round by Gene Fullmer. That year his head rocked like a bobblehead doll's.

Then came his date with Griffith in the Garden: March 24, 1962.

A lot has happened to Lucy Paret since then. She gave birth to another son, Alberto. She returned to Miami. She sold the house and bought a trailer, only to have Hurricane Andrew take it away.

She made no money off the Paret name, because it resurfaced only in gauzy recollections of prizefight rivalries—Louis-Schmeling, Graziano-Zale, Griffith-Paret—or on death-by-boxing checklists. So she worked at a thrift store, and then as a cashier at a supermarket.

Now Lucy Paret is back in New York, a retiree, not a dancer. Her nails are done and she wants to find an outfit for the premiere. With cheeks wet from tears, she says she has forgotten a lot about those days but nothing of that night, of her Benny, falling.

DECEMBER 1, 2004

A Death So Public, in the End So Forgotten

The young man walked into the soaring building that reduces us all to specks. He took the only way up: past the ticket taker, past the security checkpoint, and into one of the elevators that rocket skyward, twentieth floor, fortieth floor, sixtieth, eightieth.

Within a few minutes he had reached the eighty-sixth-floor observatory of the glorious Empire State Building, the tallest building in New York City once again. Before long, he had made his way through the souvenir shop, past the King Kong coffee mugs and next year's calendars, and out onto the deck, nearly a fifth of a mile above street level.

On this crisp and mostly clear November morning, on this day after

Thanksgiving, the world stretched out before him. Below, the flesh-and-concrete experiment known as Manhattan; above, the cerulean blue.

He pressed his back against one of the building's walls, witnesses later said, and then rushed toward the ten-foot silvery fencing whose rods curl inward and end in knifelike blades. He clambered up and over to the other side, they said, so quickly that no guard could catch him.

Now the young man was on the outside rather than the inside, his feet planted on a ledge. He paused for a moment, witnesses said, then spread open his arms to become a falling human star.

Perhaps in another city this very public form of suicide would be considered spectacular and would feed news reports for days. But in New York, death by Empire State Building has long since lost its novelty, its shock. This is partly because it has been done many times before, partly because suicides are too sad, and partly because, well, discussing suicides might encourage more.

That is why the city has a kind of procedure for Empire State Building suicides. Witnesses recount the last words and gestures of the dead. The building's managers express sympathy but point out that nearly four million people visit the site a year. And some newspapers illustrate the tragic leap with a graphic of descending dots that often end with an X—as if to say, enough.

Many of the facts and statistics about the Empire State Building are cemented in city lore: that it rises 1,250 feet in the sky, weighs 365,000 tons, and has 103 floors, 6,500 windows, and 73 elevators. In 1933 a make-believe King Kong clung to its side while swatting pesky airplanes, and in 1997, a real-life gunman killed a tourist, wounded six others, and then killed himself on the observation deck.

But statistics regarding the number of people who have jumped from the building's Olympian perches are less certain. Its owners say they do not keep a tally, but according to newspaper reports, the suicide last week was either the thirty-first or thirty-fourth at the Empire State Building since it opened in May 1931.

And it is primarily in newspapers that those who leap are memorialized. The brooding young magazine researcher who pushed off from the observation deck's concrete wall, calling out, "Well, so long, folks." The office clerk who scrawled several suicide notes, including one to an associate that read: "Jack, please call Mrs. T. I've gone out the window," and another to his wife, Mrs. T., explaining that he had "gambled on someone's say-so and lost."

"Get your insurance and take good care of it," he wrote. "Get married again by all means, but I certainly hope not. Love, Doll."

Another man, unremarkable save for his loud checked sport coat, dropped a quarter on the observation deck's floor. A young boy picked the coin up and offered it to the man, who said: "You keep it. I won't need it." The boy dropped the coin in a pay-per-view telescope, just as the man climbed onto the parapet—and vanished from view.

Of the others who vanished over the years, only a few received more than passing notice, notwithstanding their very public deaths. In 1947 a World War II veteran fell eighty-six floors to land on Mrs. Mervin Sylvester Coover, visiting from Iowa. In chronicling her long recovery, newspapers had no choice but to repeat the veteran's name.

Most, though, are forgotten as quickly as if they had killed themselves at home, no matter that they twirled through the air, drew upward gazes, landed with a resounding thud. The young man who died last week lingers on the fringes of the news only because his body has yet to be attached to a name.

He was carrying no identification. And the police have little to go on, other than a souvenir photograph of him, taken that day at the world-famous Empire State Building.

APRIL 22, 2006

Two Lives, and Two Kinds of Vision

In Chelsea, on West Twentieth Street, in the Andrew Heiskell Library for the Blind and Physically Handicapped, on the second floor, bolted to a pillar, a small plaque. It reads THE IRVING AND SARA SELIS READING ROOM.

People's names adorn nearly every inanimate object in this city, from pristine hospital wings to weather-beaten park benches. Some names are of average people who died in the service of others; others are of affluent people who would name St. Patrick's Cathedral after themselves if they could.

Many are of people you never heard of, and as you study their names, perhaps running your fingers over the letters, you try to conjure the life stories behind them.

Irving Selis grew up poor, blind, and determined not to allow either condition to thwart him. In the mid-1920s, when careers for the blind were few, he opened a newsstand at Sheridan Square in Greenwich Village. He then helped to form the New York Protective Association of Blind Newsdealers—an organization that, in retrospect, suggests the large number of blind people working at newsstands back then.

No wonder that in *City for Conquest,* a 1940 movie starring Jimmy Cagney, a promising boxer who is blinded in the ring winds up running a newsstand. At least he could count change by recognizing the size of the coins placed in his hand.

Irving had aspirations. First, though, came his courtship of Sara Neufeld, whom he met at a dance for the visually impaired. They married in 1931; two years later, she lost the little vision she had during an operation intended to improve her sight.

The Selises operated their newsstand through most of the 1930s, but newspapers did not define them. They loved to listen to music and to the talking books they would order from the Library of Congress. Sara collected cameos because she could feel the raised profiles; Irving assiduously followed the stock market, investing some of those coins he collected.

In 1938 the couple gave up the newsstand to help found the Associated Blind Inc., a nonprofit organization that promotes autonomy and self-determination for the blind and physically disabled. Irving became its executive director, and Sara set up its social services department.

They adamantly believed that the blind could lead the blind— who better?—and demonstrated in their own quiet way that the blind were like anyone else. Sara got on hands and knees to play with nieces and nephews. Irving joined the Lions Club. They vacationed in the Catskills.

"And everything had a sound" in their apartment, recalled Carol Heller, a niece. Music boxes sang from every corner. When Irving opened the component of a wall unit reserved for liquor, guests would hear the strains of "How Dry I Am."

Michael Robbins, a nephew, particularly remembered Irving's investing acumen. Here Mr. Robbins was, fresh out of Princeton, class of '55, working on Wall Street and destined for a seat on the New York Stock Exchange—and a blind former newsdealer was telling him about Benjamin Graham, the Wall Street guru and so-called father of value investing.

"He was not a speculator," Mr. Robbins said of his uncle. "He knew intimately the details of his companies—the cash value, the book value."

Irving spent many years designing and championing an apartment building for the blind and others with physical disabilities. He finally obtained a federal construction loan and opened Selis Manor, a two hundred-unit apartment building in Chelsea, in 1980. Irving and Sara moved in.

Irving's role as landlord sometimes exposed his irascible side. As Mr. Robbins put it: "He was gentlemanly, he would listen—and then he would do it his way." Ms. Heller agreed. Tough, she said. They were both tough—with a right to be.

Irving died at seventy-nine, in 1985. Sara died at ninety-three, in 2003, but not before decreeing that her cameos be distributed among the women and girls in her extended family.

Also to be distributed: the couple's $3.5 million fortune, which began with the grasp of a few coins in Sheridan Square.

Before she died, Sara established the Irving and Sara Selis Foundation that she and her husband had always dreamed of, and put Ms. Heller, Mr. Robbins, and his wife, Lois, in charge. That foundation recently presented the Heiskell Library, which is part of the New York Public Library system, with a $400,000 donation.

This is why, in that library, on the second floor, the names of two former newsdealers appear on a plaque, in print and in Braille.

MARCH 18, 2006

Swallowed in a Sea of Green

In the air the bagpipes sounded, on the pavement the feet pounded, and by chance did you see Rosemary Cosgrove? In yesterday's green-and-gold flow up Fifth Avenue, among the hundreds of thousands celebrating St. Patrick's Day, did you see her?

Was she basking in the late-winter sun along the edge of Central Park, marching in place as the pipes and drums played "The Minstrel Boy"? Did she slip into Langan's or O'Lunney's for some brown bread and tea, only to meet an impenetrable wall of drinkers? Or was she hunched in the Midtown shadows all along, unnoticed, unwell?

When last seen three years ago today, Rosemary was five foot six and 120 pounds, with short-cropped hair so dark as to be nearly black. Chances are that she looks different now, and that her Pick's disease, a rare form of dementia, has transformed her, at fifty-four, into a sort of adult toddler. That is, if she's still with us.

Lord knows her family back in Scotland tried to reason with her. But she was naturally stubborn even before the onset of the disease. She packed her burgundy-red suitcase and boarded a plane in Edinburgh. On to Amsterdam, then to Newark, and finally, to a city she had never seen, a city that would swallow her.

She was determined to attend the St. Patrick's Day Parade of 2003. The Cosgroves of Scotland can trace some roots back to County Mayo, but they were never ones to pine for the big parade in New York. Still, the notion became lodged in Ms. Cosgrove's deteriorating mind, and without telling anyone, she booked a flight and accommodations.

Looking back, family members say they were helpless to stop their beloved Rosemary. A doctor had said she was still a functioning adult, able to make her own decisions, well enough to travel. The family knew better.

They had seen the insidious disease, not unlike Alzheimer's, overtake Rosemary's mother and sister. Fastidious Rosemary was now unkempt. Opinionated Rosemary now sat at the dinner table, disengaged. Her older sister, Margaret McGuire, recalled regularly telephoning her to ask: "Have you had your tea? Have you had your tea?"

Problems greeted Rosemary as soon as she landed. She arrived at the Belvedere Hotel missing a shoulder bag containing her passport and return ticket.

A hotel manager tried to help her, and later told family members that she had seemed disoriented.

That night, after dinner, she entered an apartment building that she mistook for the Belvedere; the police had to escort her back to the hotel. Another night she never returned to the hotel at all. And on the eve of the parade, the police found her wandering near the West Side Highway and West 116th Street, in a summery outfit not fit for March.

No one knows whether Rosemary made it to the parade she was so intent on seeing. What is known is that on the morning after, she stood in the hotel lobby, planning to take a bus back to Newark Liberty International Airport, in hopes of finding her lost bag. Out the door she went, gone.

A few months later, her niece and nephew, Lorraine Dalgetty and Eamonn McGuire, flew to New York. On the ride in from the airport, Ms. Dalgetty saw Manhattan for the first time, in all its sprawling majesty, and despaired.

How would they ever find Aunt Rosemary in this vastness?

With the help of the city's chapter of the Alzheimer's Association, they made a televised appeal, distributed leaflets bearing Rosemary's photograph, and found some summery clothes in the burgundy-red suitcase left behind at the Belvedere. They returned home and waited for telephone calls that never came.

The passage of time has produced no good leads in morgues, hospitals, anywhere. "No Jane Does, nothing," said Terry Daniels, the New York police detective handling the case. Given Rosemary's disease, he added, "Anything could have happened."

Another St. Patrick's Day Parade visited Midtown yesterday. The proper and the silly, the sober and the not so, those with connections to Ireland and those who couldn't find it on a map of the Irish Sea, they came from around the world—and no matter how unlikely the possibility, you scanned the humanity for a woman fitting a three-year-old description.

Did she pause to watch the young step dancers kicking with feet of feathers on West Forty-fifth Street? Did she see the bagpipers, as big as Finn MacCool, striding up the avenue as though they owned it? Did she notice the flapping banner of County Mayo, and feel a distant pull to join the march behind it?

Rosemary Cosgrove, now where did you go?

PART V

Edward Keating

New York, After

SEPTEMBER 25, 2001

A Nation Challenged:

Messages; From a World Lost, Ephemeral Notes Bear Witness to the Unspeakable

Perhaps a formal memorial will be built someday. For now, there are the walls and windows of Lower Manhattan, where thousands of messages have been inscribed in the gray snow of destruction that fell two weeks ago today, when the World Trade Center collapsed in the wake of a terrorist attack.

Some are angry vows to kill every terrorist responsible; others are gentle reminders of God's eternal love. Then there are the simple pleas for some of the thousands missing to please come home, please.

"Vernon Cherry Call Home"—Greenwich Street, just south of ground zero

"Come Home Steve + Tommy"—Barclay Street, just north of ground zero

Someday soon, the workers will come to hose down the facades, and the messages will be washed away. Until then, they lend voice to a corner of the city rendered speechless—a ghostly corner where the smell of rotting fruit and cheese emanates from the Amish Market on Washington Street and where every advertisement seems disturbingly out of place. (Free Delivery. Luxury Loft, Apartments for Rent. Yes!! We Have Beer!)

But the messages scrawled on the wall of, say, 71 Murray Street, seem to be exactly where they should be:

"The Towers Will Rise Again"

"God Bless America"

"Avenge Them"

A few days ago, Dennis Nichols, a National Guard sergeant from a town near Buffalo called Angola, sat sentry outside the deserted but already-looted O'Hara's Pub, on Cedar Street. Over his shoulder hung a chalkboard sign listing the lunch specials for Tuesday, September 11: chicken noodle soup; chopped sirloin steak; cheese ravioli marinara; ham-and-cheese wrap with soup or salad.

"I try to tell my wife," said Mr. Nichols, who is forty-nine. "There's just no words." Except for those scrawled in the dust of all that is gone.

The dust infiltrated ventilation systems to blanket furniture, countertops, and items for sale. In the window of the Hallmark store at Barclay and Church streets, the dust has settled on six miniature Statues of Liberty, the hats of firefighter and police figurines, and on the feathers of an angel doll.

It also blew through windows shattered in the collapse. In the once-elegant lobby of the damaged Millennium Hilton Hotel, at Church and Fulton streets, a dust-coated sign near the elevator announces that Canadian National Freight and Aon Corporation had boardrooms reserved for the morning of September 11. In the gift shop, where a statue used to smash down the door lies on the glass-covered floor, stacks of that day's newspapers are piled by the cash register. And on the dark-wood walls are more messages:

"Our Tears Will Be Their Blood"

"Those Who Perish Shall Rise To Heaven On Our Love"

"New York—Chicago Shares Your Grief"

It was unclear whether another message in the lobby was intended for the catastrophe's victims or its perpetrators: "We're Coming 4 Ya."

Not all the messages are written in dust. On virtually every building in the sixteen-acre disaster site, huge Xs, along with hasty summaries, have been spray-painted to signal that rescue workers have already searched inside. One building on Greenwich Street, just south of the trade center plaza, bears a fluorescent-orange X and the inscription: "9/16/01, some floors collapsed, 0 victims."

There are other remnants to be removed or washed away. The cars in the twenty-four-hour parking lots at Vesey and West streets, including several that were scorched into rusty shells. The strips of aluminum that dangle like silvery confetti from the lamppost at Greenwich and Barclay streets. The melted parking meters on Barclay Street. The flier taped to a phone bank at Church and Vesey streets that includes a photograph of a missing blond woman ("Any information please contact her sister").

But the most ephemeral seem to be those messages in dust, often unsigned by authors who could have been rescue workers, construction workers, or even family members who managed to get near ground zero in the first hours and days.

Some have used this means of communication to let the world— at least that fraction allowed inside the restricted zone—know that they were there, have borne witness, have tried to help. The Passaic County Sheriff's Department. The Elberta, Alabama, Fire Department. "Romeo's Crew," from the City Department of Sanitation. Local 52 of the International Alliance of Theatrical Stage Employees ("Bringing Light to the Darkness").

Others have expressed their opinions, in particular, about Osama bin Laden, whom the Bush administration has described as the primary suspect in the terrorist attack. "Ben—You in a Heap of Trouble Boy"; "RIP Sammy"; "Osama Been Hiding."

Most people, though, have paused to honor in some way the missing, especially some of the more than three hundred firefighters who responded to a calamity only to be swallowed by it.

"E90/L41—Rest in Peace"—50 Park Place

"God Bless John Burnside, Ladder 20—Inwood Boy"—Albany Street

"We Miss You, Richie Allen"—Albany Street

"We Miss You Ronnie Geis Come Home"—Barclay Street

Perhaps a formal memorial will be built someday. Perhaps the skeletal remnants of the twin towers, rising so high from the smoky ruins, will be preserved somehow and placed behind a marble wall inscribed with the names of the dead. For now, though, there are the messages scrawled in dust on a building at Park Place and West Broadway.

"God Be With You Dana—Love, Mom"

"Bye Bye"

OCTOBER 3, 2001

A Nation Challenged: Circle Line Somberly Views Altered Skyline

With its foghorn sounding farewell to Midtown, the ship edged away from the pier and pushed south along the Hudson River. The waters that surround Manhattan Island are uncertain these days, but life must go on, and so must the Circle Line. There are things to point out, things to see.

The Coast Guard cutter *Tahoma,* for example, guarding the mouth of New York Harbor. And the wave-skipping patrol boats, packed with armed soldiers. And the military helicopters whock-whock-whocking from above. And, of course, the standing remnants of the World Trade Center, including the silvery skin of the south tower— "the building you saw in all of the pictures," as Chris Mason tells tourists.

What had once been an ooh-and-aah celebration of Gotham in its glory has now become a somber glide past a communal burial ground, as well as a dramatic reminder that for all its skyscraping splendor, New York City is so naked and vulnerable that it needs soldiers and gun tur-rets to guard its shores.

These are awkward times for Mr. Mason, a tour guide for Circle

Line, the city's oldest and perhaps best-known sightseeing cruise operation. For the last fifteen years he has generally followed the Circle Line script in describing the landmarks that can be seen from the Hudson and East rivers: historical summaries of the Empire State Building and the Woolworth Building, tributes to the Brooklyn Bridge and the Statue of Liberty, a couple of New York wisecracks, and he's done.

But now a centerpiece of the standard tour is gone; in its place is a seamless cloud of smoke rising from Lower Manhattan. And Mr. Mason, thirty-eight years old and a son of Brooklyn, has to rely on words like "devastation" and "attack" to touch upon what the sightseers already know. Sometimes, he said, mere silence works best.

"It depends on the mood of the trip," he said.

When the second tower of the World Trade Center collapsed on that sunny morning of September 11, the Circle Line was one of several ferry and sightseeing operations that spontaneously began to take panicked people across the Hudson River free. By nightfall, the Circle Line had ferried about thirty thousand people—six hundred at a time—to Weehawken, where they set foot on suddenly blessed New Jersey soil.

For several days after the attack, the company's ships remained moored at Pier 83; it was not the time for sightseeing, no matter how respectful. Even the upbeat Circle Line brochure had become a glossy remnant of the time before, with its ten pictures of the twin towers and its promotion of a "sea and sky package" that included a trip to the top of one of the towers.

On September 20, Mr. Mason was the tour guide on the first post-attack three-hour cruise around Manhattan. It was a gray day, he recalled, with only about hundred passengers, many of whom were interested in where he was when the planes struck the towers. Like so many others in the region, he explained, he was in the midst of the mundane: sitting in his home in Bay Ridge, Brooklyn, listening to traffic reports on the radio before he commuted to the city.

As that first ship glided past the site, Mr. Mason said, "I did sort of a moment of silence."

"Now we're getting on three weeks later, and there's more of a getting over the tragic part of it," he said. "They're taking lots of pictures, and they should go for it, because it's definitely part of history."

On Monday afternoon, 151 tourists—one quarter of the ship's capacity—lined up in the drizzle to board Circle Line XVII for a two-hour tour. They were immediately greeted at the gangplank by an armed security guard, who checked their bags and, in some cases, patted them down—all part of new Coast Guard restrictions, explained Peter Cavrell, the Circle Line's senior vice president for sales and marketing.

Once onboard, they were greeted by the knowing and mellifluous voice of Mr. Mason, whose father, John, has been a Circle Line tour guide for four decades. Wearing a white shirt with epaulets and holding a cordless microphone, the guide explained that after passing a few Midtown sights, "we'll be down at ground zero, where we'll see some of the devastation, and then on to the Statue of Liberty."

As the ship nudged south along the Hudson, in waters as gray as the overcast sky, Mr. Mason generally followed a time-honored patter: to the right was Hoboken, "the birthplace of Ol' Blue Eyes, Frank Sinatra"; to the left, Greenwich Village, "the so-called bohemian part of the city." Now and then, though, his ad libs reflected how much life had changed in three weeks; he told his listeners, for example, that builders of a riverfront park in Manhattan had "shut down operations due to the attack."

Moments after Mr. Mason explained that TriBeCa meant "triangle below Canal," the captain of the Circle Line XVII cut his engines and the ship fell silent. Every passenger looked to the east to see the smoke, the police helicopters, the blackened wreckage—the void.

One of the sightseers, Jane Rogers, later began to cry while describing how she felt at that moment, looking eastward as the waters of the Hudson gently rocked her. She said she and her husband and their three children had driven three days from Parker, Colorado, to stick with a months-old plan to visit New York City in early fall. But now, the forty-year-old woman could not shake an image from a twelve-year-old photograph: a much younger Jane Rogers, smiling, with the World Trade Center towers gleaming behind her.

"It was just very hard for me," she said.

After the moment of silence, which was never requested but uniformly understood, Mr. Mason described which wreckage used to be which building. "When we turn around later on," he said, "we'll get some different angles of Lower Manhattan and the devastation."

The Circle Line glided past the *Tahoma,* the 270-foot Coast Guard cutter that has become a kind of New York landmark in its own right. Mr. Mason made no reference to it, nor to the patrol boat that skipped past just thirty yards away, a half-dozen soldiers in camouflage standing in its hold, their weapons in plain view.

But he did point out Governors Island—"fifteen hundred National Guard have been stationed there since the attack"—as well as Battery Park, which he described as now looking "almost like a scene from *M.A.S.H.*" And he did turn the tourists' attention to the dull-green military-transport helicopters that cut across the sky before disappearing behind the Lower Manhattan skyline.

The Circle Line sliced past Ellis Island and the Statue of Liberty, which Mr. Mason said were closed because of the attack. It then went up the East River to about East Twenty-third Street before turning around and swinging once again past the tourist attraction now called ground zero. The captain cut his engines again, but this time Mr. Mason's words broke the silence:

"That's the American Express tower, which took a real big hit. . . . Such a tough sight to see. . . . It's amazing how many buildings were not affected. . . . Just all the devastation and horror. . . . According to the mayor, the cleanup here might take up to a year."

Camcorders whirred and cameras clicked. But Frank and Margaret McGrath sat still as they stared out the Circle Line window, like a pair of churchgoers searching for meaning in a stained-glass design. The camera that they had brought from Dublin for their first visit to the United States stayed packed away in a bag at their feet.

Taking pictures, they had decided, would be inappropriate.

SEPTEMBER 12, 2002

A Day of Tributes, Tears, and the Litany of the Lost

They followed one another down, down into a seven-story hole in Lower Manhattan yesterday, thousands of them, filling with their sorrow the space where their husbands and wives, mothers and fathers, sisters and brothers, sons and daughters, had died a year ago to the day. Some left cut flowers on the hard earth; some left photographs; some left whispered words.

They lingered for a long while; a few even collected stones. And then the people who have become known as the "family members"— as though they belonged to one international family—trudged back to level ground, to the living.

There, a city and a country were commemorating a date so freighted with emotion and imagery that simply uttering it seems to say everything: September 11, 2001. The day that as many as 3,025 people died in terrorist attacks that destroyed the World Trade Center, damaged the Pentagon, and crashed a jetliner in rural Pennsylvania.

With moments of silence and recitations of familiar speeches, with the tolling of bells and the lighting of candles, with peaceful music and vows of military retribution, the United States observed that day's anniversary, joined by countries around the world that honored the date in their own, distant ways.

President Bush led the country in a moment of silence at 8:46 in the morning, Eastern time—the moment of the first strike, when American Airlines Flight 11 cut into the trade center's north tower at more than four hundred miles an hour. Then, visiting the repaired Pentagon, the president spoke of a renewed commitment to the war against terrorism.

"The murder of innocents cannot be explained, only endured," Mr. Bush said. "And though they died in tragedy, they did not die in vain."

A short while later, in Lower Manhattan, Governor George E. Pataki read Lincoln's brief but powerful Gettysburg Address; Mayor Michael R. Bloomberg succinctly described the dead—"they were us"—and former mayor Rudolph W. Giuliani began the invocation of the names of every one of the 2,801 victims on the city's official list.

It was Lower Manhattan that held the unfortunate claim as host to the largest, most elaborate observance, with foreign dignitaries—including Hamid Karzai, the president of Afghanistan—paying their respects. On a day almost as clear as the early Tuesday morning of a year ago, tens of thousands of people surrounded a sixteen-acre pit and watched the wind spin eye-stinging twirls of dust from the place where two 110-story towers once stood.

All the while they listened in virtual silence as a riveting, two-and-a-half-hour story was read to them. The story, whose words leapt from loudspeakers to ring through surrounding streets, had no verbs or adjectives; in a way, it was one epic paragraph. It began with "Gordon M. Aamoth Jr.," ended with "Igor Zukelman," and in between contained the names of 2,799 other people—bond traders and secretaries, firefighters and assistant cooks.

They have been dead, now, a year.

A year may seem an arbitrary measure, but experts in the human condition say that first-year observances of cataclysmic events are fitting, even necessary. "The date itself is emblazoned in memory," said Robert A. Neimeyer, a professor of psychology at the University of Memphis. "The same ritual that allows us to remember also releases us to live."

Yesterday's ritual began in the first hours of this September 11, in the darkness. In each of the city's five boroughs teams of bagpipers began their miles-long march toward the disaster site, the wail of their instruments summoning city residents to their apartment windows for predawn reflection.

As the Manhattan contingent made its way down Broadway, people in Washington Heights raised flags, fists, and candles; some held their hands over their hearts. James Leyden of Yonkers was at the corner of West Ninety-sixth Street well before five o'clock, in time to see the lights in a nearby apartment building flick on as the loud procession passed. It gladdened him, he said, because he lost a nephew in the trade center calamity.

"I just liked the notion of marching down all the boroughs, and basically waking people up," he said. "It's just such a bad day, a bad day for families to relive."

The bagpipers, all employees of various city agencies, were slowly marching through a changed Lower Manhattan, part of a changed city. Those changes go beyond the eighty-nine-year-old Woolworth Building reclaiming a dominant piece of the city skyline. They are also in the unclaimed pairs of resoled and polished shoes, dozens of them, at the Shoetrician shop on Fulton Street. The manager said he keeps the shoes because what else can he do.

The bagpipers converged like skirling streamlets into a sea of people already gathered at the bottom of Manhattan to honor the dead. By eight A.M. the people were four deep along Church Street to the east, a dozen deep along West Street to the west, and thick through every alley and side street. Gone, for now, were the vendors selling mass-produced photographs of the World Trade Center in distress; in their stead, family members—distinguished by their ribboned pins— holding aloft photographs of their lost loved ones.

The photographs of the dead bobbed upon the swells of the living. Over here, one of Charlie Murphy, with the reminder to "Remember Me"; he had four older sisters, a fiancée, and a deft sense of humor, and he was thirty-eight. Over there, Shannon Fava; her son is four now, and she would have been thirty-one.

Then, suddenly, it was time: 8:46. Silence settled over Lower Manhattan and other corners of the world. In London, thousands paused during a memorial service at St. Paul's Cathedral, while in Dublin, the government asked for a minute of silence in factories, offices, and schools.

At the Dallas Market Trade Center employees held a moment of silence around a reflecting pool surrounded by votive candles for each victim. At Logan International Airport in Boston—where the airplanes that struck the trade center took off—operations halted for one minute.

That minute of silence, in a section of Manhattan not accustomed to silence, was followed by Governor Pataki's reading of the Gettysburg Address. Then up stepped Mr. Giuliani, who has been applauded for his leadership in the weeks after the terrorist attack and who a day earlier had attended the funeral of his ninety-two-year-old mother, Helen.

"Gordon M. Aamoth Jr.," Mr. Giuliani said, reading the first name on a list of 2,801 that would take the rest of the morning to read. Mr. Aamoth, of course, was more than just the first name: He was an investment banker, just thirty-two, and there is now a football field named after him in Minnesota.

Mr. Giuliani was the first in a long line of dignitaries, city officials, and family members to invoke names, while Yo-Yo Ma and other musicians played "Avé Maria" and other selections in the background. Now and then, the wind would blow so hard that it would rumble like thunder through the microphones; now and then, brown billows would rise from the pit to anoint listeners with dust.

David Hochman, a master electrician who a year ago lost more than a dozen friends and co-workers, watched quietly from a raised vantage point in the World Financial Center's recently restored Winter Garden. Then, pointing his hard hat at the scene, he said: "You see that tremendous hole? That was New York."

The invocation of names paused at 9:04 so chiming bells could mark the moment that United Airlines Flight 175 hit the south tower, when, everyone present knew, a year earlier thousands were fleeing for their lives while hundreds of firefighters and emergency workers were filing in.

Family members would later say that it was important to hear the names of their loved ones read, though they could not say exactly why. Monica Ianelli, dressed in black and with head bowed, held a portrait of her fiancé, Joseph Ianelli—whose name she took—close to her body, now and then wiping away the dust. When his name was read at 9:53, she looked up and smiled.

At 10:29, the moment when the second tower collapsed, the readings paused again, while bells chimed and the foghorns of boats on

the Hudson sounded. An hour or so later, the last name was read;
Governor James E. McGreevey of New Jersey read the Declaration of
Independence; and family members began filing down a ramp and
into the pit.

They went down together to be alone, it seemed, as people sym-
bolized their grief in individual ways: a funeral wreath here, a photograph there. Many built small, almost primitive memorials by propping
up photographs with mounds of pebbles; many took pebbles or fistfuls
of dirt to bring with them.

Kathleen Shay, of Staten Island, later said that the death of her
twenty-seven-year-old brother, Robert J. Shay Jr., a bond broker at
Cantor Fitzgerald, did not really sink in until she had descended into
the pit. Her sister, Leanne, said that in building a small memorial
there, they "tried to figure out where his office was."

Remembrances and services and seminars continued throughout
the day in New York City, ensuring that year-old memories remained
fresh. At St. Patrick's Cathedral in Midtown, for example, Cardinal
Edward M. Egan concluded a memorial Mass by introducing four
brothers who had served as altar boys—all sons of Firefighter Vincent
Halloran, killed in the trade center collapse.

Meanwhile, in Brooklyn, the Arab-American Family Support
Center sponsored a silent vigil at Borough Hall to honor the victims,
as well as to highlight what it said were the difficulties that the Arab
American and Muslim communities have faced in the last year.

In the late afternoon President Bush and the first lady, Laura Bush,
paid their respects at the disaster site. Mr. Bush seemed at ease amid
the crush of grieving family members. He listened, occasionally
smiled, rubbed the back of the neck of a father of a dead police officer. Someone handed him a palm-size photograph; he tucked it in
a pocket.

As dusk came to the city, dignitaries representing the dozens of
countries that lost citizens began to file into Battery Park, at the bottom of Manhattan, for a memorial service that would include the
lighting of an eternal flame in front of *The Sphere,* a battered sculp-
ture that once graced the trade center plaza. Aaron Copland's "Fanfare
for the Common Man" was performed; Mayor Bloomberg read the
Four Freedoms speech of Franklin D. Roosevelt; vigil candles were
clutched.

Meanwhile, back at ground zero, all of the dignitaries and invited guests had left. It was dark now, but the wind was still gusting, and throngs of people were still lingering. They snapped photographs, trying to capture the emptiness of it.

A petite woman named Marianna Dryl pressed her face against the chain-link fence along Liberty Street and looked north into the pit, set aglow by stadium-style lights. She said she was fifty-three, an accountant from Kew Gardens, Queens; she said she had not been to the site since the first weeks after the disaster.

"When I first came, it was such a horrible pile," she said. "I thought they could never take it all away. Now it looks so empty and clean. It is almost beautiful."

SEPTEMBER 10, 2003

For One 9/11 Family, Five Waves of Grief

You know the Petrocellis. They live up the block, around the corner, or across the hall. They are a Staten Island family, a New York family.

The other day Al and Ginger Petrocelli learned that some remains of their son, Mark, had been identified. Again. Which meant that it was time to visit the funeral home. Again. Time to cremate. Again.

This was the fifth time in the last two years that parts of Mark Petrocelli had been identified. Mark Petrocelli, twenty-eight: husband of Nicole, son of Al and Ginger, younger brother of Al Jr., uncle of Emily, friend of many. The fifth time.

His father, Al, sat at the dining room table in the family home, a home where the cappuccino maker is no longer used because so many cups had been shared with Mark and Nicole. He looked at his handwritten notes on a yellow pad; this is one of the ways he tries to make sense of things.

"This time," the father said, "from his left knee down to the top of his foot. Right femur with right lower leg and kneecap. Some skin. A piece of skull bone. Soft tissue. Muscle."

Ginger Petrocelli sat beside her husband as he read, her eyes trained on the plates of cake and rolls that she had laid out for guests. As odd as it may sound, she said, some good came from this latest call from the medical examiner's office. She did not touch the remains the first four times and she regretted it; this time, though, she laid her hands on the zippered white bag and felt a profound maternal connection.

"I have to say," she said, her eyes welling, "I did get comfort in touching him."

The phrases we rely on to make sense of grief have always failed to convey the ache of the irreplaceable. But even with the grace of two years, the World Trade Center collapse continues to render meaningless such terms as "closure" and "moving on."

Acceptance may be a better word, acceptance of how the event has become incorporated into our everyday lives—into who we are. At least that is how your neighbors the Petrocellis see it. The Petrocellis, one wounded family among thousands.

Before the catastrophe, Mr. Petrocelli said, "everything was like—"

"The way it should be," said Mrs. Petrocelli.

That meant Sundays, when family members would gravitate to the homestead in Staten Island's Huguenot neighborhood, and Mrs. Petrocelli would put on the meatballs and the macaroni. Al Jr. and Andrea would bring Emily, the in-laws would stop by, and Nicole and Mark always seemed to be about.

"Mark sits right there, where you're sitting," said Mr. Petrocelli, motioning to the chair to his immediate right. "That's his spot."

Mark Petrocelli, a commodities trader for Carr Futures, was attending a meeting on the ninety-second floor of the north tower, which says it all in the parlance of post-9/11. But the Petrocellis did not know this on that day. Al Petrocelli, a retired battalion chief with the Fire Department, and Al Jr., also a firefighter, raced to Lower Manhattan after the attack.

The father remembered feeling a can-do sense of mission, an echo from his days as a firefighter and as a soldier in Vietnam. "I thought that 'I could go down there and I'll find Mark,'" he said. But reality set in with the rain that fell two days later, he said. "I came home and said, 'No way.'"

At some point, the Petrocellis instructed the medical examiner's office to notify them whenever any of Mark was recovered. They could not imagine allowing parts of Mark to go unclaimed. No matter how painful, they felt a responsibility—a primal need, really. Mrs. Petrocelli could just imagine her son meeting her in heaven and asking, "You left me there?"

On September 25, 2001, the Petrocellis learned that Mark's death had been confirmed through dental records. On October 26, they were told that his upper torso had been identified. On November 11, some soft tissue and muscle. On March 21, 2002, four parts, including his heart.

"They found his heart," Mrs. Petrocelli said. "What do you say?"

The cremated remains of Mark Petrocelli were buried on August 10, 2002, at the Cemetery of the Resurrection, not far from where he grew up, not far from where he lived with Nicole. The first anniversary came and went, and his parents searched for distraction and solace, renovating the bathroom, painting the living room, attending Tuesday night group sessions with other parents who lost sons on September 11.

The other night, in telling the group that more of Mark had been found, Mrs. Petrocelli expressed the belief that her son had not even had the chance to say, "Oh my God." Afterward, one of the other grieving mothers went up to her and said, "I would like to say that about my son."

Another way the Petrocellis cope is by tending to the memorial that the father has erected in his front yard. He has replaced most of the grass with brick, and has installed a flagpole from which he flies flags that honor 9/11 victims. Around its base, amid the statues of angels and bursts of impatiens, he has carefully arranged a piece of trade center I-beam, a small cross made of trade center steel, a portrait of Mark on his wedding day, and a Mass card.

"I see it as always being there," Mr. Petrocelli said of his memorial. "I would never think of not having it looking prim and proper all the time. It gives me satisfaction and comfort to do it—to talk to Mark."

Mrs. Petrocelli agreed. "You pull the car out of the garage, you say, 'Hi, Mark,' and you go about your business," she said. "It doesn't make me sad to see it."

Tomorrow, on the second anniversary of his death, more of Mark

Petrocelli will be buried at the Cemetery of the Resurrection. And the Petrocellis—all of them—will continue on with his absence an integral part of their lives.

"We're new people now," Mr. Petrocelli said.

You might see them someday in the shops and restaurants of this city and notice what they are wearing: Al's bracelet that bears Mark's name, Ginger's pin of the steel-girder cross found at ground zero. Or you might pass them on a highway—the BQE, or maybe the Belt—and see the silhouette of the World Trade Center skyline adhered to their back windows, along with Mark's name and the inscription "We Love You, We Miss You."

They are the Petrocellis of Staten Island. Of New York.

MAY 5, 2004

Stinging Eyes as the PATH Hits Daylight

World Trade Center, next and last stop."

As if summoned to life by the conductor's chant, the train lurches deeper into the darkness. It creaks and cries as it slinks beneath the Hudson River, lured ever forward by the promising green lights that disrupt the underworld dusk. Here, on the PATH train, unnatural light feels natural.

A few dozen yards from the last stop, though, the silvery train emerges into the invasive sunlight that shines upon ground zero. It snakes across the space where the twin towers once stood to provide a close-up view of men in white construction helmets, of steel girders on the ground, of massive spools of wire. Aboard that train, you feel the shiver of inappropriate intimacy, of psychic trespass.

It doesn't matter whether you take that ride once or a thousand times, you never quite get used to it. So says the conductor.

"That's because I never saw daylight before," he says.

Six times a day, five days a week, Eugene Rogers is the conductor on one of the PATH trains wending their way to the renovated World Trade Center station. And just about every time, he finds himself gazing in silence at the ground zero panorama, until the train comes to a stop with an exhalation like a sigh.

"I knew so many people over so many years," he says. "My riders."

Mr. Rogers, fifty-eight, has been with the Port Authority of New York and New Jersey for his entire adult life, save for a two-year hitch in the Army that included three months in Vietnam. He started as a token clerk, and then moved up to conductor just as the finishing touches were being put on the trade center.

For more than twenty years of weekday mornings now, he has worked exclusively on the Newark–to–Trade Center line. That is by choice: He's the kind of man who thinks about the Hudson River when he's under it, and he liked how the Newark stretch of the trip stays aboveground. He also wanted a schedule that would allow him to get to know his passengers.

"That's what makes my day go fast," he says. "I'm a sociable train."

On that Tuesday morning, around nine o'clock, the trainmaster back in Journal Square called him on his walkie-talkie. Evacuate your train at Exchange Place station, he recalls the boss saying. Pick up anyone at the trade center stop and get out. There's been an explosion of some kind.

Mr. Rogers and the train's engineer, Noel Roman, did as they were told. They picked up a maintenance man, a couple of PATH employees, and a homeless man that Mr. Rogers roused from a bench. Theirs, he says, was the last PATH train to leave the station before the towers fell.

Who knows how many of his riders died that day. Riders who would nod to him, call him by name, wish him a good day. Whenever photographs of the victims appeared in print, he would look closely at their features and, occasionally, feel the pang of loss.

Mr. Rogers worked for two years as a conductor on the trains going to West Thirty-third Street, while construction crews tried to reconnect the PATH line to lower Manhattan. When his superior called to ask whether he would read some of the victims' names at the memorial service marking the first anniversary, he said that he would be honored.

"I read fourteen names," he says. "I read in the *P*'s."

Six months ago the PATH trains finally returned to the World Trade Center station—or, rather, an approximation of that station. Where there had been shops and bustle all cast in the false light beneath the towers, there is now an eerie grayness—in the concrete, in the escalators, in the exposed steel, in the stray pigeons pecking about.

And there is daylight.

Sometimes, especially after rush hour, Mr. Rogers has a few minutes until the train returns to Newark, so he stands on the barren platform, staring at the absence in daylight. Everything is so strange, he says, that he has yet to pinpoint where the conductors' locker room used to be.

Most of all, he says, he thinks about seats unfilled on his sociable train.

A couple of weeks ago, Mr. Rogers noticed a passenger staring at him. After a while, the man broke into a smile and said, "Gene." The man went on to explain that it was his first trip back to the trade center station since the collapse, and that he had remembered the conductor's name because it was the same as his own.

The man stood to shake the conductor's hand. Then the two Genes embraced, as another PATH train groaned toward daylight.

JULY 10, 2004

What's Scary and Buried in the Refuge?

Late afternoon had come to that sprawling urban wonder known as the Jamaica Bay Wildlife Refuge. Time to stop trimming the overgrowth along Cross Bay Boulevard. Time to bid good night to the box turtles, to the egrets, to the rufous-sided towhees warbling farewell from the trees.

While a park ranger, Chris Olijnyk, stored the tools, his brother and fellow ranger, Steve Olijnyk, decided to check some open space about fifty feet off the road. Maybe someone was cultivating cannabis on federal land again, in an overly broad interpretation of the refuge's commitment to biodiversity.

Instead of marijuana, Steve Olijnyk (pronounced OLE-nik) found something else that did not belong among the bayberry shrubs and cherry trees: the soft edge of a suitcase, jutting from the sandy ground. Curious, he and an intern began digging at the yielding earth.

Soon he was reaching for his walkie-talkie. Chris, he called. You've got to see this.

As The Wave, a weekly newspaper in Rockaway Beach, recently re-ported, they had uncovered a suitcase and a plastic garbage can, both crammed with items that one might bury in apocalyptic anticipation: clothes, sunglasses, flashlights, batteries. More digging turned up more plastic containers, each one brimming with—more stuff. "And when we saw the two-way radios," Chris Olijnyk said, "we decided it was a police matter, and called it in."

If the park rangers had made this discovery on, say, September 10, 2001, they might not have immediately contacted the police. But this was in the early summer of 2004—a new time, a time in which we are advised to report anything out of the ordinary. In New York, of course, this raises the question of what constitutes ordinary.

Three years ago the Jamaica Bay Wildlife Refuge was 9,155 acres of wetlands and woodlands, protected by the mainland of Brooklyn and Queens to the north and the Rockaway peninsula to the south. Today it is that, and more: 9,155 acres of wildness in close proximity to a possible terrorist target, Kennedy International Airport.

The United States Park Police adorned the area with crime-scene tape. While officers in plastic gloves tried to make sense of the dis-covery, the park rangers noticed certain patches that did not look quite right. "The vegetation on the ground wasn't as dense," Chris Olijnyk said. "The plants weren't as vigorous."

David Taft, the district ranger for the refuge, said that such obser-vations fall within a discipline that he calls "vegetative forensics."

More digs of a shovel uncovered more bins and more belongings: a portable radio, two fishing rods, running shoes, and a meticulous, handwritten inventory of what had been buried. The list was both helpful and a bit unsettling, said Lieutenant David Buckley of the Park Police. "The concern was not so much with what was on the list as what was not on the list."

"It got weirder and weirder," recalled Ranger Taft, who was worried that any digging would disturb the sickle-leaved golden aster and other vegetation. "We wanted to make sure that if we sacrificed the refuge, it was for national security."

The FBI-NYPD Joint Terrorist Task Force was notified. Its agents quickly determined that the material had been buried not by a potential terrorist, but by a man "in the throes of some kind of religious zeal," as one FBI agent put it.

Informing this determination were the many buried papers that included names, addresses, and hints of one man's singular philosophy. With this documentation they tracked down his wife, who described her husband this way:

He likes to bury things.

The man, it turns out, has buried survivalist caches in a few places, including Florida, where he now lives, and New York City, where he used to live. In a city of eight million, where better to stake an end-of-civilization claim than in a hidden sanctuary with a water view?

With the threat level considerably reduced, park officials used the man's inventory to guide them in finding nearly twenty buried treasures in all, containing everything from two jars of honey to a bicycle with a container of water in its bottle holder.

The clothes were musty, the food was unappetizing, and the bicycle did not strike anyone as particularly functional for postapocalyptic roadways.

Out at the clearing the other day, a rufous-sided towhee called, towhee, towhee, while flocks of jetliners gathered in the distance. Standing over holes that formerly contained one man's plans for the future, two park rangers talked of their own plans: fill in the holes, and wait for wildflowers to take root.

SEPTEMBER 1, 2004

Serving Canapés, Then Recalling the 107th Floor

To be a banquet worker is to be invisible. Do not engage customers in chitchat. Just collect the discarded shrimp tails, keep the cheese platters fresh, and know how to pose simple questions—"Hors d'oeuvre?"—so unobtrusively that you might as well be a phantom.

These rules hold true no matter how often out-of-town customers turn a certain jagged phrase into a political rally cry, and no matter how often their bar-banter invocation of that phrase, September 11, sends you back. You ask if they'd like another mojito, and you say nothing more.

Monzur Ahmed, who has been managing a buffet table this week for several Republican National Convention parties at the Noche restaurant in Times Square, says nothing as speakers use September 11 to justify four more years for their candidate. He tells no one about his life at Windows on the World, the glittery restaurant on the 107th floor of the World Trade Center's north tower, or about the seventy-nine friends and colleagues who died, including a beloved uncle.

James Johnson, a former Windows employee who has been serving mojitos and hors d'oeuvres at Noche, never shares how he could not work for nearly a year afterward. Ahad Ahmed, another Windows veteran at the buffet, keeps to himself the memory of a colleague's little girl crying—oh was she crying—because Daddy wasn't coming home.

And Victor Rojas, the bartender in the restaurant's penthouse, serves margaritas to out-of-towners, but never talks about the sunrises and sunsets he witnessed from the top of the world with people who are no longer here.

As Republicans rally and party in New York this week, they have frequently raised the subject of the terrorist attacks of September 11, some more delicately than others. That day is history, of course. But in the city they have chosen for their political coronation, it is also personal—so personal that they may be closer to the tragedy than they realize, in the form of that silent person before them, offering tenderloin tips on a tray.

At Ben Benson's steakhouse in Midtown, their waiter might be Magdi Labib, once a dining room captain at Windows on the World who earned twice what he is making now. Standing in his white apron in the restaurant's mostly empty patio on Monday's muggy night, he watched as Republican delegates dined inside in air-conditioning, and he remembered. "So many stories," he said.

How fifteen or twenty Windows employees would head after work to a Chinese restaurant in Queens, and eat like one big family. How an enthusiastic new waiter named Telmo Alvear worked the breakfast shift that Tuesday to help out a colleague, and died for it. How, after the calamity, a certain former dining-room captain returned to his native Egypt for a few months to clear his head.

Mr. Labib said that he became an American citizen more than a decade ago because he wanted to vote. Now, as politicians dither and Iraqi battles continue and the third anniversary approaches, he said he cannot shake his anger. "I love what this country stands for," he said, but now, "I don't believe anybody."

Hurt is more in evidence than anger among the Windows workers now at Noche, just a few blocks west from Ben Benson's.

No place has stronger ties to Windows on the World than Noche. It is managed by some of the same people who managed Windows. It had sixty former Windows employees when it opened in 2002, thanks in part to the involvement of Local 100 of the Hotel Employees and Restaurant Employees union and a group called the Restaurant Opportunities Center of New York. Whenever the police identified Windows effects among trade center debris, they called Noche.

Noche now has about fifteen former Windows employees, from Ramon Lorenzo, a dishwasher, to Joe Amico, the general manager.

They listened quietly to September 11 chatter at Sunday's gathering of Missouri Republicans, and at Monday's Republican Governors Association party, where Mr. Johnson served wine, Mr. Rojas worked the penthouse bar, and Monzur Ahmed and Ahad Ahmed kept the buffet tables clean and inviting.

After Monday's party they walked over to Ben Benson's, where Magdi Labib, the former dining room captain, greeted them with hugs. While the lights of a Con Edison truck flashed ominously down West Fifty-second Street, they sat and talked about what they would have said.

Monzur Ahmed would have spoken of his uncle, Shabbir Ahmed, a Windows banquet server whose remains have never been found. To this day, he said, when he goes fishing in Brooklyn, he imagines his uncle beside him, saying what he always said: "Coffee's ready, Monzur. Doughnut's ready."

Mr. Johnson would have recalled speaking by telephone to Christine Olender, the assistant to the general manager, that morning. Mr. Rojas would have remembered a banquet server named Gomez. Ahad Ahmed would have talked of a manager named Jupiter. Other names were mentioned, out of respect.

A few minutes before Rudolph W. Giuliani began talking of September 11 at a political event down at Madison Square Garden, they decided to go home, to places that most delegates would not be visiting: Harlem, and Woodside, and Elmhurst.

Noche will close for good this week; its owners have other plans. But there was still another Republican party to work last night, a lunch and dinner scheduled for today, and a final lunch on Thursday. After that, some Windows on the World veterans will be looking again for another restaurant.

September 11, Yet Nothing Stops the Tides

New York has its ends of the earth, odd little places so psychically removed from the rest of the city that they barely heed the urban scat. Places like City Island, that Bronx curio of a community lingering like an afterthought in the chop and sway of the Long Island Sound.

And within these odd little places like City Island, there are odder, littler places still, so self-contained that they could just as well exist in Oregon or Maine. Places like Barron's Boat Yard, a scrappy marina where the rhythms of the tide matter more than the schedules of any city bus.

Even so, the denizens of Barron's marina still follow the New York clock. They know that it is the second week in September when the final exhalations of southern storms create weather that matches the city's mood: one minute sunny bright, the next minute dark gray, as though neither the sky above nor the people below know whether to smile or to cry.

If you think about it too much, a kind of paralysis threatens to set in. You can stand at the boatyard's pier, under uncertain skies, and feel the tug of melancholy so easily found at water's edge. The clang of wind-whipped rope against the mast. The twirl of arrow-shaped weather vanes. The sight of Hart Island a half-mile away, where inmates of this city bury its unclaimed dead.

Or you can think about it in the manner of the marina's owner,

John Barron. Honor that September day by living in this September day. Push your wheelbarrow. Protect your customers' boats. Repair your seawall. Get through it, in part by finding reassurance rather than sorrow in the lapping waters before you.

"I find it soothing," he says.

Mr. Barron, a City Island native, looks the part of marina operator, with an oil-stained cap pulled low on his head, a slight limp in his walk, and a leathery wear to his face that suggests fifty-five years spent on or near the water. His father opened this boatyard in 1934, and now he finds himself relying more and more on his own son, Jason, to keep things running.

Sitting in his glorified shack of an office the other day, musing about September in New York, Mr. Barron explained that other matters vie for his attention. "Look at this," he said, brandishing a printout of a map that showed Hurricane Ivan engulfing Jamaica and moving toward Florida.

With Charley, then Frances, and now Ivan roiling the waters, Mr. Barron said he felt acute responsibility for the dozens of boats entrusted to him by customers, boats that are bucking like mustangs just off his pier. Word is, three boats on the other side of the island broke free of their bridles.

He also feels the pressure of his other duties: ferrying customers to and from their boats, shoring up that seawall, and—well, just look around the boatyard, cluttered with dry-docked boats needing attention. More than enough to occupy the mind, he said. More than enough.

But it is the second week in September, the third anniversary, and remote City Island is still New York City. As with any of us, Mr. Barron has his story: of hauling in a boat when word came; of taking his own boat to see for himself, but turning back at the sight of the rising dark plume ("Too sad"); of the stricken City Island faces; of the familiar names among those of the missing, including that of Chris Kirby, his son's close friend, a carpenter, twenty-one.

With Chris Kirby gazing down from a memorial card tacked to the wall of his shack office, Mr. Barron explained again his approach to this awkward moment on the city calendar. "You can honor the fallen by fulfilling your role in society," he said. Work hard, but remember to pause before the water.

This morning on City Island, known to itself as the Seaport of the Bronx, the Torah study group will resume at Temple Beth-El. Throughout the day, people will be dining at the Crab Shanty, the Lobster Box, and Sammy's Fish Box. Tonight means karaoke at one of the local yacht clubs. High tide will be at 10:31 in the morning, and then again at 10:43 at night.

At Barron's Boat Yard, Jason Barron will be working all day, but he expects to see his girlfriend, Annie Mataraza, tonight. They met nearly three years ago at a candlelight vigil for their mutual friend, Chris.

As for the owner, he is gone. Seeing opportunity in the good weekend weather reports, John Barron sailed away from the city on Friday, borne by the waters that soothe him.

NOVEMBER 24, 2004

A Bond of Loss, Now Bundled with Joy

John Duffy and Kieran Lynch lived their lives sharing a deep fraternal bond, but they did not know each other. Not until last night.

They both grew up on Long Island, in Irish-American homes. They both shared bedrooms with beloved brothers. They both went to Catholic grammar schools, high schools, and colleges. They both work in bonds. They both know loss.

And they both know a guy named Paul Murphy, a guy they just call Murph.

But Mr. Duffy and Mr. Lynch did not know each other, not until last night, when Mr. Murphy brought them together for a couple of beers at Smith & Wollensky steakhouse on the East Side. You two have got to meet each other, their friend Murph kept saying. You have to meet each other.

And he was right.

This story demands the reader's attention, because the short Irish surnames of the three principals—Duffy, Murphy, and Lynch—might evoke thoughts of three tenors, or a firm specializing in immigration law. This story also illustrates how, in the end, imperceptible threads hold together this massive city of steel and concrete.

It begins, as so much does now, with what happened after the towers fell. Mr. Murphy and Mr. Duffy, acquaintances then, were working in the trading room at J. P. Morgan in Midtown. Everyone lost that day, with Mr. Duffy losing his younger brother, Michael, in the dust of the World Trade Center's south tower.

In the months before, John and Michael and their sister Mary Kay would leave Manhattan to spend weekends with their father, Jack, who was gradually dying, in the family home on Long Island. "In fact," John Duffy says, "it turned out we were being together with my father and Michael."

Michael Duffy was just short of thirty, with a girlfriend named Allyson and a way about him that made you want to be by his side at all times. How many nights had two brothers lain in the darkness of that bedroom back in Northport, talking of life.

After the catastrophe, two acquaintances in the J. P. Morgan trading room, Duff and Murph, became friends.

Mr. Murphy left J. P. Morgan last year for a similar job with UBS Securities, the investment bank, in Stamford, Connecticut. He soon learned that a co-worker sitting twenty feet away, Kieran Lynch, had lost his two older brothers in the trade center collapse.

There was Farrell Lynch, thirty-nine, father of three, and Sean Lynch, thirty-six, father of two with a third on the way, both working for Cantor Fitzgerald on the same floor in the north tower. Kieran talked with Farrell by telephone that last morning about the early, confusing reports of what was happening. "He said that he was going to get Sean," Kieran Lynch remembers. "And he said, 'I'll call you when I get down.'"

With that, the Lynches of Merrick became five instead of seven, and funny family stories about the four boys—Farrell, Sean, Kieran, and Brian—sleeping together in the attic bedroom were tempered with tears. How many boyish whispers rose like prayers from those attic beds, about basketball, about girls, about what comes next?

When the opportunity presented itself years later in a trading room in Stamford, Mr. Murphy expressed his condolences to his colleague, Mr. Lynch, and another friendship took root.

So Mr. Murphy saw Mr. Lynch every day, while keeping in touch by telephone and e-mail with Mr. Duffy. At some point, while once again discussing September 11 and its aftermath, he asked Mr. Duffy if he knew a Lynch, a Kieran Lynch.

No, Mr. Duffy answered, but added that he knew his brother Farrell quite well. He was an outstanding figure in the insular world of bonds, Mr. Duffy said—and a hero of his. In fact, he said, he was going to name his first child, boy or girl, after Farrell.

Well, then, Mr. Murphy said, you have to meet my friend Kieran.

Last night, while waiting at the bar, Mr. Duffy talked with someone about what it is like to live in a city where 9/11 loss is commonplace. Sometimes he wants to say: "Did you hear what I just said? I lost my brother."

At six on the dot, Mr. Lynch and Mr. Murphy walked in with a swish of cold wind behind them. The place was warm and inviting, the way bars can be at holiday time.

Someone ordered beers, and soon the men were clinking bottlenecks.

"Nice meeting you," Mr. Lynch said.

"Kieran, nice meeting you," Mr. Duffy said.

A conversation began, about loss and connection. Then Mr. Duffy held out a small green photo album filled with snapshots of a newborn girl: Farrell Ann Duffy.

"I've got some pictures," he said.

JUNE 25, 2005

"Remember When," but Also "Never Forget"

The distribution of yearbooks the other day made it official: Adulthood had come to the seniors of Stuyvesant High School. They cracked the binding and pored over four years of snapshot moments that began when they were thirteen, fourteen; children, really.

Here was Vicky, wielding her tennis racket. Here too was Lisa, smiling with friends on the track team. Here were Jason, and Chun Che, and Soleil. Remember Halloween, when that boy came dressed as Marilyn Monroe? Remember Pajama Day? Remember?

In a way, though, these seniors became adults just days into their freshman year. Nearly eight hundred students will graduate on Monday as the Class of 2005, but once you do your math, and remember that Stuyvesant is just north of what was the World Trade Center, you realize that theirs was also a Class of 2001; September 11, 2001.

Their jumbled high school memories are both sweet and shocking, funny and not. Remember the junior prom, and physics class, and that first loud boom, and those car alarms going off? Remember the ballroom dancing, and the song-and-dance competitions, and seeing the debris falling from the towers? Was it debris? Remember?

But as some of these seniors recall their high school careers, strands of resilience weave through their stories. They refuse to allow a catastrophe outside their schoolhouse doors to define these four precious years of theirs. They remember the downwind whiffs of death, but they also remember biology tests, free periods, and the zing of first kisses.

It was the first Tuesday of their first year at Stuyvesant, an intensely competitive high school that attracts students citywide. Jason Hsu was putting a cover on his Spanish textbook when he heard a boom—the sound of the first plane hitting the north tower.

Lisa Cao heard a chorus of car alarms while sitting in art appreciation class. Soleil Ho was in English, trying to get lost in a poem she was writing.

Then the lights flickered. Vicky Porto was in math class on the fourth floor when she saw debris spewing from the south tower after the second plane hit. "I really wasn't sure what was going on," she recalled. "I remember one girl in my class starting to cry."

Some watched televisions; others watched from the windows. Jason saw "stuff" falling from the towers, but he says he doesn't think it was people; "at least I hope it wasn't." Chun Che Peng remembers a teacher telling students to focus on their work, but no one could.

A voice on the public-address system directed students to their homerooms and then out the north side of the building to West Street. Behind them, a billowing curtain of smoke; in front of them, crowds fleeing north. Lisa remembers giving a bottle of water she had to a firefighter heading south.

While some students gathered at Chelsea Piers, others set out to find pay phones, food, home. Soleil walked to Union Square with a friend, and remembers being annoyed that Urban Outfitters was closed. Chun Che had a burger at a McDonald's in Midtown. Jason walked all the way home to East Sixty-third Street.

With their high school taken over by rescue and recovery workers, Stuyvesant students attended truncated classes at Brooklyn Technical High School in Fort Greene, then returned in early October to a school that had been scrubbed clean, but was still just four blocks from the smoldering trade center pile. The air smelled of it.

"It felt like we were coming back to a strange land," Chun Che said.

"I think I was confused the whole time," Vicky said. "I'd come home and on the radio they were talking about how the air around here was not great."

Vicky and Lisa carried surgical masks in their backpacks, and people in orange vests interrupted classes to test the air quality. They became so much a part of Stuyvesant life, Lisa says, that two students dressed up as air-quality testers for Halloween.

Meanwhile, counselors gently discussed post-traumatic stress, though few students accepted their offers to talk privately. Instead, art appreciation helped, as did new friends, English homework, track practice.

From some windows the students could see the debris-laden trucks rumbling to barges on the Hudson. But they also had teachers before them, demanding answers to questions about other things. "Not really block out, but accept," Soleil said. "It happens. People died. They're still down there. Gotta go to school."

Sophomore year arrived, then junior year, and then they were seniors, Stuyvesant seniors. Some outsiders have connected 9/11 to a supposed drop in the number of those receiving early college admission. "That's a stretch," said Vicky, who is going to Columbia in the fall. Lisa agreed; she's going to Cornell.

The two young women sat in a coffee shop near Stuyvesant yesterday, flipping through a yearbook that dedicates two pages to 9/11, and the rest to smiles and inside jokes and senior portraits. They are both seventeen. .

Under Vicky Portnoy's photo, it reads: "Life may not be the party that we hoped for, but while we are here, we might as well dance." And under Lisa Cao's, this: "Life is short—eat dessert first."

JULY 27, 2005

What Does "Suspicious" Look Like?

Police officers stopped a sightseeing bus in Times Square on Sunday morning, and not because they suddenly desired to see the South Street Seaport. Urgent word had come to them of suspicious men onboard, acting suspiciously in these suspicious times.

Within seconds, the tourists on the double-decker bus had their hands raised high, in pantomime of thrill-seekers riding the Cyclone. And within minutes, five of those tourists, all dark-skinned men, had their hands in cuffs and their knees on city pavement, in pantomime of new immigrants worshiping the ground of this freedom-loving country.

It quickly became clear that those five suspicious-looking, dark-skinned men, who suspiciously had bought their tickets in advance, were just British citizens on holiday, with vacation snapshots that now will include newspaper photos of their public humiliation. Mayor Michael R. Bloomberg issued a public apology—on behalf of the city, not the police—and the city lurched toward its next uneasy moment.

But the bus incident warrants pause; it has meaning, as do the random checks being conducted in transit hubs. They reflect a city struggling to find balance in a trembling world: a city that embraces personal freedom, a city whose motto could be "It Takes All Types," and yet a city that sees its troubled reflection in the news images from besieged London.

People with their hands up. On a tourist bus. In Times Square.

"We're struggling with this transition from a pre-9/11 world to this new world," said Dr. Irwin Redlener, director of the National Center for Disaster Preparedness, at Columbia University. "On the one hand, we want to be protected. In the immediate aftermath of the bombings in London, there's a certain acceptance of tourists with hands raised on a sightseeing bus."

But on the other hand, he said, the question looms: "How far do we actually have to go?"

According to the police, a supervisor for the Gray Line bus company notified a police captain that five suspicious-looking men with backpacks had boarded one of its tourist buses, Number 320, near the Waldorf-Astoria. Mike Alvich, Gray Line's vice president for sales and marketing, said yesterday that the notification reflected the "extensive training" that Gray Line's employees undergo for "situations like this."

More training may be in order, though. Based on the bus company's tip, the police directed bus Number 320 into an area near Broadway and West Fifty-first Street that was already cordoned off—because of another security scare!—and conducted a dramatic frisk-and-hunt. Its quick conclusion: The five men had no backpacks, no fanny packs, nothing.

On Monday, the *Daily News* published a front-page photograph of scared tourists with hands raised, as if re-enacting a stagecoach holdup. That afternoon, Mayor Bloomberg apologized, but he said that the police had no choice but to take "total control." And, in a subtle slap at Gray Line, he urged people to use "some common sense" in reporting suspicious behavior.

But what is common sense? And in this metropolis of tolerance and eccentricity, what constitutes suspicious behavior?

"This is a disturbing event because it raises the question: 'What would you have done?'" said Dr. Rachel Yehuda, a professor of psychiatry at the Mount Sinai School of Medicine with expertise in posttraumatic stress. "If the main goal is to make sure that no one gets killed by an act of terrorism, then this may come at a cost of overreacting to perceived threats that are not real. The area that needs refining is: What is a credible threat? How do we know someone is suspicious?"

In what might otherwise be a compliment, New Yorkers generally do not question the behavior of neighbors. "We can't really point out who's different, because everyone is," Dr. Yehuda said. "Who in fact are our enemies? And what behavior will distinguish them as such? That's the difficulty."

Were there enemies at the Gray Line storefront on Eighth Avenue in Midtown yesterday morning? Red double-decker buses idled on the street, while dark- and light-skinned employees of the company encouraged dark- and light-skinned tourists to take the downtown loop, or the uptown loop, or the Brooklyn loop.

See the Empire State Building. See the Museum of Natural History. See City Hall. Each a landmark, each a potential target.

A woman mentioned to her companion how she had always wanted to see the Cloisters. Another woman hustled her family to a bus on which the wonders of Lower Manhattan would be described in German. And the rest of us carried on, hands raised in outrage, submission, or both.

SEPTEMBER 10, 2005

In New Orleans, as It Did in New York, X Marks the Pain

New Orleans

A crude symbol has surfaced in New Orleans to displace for now the fleur-de-lis, the crescent, and the string of beads. It is a large X sprayed with neon-orange paint onto the emptied homes, the violated stores—even the city buses that litter streets like giant discarded milk cartons.

The fleur-de-lis reflects the enduring French influence on life here. The crescent symbolizes the bend in the nurturing Mississippi River. The beads evoke Mardi Gras, though these days they dangle from trees like gaudy nooses. And now, scrawled across all of that, a large X the color of Halloween: the postcatastrophe symbol used by search-and-rescue units to signal that the space inside has been checked for signs of life or the remains of death.

On Tuesday—was it Tuesday?—a task force from Texas, armed with guns and spray cans, decorated the Bywater section here with the macabre graffiti. At the top of the X, the date (9/6); to the left, the unit that conducted the search (TXTF); to the right, the number of hazards, structural and otherwise, within (0); and at the bottom, the number of dead (0).

The symbol has haunting resonance for those who walked the gray-powdered streets of Lower Manhattan in the first days after 9/11. Four years later nearly to the day, you notice that X on a deserted storefront on St. Claude Avenue here; you take comfort in seeing zeroes; and in a finger's snap you are back there on Vesey Street, or Liberty, or Church. What's more, the skies over southern Louisiana have been a baby blue the last few days, as they were over New York on that Tuesday morning.

So many images here set off dormant memories. The National Guard encampment in Audubon Park recalls the National Guard encampment in Battery Park, where a thunderstorm one night had people imagining another attack. The whiff of rotting food in a market on St. Charles Avenue brings back the pungency of that dusty still-life display of food rotting in the Amish Market on Washington Street. The fear of contaminated water now; the fear of contaminated air then.

A disturbing question comes too quickly to the mind. Which was worse: the attacks of September 11 or the attack of Hurricane Katrina?

The question reflects our strange desire to quantify disaster. Any time a jetliner crashes—in Lockerbie, outside Pittsburgh, off the Moriches—the news media rush to point out its standing in terms of the number killed, as though measuring its worthiness for some sorrowful hall of fame. Sometimes newspapers will even publish an accompanying graph: Five Deadliest Plane Crashes.

From the acrid-smelling streets of this fresh horror, near the fourth anniversary of another horror—still fresh in its own way—such calculus seems fruitless, inappropriate, and akin to comparing a wounded apple to an injured orange. They are distinct in their own awful ways.

The hurricane was a natural disaster. The disaster of 9/11 was madman-made. The hurricane exploded across hundreds of miles, devastating cities, towns, and obscure places that many people here barely knew of; Happy Jack, for one. The jetliners that became bombs on 9/11 devastated a corner of Manhattan, and brought down two of the most famous buildings in the world.

On and on the distinctions go: 9/11's fire to the hurricane's water; people dying at work and people drowning at home; congregations mourning in places of worship and congregations mourning for places of worship that are now inaccessible, underwater, destroyed.

Rather than wasting energy and emotion on that awkward question of which is worse, those profoundly affected by 9/11 might consider what now forever binds the New Orleans of 2005 to other American cities: the Johnstown of 1889; the Galveston of 1900; the San Francisco of 1906; the Oklahoma City of 1995; the New York of 2001.

The overwhelming loss of life, of course, and the crippling tolls to the economy, to the infrastructure, to the community's sense of self. But more than that: the denial of that basic, sacred need to claim and bury the dead. Four years have passed, and 1,152 of the 2,749 victims of 9/11 have not been identified. Two weeks have passed, and who knows how many bodies still bob in dark waters.

Which is worse? Let the question go.

Just know that emergency telephone numbers and wrenching news updates trickle across the television screens here, just as they did then. That volunteers from across the country are here to help out, just as they did then. That people here vow to rebuild, just as we did then.

One night four years ago, a city sanitation worker started sweeping the debris of chaos from Church Street. And one afternoon this week, a shopkeeper on deserted Royal Street did the same.

MAY 17, 2006

Hope, Saved on a Laptop

For a long time, Ann Nelson's laptop computer remained dark.

It had been returned to her family in North Dakota, along with the other belongings she left behind in that great city 1,750 miles to the east. She was thirty, lively, working near the very top of the World Trade Center, and—you already know.

In the small town of Stanley, halfway between Minot and Williston, a fog thick enough to blur time's passing enveloped the Nelson home. Amid the many tributes to Ann, amid the grieving and the absence, it became hard to remember just when and how the laptop wound up in the basement of the one-story bank that the family owned.

There the laptop sat, for years, tucked away from sight in a black case. It was a Dell Inspiron 8000, bought shortly before Ann called home that day in early 2001 to say she had gotten a job as a bond trader at Cantor Fitzgerald—in New York! Soon she was living near the corner of Thompson and Spring, and working in an office 104 stories in the air.

Ann's parents, Jenette and Gary Nelson, say the laptop remained unopened because they are not computer savvy. But it was more than that, Mrs. Nelson admits. "To tell you the truth, it was just too painful."

Three summers ago, during an art class Mrs. Nelson was teaching in that basement, a couple of students showed her how to use the computer. After the class, she says, "I just left it there."

Who knows why never becomes someday, and someday becomes

today. One day last fall—"when I got to feeling stronger," she says—Mrs. Nelson finally opened her daughter's computer. She pushed its power button and started by looking at the photographs stored in its memory.

Soon Mrs. Nelson was learning how to play the computer's games, including solitaire and hearts. These distractions both relaxed her and reminded her of the games she used to play with Ann. Somehow, this little black machine made Ann seem present, there beside her.

Getting lost in the computer became part of Mrs. Nelson's after-work ritual, though she never bothered to open a file that said "Top 100"; probably some music, she figured. Then, two months ago and who knows why, click.

What she found was a catalog of goals, humanly incomplete: a list that reflected a young woman's commitment to the serious, to the frivolous, to all of life. That night, Mr. and Mrs. Nelson sat down with the list, and were with their daughter again.

1. *Be healthy/healthful.*
2. *Be a good friend.*
3. *Keep secrets.*
4. *Keep in touch with people I love and that love me.*
5. *Make a quilt.*

Mrs. Nelson used to sew all the time, until it simply became too hard to guide a needle properly with a joyous little girl frolicking in her lap. Then, when Ann grew older, mother and daughter decided to sew a tablecloth.

"I don't think we ever finished," Mrs. Nelson says, laughing. "She had to be doing a hundred things at a time, and consequently some of them didn't get finished."

As for this goal of making a quilt, she adds, "I'm sure that I would probably have been deeply involved in this process."

6. *Nepal.*
7. *Buy a home in North Dakota.*
8. *Get a graduate degree.*

9. *Learn a foreign language.*
10. *Kilimanjaro.*
11. *Never be ashamed of who I am.*

"Ann was in many environments where being a girl from North Dakota may not have been the most sophisticated label to wear," Mrs. Nelson says, recalling that her daughter had traveled to China and to Peru, and had worked in the high-powered environments of Chicago and New York.

Even so Ann always conveyed pride in who she was, who her parents were, and where they came from—though never in a boastful way. "It's an important point about her personality," her mother says.

12. *Be a person to be proud of.*
13. *Always keep improving.*
14. *Read every day.*
15. *Be informed.*
16. *Knit a sweater.*
17. *Scuba-dive in the Barrier Reef.*
18. *Volunteer for a charity.*
19. *Learn to cook.*

By her late twenties, Ann had actually become a fairly decent cook. Still, her mother laughs in recalling late-night calls, like the one that began: "Mom, what's drawn butter?"

20. *Learn about art.*
21. *Get my C.F.A.*
22. *Grand Canyon.*
23. *Helicopter-ski with my dad.*

Then Ann Nelson's list repeats a number.

23. *Spend more time with my family.*
24. *Remember birthdays!!!!*

Birthdays loomed large in Ann's life. She would celebrate her birthday not for a day, but for a week—in part because her father's birthday came the very next day, in part because she was proud to have been born on Norwegian Independence Day—which is May 17, today.

"Ann would have been thirty-five," says Mr. Nelson, who turns sixty-five tomorrow.

25. *Appreciate money, but don't worship it.*
26. *Learn how to use a computer.*
27. *Visit the New York Public Library.*
28. *Maine.*
29. *Learn to write.*
30. *Walk—exercise but also see the world firsthand.*
31. *Learn about other cultures.*
32. *Be a good listener.*
33. *Take time for friends.*
34. *Kayak.*
35. *Drink water.*
36. *Learn about wine.*

Ann was supposed to attend a wine class the evening of September 11, in keeping with Numbers 13, 19, 31, 36—the whole list, really. After 36, there is a 37, but it is blank.

Mr. Nelson reads the list as an inventory of his daughter's values. "You don't see any Corvettes in the garage or any of those material things you might expect from someone that age," he says. "She recognized that you appreciate a few things and kind of live your life wisely."

Mrs. Nelson interprets the list as another way in which Ann seems to communicate with her when she is most in need. So, just about every day in a small North Dakota town, halfway between Minot and Williston, the screen of a laptop computer goes from darkness to light.

PART VI

Susan Farley

Congress of Curious
New York Peoples

JULY 2, 2003

Conjuring Hamlet in a Hard Hat

The skull kept staring at Al Zabroski. He tried to get on with his work, but he could feel its eyes—or maybe its eye sockets—boring through the back of his own cranium. Whenever he looked, the skull looked back, wearing its great death mask of indifference.

Ask me, the skull seemed to say. Go ahead, Al. Ask.

Mr. Zabroski obliged. He picked it up, returned its hollow gaze, and silently posed the questions that any person might ask of a skull found in New York City muck.

Who were you? How did you die? And, although it might be a tad late, is there anything I can do?

The loam of this city offers up ghostly fragments of its past with fair regularity. Sometimes it renders pottery shards; sometimes, human remains. Each piece dares the finder to determine its placement in the cosmic jigsaw puzzle of New York.

It is a fool's challenge, of course; there are never enough pieces, and those that surface never quite fit. Still, our humanity all but requires us to think big thoughts about the present and future when confronted with a sacred piece of the past. It is the Hamlet in us; it is the Al Zabroski.

"It was very out-of-body," said Mr. Zabroski, thirty-four, who protects his own pate with a bandanna.

Mr. Zabroski's Yorick moment occurred last week in a fifteen-foot hole on a construction site in East Harlem, where the foundation for a housing development for the elderly is being laid. He and a colleague were drilling into the bedrock under an unforgiving sun. The machinery they were using was spraying water all over the pit, turning everything to mud. Lunch break seemed a lifetime away.

The two men suddenly noticed that the wet rock to their left wasn't a rock at all; it was a skull. Mr. Zabroski's workmate poked at it with his gloved hand, then backed away.

Al, the skull seemed to call. A-a-a-l?

Mr. Zabroski picked up the incomplete skull, which was missing pretty much everything below the eye sockets. It humbled him, filled him with questions about how the life of this skull's owner was lived and how it concluded.

He put it down and returned to work, but kept glancing over his shoulder to ask: Who were you? The more he thought, the more he suspected foul play. He found himself asking: Who did this to you? Who?

"I wanted to know so bad," he said.

The police officers who answered the call asked him to carry the skull up out of the hole—and to please put it in something. He found a used plastic bag and a discarded box, placed the piece of a person inside, and hauled it up to curbside. Then they asked him to put it back in the pit where he found it.

Amy Zelson Mundorff, the city's forensic anthropologist, arrived with an assistant. They took photographs and measurements, asked a few questions, and drove off in a sport utility vehicle, skull aboard.

Ms. Mundorff declined to discuss this case, but she said complete skulls provide much better data about sex, ancestry, and approximate age. She knows these things: a dozen times a year she is summoned to a place where the living are asking the unanswerable while standing before newly discovered bones of the dead.

"Sometimes they're full skeletons," she said. "Those are a lot easier to work with."

If the skull's incompleteness thwarts deeper inquiry, then what

about where it was found—at the southeast corner of East 127th
Street and Lexington Avenue? Alas, it was nothing more than a vacant
lot. And before that, a community garden. And before that, the longtime home of the old Harlem Eye and Ear Hospital. Not eye, ear, and
skull; just eye and ear.

It seems that the inquisitive Mr. Zabroski may never know to
whom the skull belonged. Most likely it will be cataloged, then
buried in the potter's field on Hart Island, along with other bits and
pieces of the New York puzzle.

After Ms. Mundorff left, Mr. Zabroski became obsessed with her
request that he keep an eye out for more; even a tooth would be helpful in identification. He drilled deeper into the earth, while searching
the muck for what else it might render.

Three o'clock came. Time to climb out of the pit and return to
flesh-and-blood living. He climbed into his pickup and began the
long ride home to western New Jersey.

Along the way, though, he decided to stop at a strip club in Elizabeth that professes to have "the most beautiful women in the world."
He told his skull story to a barmaid, who began firing off those cosmic questions. Who was it? Who did it? Who?

Exactly, said Al Zabroski.

OCTOBER 18, 2003

Taking Down Savage Beast,
Via Elevator

Never poke a tiger with a stick.

This would appear to be one of the basic rules of survival that are
known to us at birth. No firsthand knowledge is necessary for one to
appreciate its wisdom. Tiger. Don't poke. Got it.

But a couple of weeks ago there arose what is known in this city
as a "situation"—code for an event in which the commingling of

prayer and epithet is permitted. This particular situation, awkward to the extreme, required that a large, affable man named James Breheny poke a tiger with a stick.

It should be noted that tigers are not indigenous to the Bronx, where Mr. Breheny was raised by humans. It should also be noted that while he is the associate general curator of the Bronx Zoo, Mr. Breheny (pronounced bre-HEE-nee) is not a professional tiger poker. He just happened to be working two Saturdays ago when the police telephoned to say they had, well, a situation: an adult tiger in a Harlem apartment.

The situation became instant city lore. How the owner fed Ming the tiger with careful tosses of butchered chickens. How the residents in the high-rise came to accept Ming as just another neighbor. How the police subdued Ming with a tranquilizing dart. And how Ming now resides in a sanctuary in Ohio.

Such a tale is worth revisiting, though, especially when seen through Mr. Breheny's wide eyes. He may be the consummate animal guy: Someone who started working at the zoo when he was fourteen, giving pony rides. He may have a graduate degree in biology. He may even have gotten married on the zoo grounds—to another zoo employee.

But a tiger in Harlem? Even in the controlled environment of the Bronx Zoo, he said, the rule is: "You never occupy the same space as the cats."

As Mr. Breheny and two veterinarians drove to Harlem in a brown zoo van, they discussed what awaited them. Do you really think it could be an adult tiger? Naah. Probably some small exotic cat.

They arrived on the scene to find hundreds of people milling about, and police officers waving them through. "They were quite happy to see us," he said. "It was like a scene from *Ghostbusters.*"

Police officials escorted them to a television monitor receiving a live feed of the goings-on in a certain fifth-floor apartment. It was an adult tiger all right, a big one. Zoo and police officials hurriedly developed a tactical plan.

First, a police officer rappelled down the side of the building and managed to shoot the tiger in the rump with the dart. The animal let out a roar that reverberated through the building, then lumbered out of the camera's view.

Now it was the zoo people's turn. Mr. Breheny and the two veterinarians—Robert Cook and Bonnie Raphael—waited and waited for the drug to take effect. After about twenty-five minutes, and with police accompaniment, Mr. Breheny and Dr. Cook ventured into the apartment, where it was quiet, too quiet.

"It was tense, and our adrenaline was flowing, but we were so focused on getting the tiger," Mr. Breheny, forty-four, recalled from the safety of his office the other day. He seemed so at home there, so at peace, with paintings of animals on his walls and a pattern of camels on his tie.

But then the absurdity of it all—the danger—returned to the fore of his thoughts. "We were not working in a controlled environment," he quickly added.

They had no trouble finding the drugged, inert tiger; its striped coat did not exactly blend. Then, with a five-foot pole, Mr. Breheny defied a cardinal law of survival: He poked the tiger.

"I just kind of, quietly, steadily, poked him once," he said. "I waited, and then I poked him two more times."

The tiger didn't move, but Dr. Cook gave it another shot for good measure. It was in good physical shape, Mr. Breheny recalled, except for a little tartar on the fangs. But that is beside the point, he emphasized.

"The sheer majesty and power of these animals!" he said. "They deserve better than to be held captive in an apartment."

The tiger team dragged the animal into the hallway, where it was fed gas through a tube and lifted onto a gurney. The elevator arrived, and several people crowded into the small car with Ming, including the man who would live to tell about poking a tiger.

Someone pushed the button for the ground floor.

But the elevator went up—to twelve. The door opened to reveal a few people waiting to go down.

"Next elevator," they were told.

After Thirty-five Years, Unburdening a Guilty Heart

Four dozen men live in the cubicles at the century-old Andrews House on the Bowery. They pay thirty-six dollars a week for a five-by-seven room that has barely enough space for the thin cot, the small locker, and any secrets they might need to stash for the night.

Each cubicle holds the epic of a transient. If he wants to stop drinking, or find a job, or feel better about himself, social workers in the building are ready to help. But if he prefers to brood in peace or work things out on his own, that's fine too.

Last week, one of the residents, a man who called himself George Cook, made a momentous decision. He was sixty-nine years old, living in a box with a failing and heavy heart. It was time to set the record straight. To begin with, his name was not George Cook.

He made his way down to Foley Square, entered one of the buildings where the business is justice, and introduced himself to federal marshals. His name was Gerald Geller, he said, and if they checked their records, they would find that he was wanted for a bank robbery in 1971. September 3, 1971.

On that morning in this city, the air was warm, the skies cloudy. Down in City Hall, Mayor John V. Lindsay was harboring presidential ambitions. Up at Yankee Stadium, Fritz Peterson was scheduled to start against the Detroit Tigers. And in Herald Square, some men were walking into the Atlantic Bank and forcibly withdrawing $63,535 of other people's money.

One of the robbers barely made it out the door before a police officer grabbed him; maybe the automatic pistol he was carrying had
slowed him down. Two others were quickly caught as well. But a
fourth robber, Gerald Geller, found his wrinkle in time, and slipped
through.

Who was this Geller? A nobody, really, from Brooklyn—"one of
these wannabe guys," one investigator said—with a couple of book-
making arrests and a fondness for betting on horses. Short and stocky,
he conveyed pride in his heritage with a distinctive tattoo on his right
bicep: an American eagle inside a Star of David.

How Mr. Geller spent the next thirty-five years is not entirely
clear. Sometimes he called himself George Cook; other times, Peter
Yannacone. He lived in New Orleans, in Tampa, Florida, and possibly
in Quincy, Massachusetts. He worked in restaurants, bars, and a book-
store. He grew a beard and shaved it off, but kept a mustache.

For more than a decade now, he has been back in New York as
George Cook, waiter in diners, resident of a cubicle on the Bowery.
Last year, though, he had a heart attack, and was no longer able to hold
his own in the coffee and souvlaki swirl. Nor was he eligible for
proper health coverage, since every day of his life began with a lie.

He was a man not well, a man not at peace—a man not even himself. So he reclaimed his name—Gerald Geller—and turned himself in.

Mr. Geller has advanced heart disease, and the need for medical attention beyond an emergency-room visit clearly figured in his decision to surrender. It seems, though, that more was at play, judging by
what he subsequently said to law enforcement officials:

I want my record clean before I pass on.

Yesterday morning, a hunched little man gingerly entered a federal
courtroom, walking as though he were stepping on broken glass.
Shrunken, not stocky, he had a gray mustache, a gray sweater, and gray
corduroy pants with a hole in one of the back pockets. Everything
about him was gray; he looked worn out from running.

When Mr. Geller went on the lam, the judge before him, Kenneth
M. Karras, was seven years old, and the defense lawyer beside him,
Sean Hecker, was not yet two. Even the federal building he stood in,
at 500 Pearl Street, did not exist.

"Your Honor, this is an old case," the federal prosecutor began.

He explained that two of Mr. Geller's convicted codefendants are dead, and the whereabouts of the third is unknown. Given the paucity of witnesses and the passing of decades, it remained unclear whether the government would be able to present a criminal case, but the prosecutor promised that it would "make every effort to go forward."

The judge set the next court date for May 5, and wished everyone a good weekend.

With that Mr. Geller, ex-fugitive, shuffled out, bound perhaps for a cubicle on the Bowery, where lately there is less clutter.

JANUARY 28, 2004

Man of Steel, Meet the Man of Staples

Sometimes, as his bus or bicycle draws nearer to Gotham, he imagines himself to be a superhero in disguise. Not Superman, no. Not Batman or Aquaman or Spider-Man. No.

Flyer Man.

"I take off my suit, and here I am," says mild-mannered Martin Forro. "Flyer Man."

Superman has his cape, Batman his cowl. Flyer Man has his enormous backpack, from which he can retrieve boxes of staples, jars of thumbtacks, rolls of tape—and multicolored reams of fliers, each one promising another way to invigorate this dreary existence of ours.

Enjoy Yoga at Home. Awaken Your Dormant Creativity Through Counseling. Learn How to Make Yourself Happy Through Buddhist Meditation. Join an Acting Workshop. And, if all else fails: Learn to Play the Five-String Banjo.

"Fliers do work," says Flyer Man, who prefers the spelling that suggests superheroic ability. "Definitely."

Fliers are the wallpaper of New York. They shout from the metal-frame doorways of bodegas, beckon from bulletin boards in laundry rooms, insinuate themselves into the idle thoughts of customers at coffeehouses. But where do these fliers come from? Does the banjo guy pause from composing his Appalachian opus to adorn Chelsea with fliers? Does the meditation master interrupt his "om" to hustle down to Kinko's?

Om-m-m, no. They call on Flyer Man.

Martin Forro, forty, was once a mere mortal. He was laid off nearly two years ago from a job selling pagers, which he had taken years earlier after being laid off from a job selling copiers, which he had taken when his planned career in real estate went nowhere. One day the answer just revealed itself: fliers.

"I almost feel like God was on my side when I got laid off," he says.

He vowed to devote himself full-time to papering Manhattan with commercial come-ons. Sitting in their home in Cliffside Park, New Jersey, he and his wife, Betty, developed a flier, what else, to announce his new purpose in life. "How do you get the word out?" the advertisements asked. "Let Martin, the Flyer Man, distribute your fliers."

Mr. Forro felt empowered by experience. He used to post fliers part-time in the early 1980s, back when he was living on the Upper West Side, back when fliers were the spam of urban existence. Those wild days are long gone, though. If Batman heeds that bat signal in the sky, then Flyer Man is duty-bound to honor that message on bare walls: Post No Bills.

Flyer Man agreed to meet with a civilian the other day at Murray's Bagels, on Eighth Avenue in Chelsea. He waddled into the store, Hulklike, as if weighed down by sheer muscle, though the weight turned out to be his unwieldy parka, other layers of clothing, and that huge black backpack. He ordered only a Diet Coke—Flyer Man is on a diet—and began to talk about his peculiar niche in this city.

A customer will benefit from all that Flyer Man has gleaned from being out there, armed with little more than a stapler. For example, he has identified about 150 high-visibility locations where fliers are permitted—and that is just between 57th and 123rd Streets. He knows which supermarkets allow fliers and which do not. He knows the preferences of stores: staples, tape, or tacks. He knows that simple messages work the best.

And he knows that he has a nemesis, a competitor who has only recently emerged on the scene. "There's another guy out there," he says. "I think he called me once and posed as a customer. He asked me how I do my job."

Mr. Forro swings his backpack onto his shoulders and sets out to begin his rounds. No gloves over his chapped hands, because he needs his fingers to be free. No radio headset, because he needs to concentrate. When he is posting, he says, "I'm thinking about what my next location will be."

He staples some fliers to the bagel shop's bulletin board, click, click, click, then shuffles across Eighth Avenue to a doorway festooned with fliers. He points to one of his old fliers, for a photographer, which is missing a few tear-off phone numbers.

"See?" he says. "Look how effective. That's amazing. One tag left."

With each stop, at this coffee shop and that laundry, Mr. Forro prunes the bulletin boards like an attentive gardener, weeding the old, planting the new and—

Holy Swingline! What's this? The flier of that competitor! Stapled over a flier for Flyer Man!

Our hero tears the offending piece of paper from the wall, and crumples it with his bare hand.

FEBRUARY 4, 2006

Raising a Family and a Bridge

Many years ago, Delonda Bates took a course on nontraditional employment for women. Maybe she would become a construction worker, or a carpenter, or an electrical technician. Who knew how fate would employ her?

The only thing certain was her need to work. Right out of high school she had taken a factory job, married a factory man, quit the factory, and given birth to four children in fairly quick succession. Now it was time to rejoin the working world.

As she considered her nontraditional options, an employment specialist for the city's Department of Transportation seduced her with a compelling pitch to introduce women into the closed male world of bridge operators. The job sounded cool; she gave it a shot.

That was in 1989. Today Ms. Bates is the only woman among the fifteen operators-in-charge who oversee the twenty-five city-owned movable bridges in New York. A few other women have come and gone, but she stuck it out, and now she is the only woman who, with a push of a button here and a turn of a switch there, can elevate tons of New York road. And it is cool.

Over the years, Ms. Bates, forty-one, has worked at many of the city's movable bridges, from the Unionport Bridge along Bruckner Boulevard in the Bronx to the Mill Basin Bridge along the Belt Parkway in Brooklyn. She has also worked at the Pulaski Bridge, which connects Brooklyn and Queens over the Newtown Creek and provides its operators with a choice view of the majestic Manhattan mirage to the west.

For the last four years, Ms. Bates has worked at the Ninth Street Bridge, one of the five bridges over the curious South Brooklyn waterway known as the Gowanus Canal. It takes some imagination, though, to find majesty in the view from her squat office tower—a cityscape that includes an old brick warren of a factory, a parking lot for a Lowe's and a Pathmark, a construction site, and Old Man Gowanus, dressed in oil spots and debris.

And directly above clatters the train that every day takes her on her way to Far Rockaway, where she lives with her husband, Vernon, now a track worker for the Long Island Rail Road, and her children, now numbering five.

The canal is not exactly a hot spot for pleasure craft, and if anything, traffic is even slower in winter. According to the red logbook that she keeps on the windowsill, the bridge rises twice or maybe four times a day—for the *Cando,* a crane barge, going in, going out, or the *Mister T,* a gravel-hauling tug, going in, going out. That's about it, give or take a vessel.

The captains will radio in, and Ms. Bates, the unseen bridge levitator, will work the control panel. An air horn honks, sending pedestrians scurrying; "Everybody in this area knows that sound," she says. Traffic signals blink. Two sets of gates lower. Massive pins within the bridge disengage, or unlock. Then an eighty-two-foot-long section of road rises, slowly, magically, some fifty feet in the air.

A tug will glide by. The bridge will lower. And six minutes will have passed.

Ms. Bates has responsibilities beyond the control panel. She has to make sure that the bridge mechanisms are free of debris, that the air pressure is fine, that the lights along the pier wall are working—that her piece of Ninth Street, of Brooklyn, of New York, is in order.

This still leaves time for the diminutive bridge operator to look out her window at the discolored, ever-moving water that rises and falls with the tide. The oddest things float past: a blue laundry basket; a green ball; a family of ducks; those shimmering oil slicks that look like passing clouds, and set you to wondering.

Last year, her second-oldest son, Kasheem, started to have seizures during his senior year at Beach Channel High School. It turned out he had a brain aneurysm that required two operations because, she says, the first one "didn't take." He gradually got better, made it through rehabilitation, and is now, his mother says, "taking it kind of slow."

But for a while there, it seemed as though the life of Delonda Bates was a constant raising and lowering of bridges and spirits. Her son was unconscious for three weeks, while family members assured him with hand squeezes and words that they were there beside him.

The operator-in-charge at the Ninth Street Bridge remembers what she would say: "We're here every day. You don't see us. But we're here."

OCTOBER 15, 2003

Tales Sweet as Ice Cream, Salty as Tears

You tell the ice cream story."

"No, you."

"No, you. You tell it best."

The daughters of Ran Kim want to share the ice cream story

because it says so much about their mother. The story is well known among Korean immigrants in New York, they say, and is very funny— but also very sad. With no daughter eager to cry in public, they set the story aside for a while.

Instead, the daughters toss other stories like flowers onto a corner table in a Korean restaurant in Flushing, creating a bouquet of loving words for their mother, who sits beside them, smiling, understanding more English than she lets on. She is wearing a black outfit with a purple blouse, and a purple ribbon in her bun of black hair.

Strangers to Flushing might not give Mrs. Kim and her purple highlights a second look. But many Koreans know that this petite woman, who sells flowers in a minimall on Thirty-ninth Avenue, is the Purple Lady, whose published writings—including a memoir— about her family's travails in New York give voice to their own immigrant experiences.

"Many people identify with her," said Yong Il Shin, an associate editor at *The Korea Times*. Elizabeth Lauriello, Mrs. Kim's youngest daughter, agreed, saying, "She's the ideal example of how to overcome the hardships of immigration."

Mrs. Kim and her four daughters arrived in Queens on the Fourth of July 1974. She was so certain of the fine living that awaited them that she had formal gowns custom-made for herself and her girls, with matching gloves and purses. Proper attire, she thought, for all those nights to come at the opera.

Life, though, was not so fine. The family lived for a while in a one-bedroom apartment in Sunnyside. The father, a high school teacher who had come to New York a year earlier, ran a small grocery store, while the mother, a floral designer, could not prettify the racism her children experienced. Playground fights were common.

But at least the girls were able to wear their formal dresses on those Sunday visits to feed the ducks in Central Park. "The tourists were taking pictures of us," recalled Sunny Kim, another daughter.

All the while, at night, with her husband and children in bed and her only companion a cup of green tea, Mrs. Kim was writing.

After winning a newspaper's essay contest, she began to file dispatches from Queens about one Korean family's New York journey. She recorded every up and down, from the success of a manufacturing business that allowed the family to buy a house in Whitestone, to the business collapse that forced the family to move to a rented apartment in Flushing.

Her stories, and the memoir that followed, turned her daughters into characters in a long-running soap opera. Daughter Number 1 is Suzanne, a social worker and a divorced mother, who defended her younger siblings in all those childhood fights. Number 3 is Sunny, a gifted fashion designer, and single. Number 4 is Elizabeth, a married business whiz now, but the baby then, always by Mama's side. And the memoir ends with the wedding in Paris of Daughter Number 2, Jasmine, a Mount Holyoke graduate.

The daughters hear from their mother's fans all the time. The cabdriver, for example, who peered at Suzanne for a long time before asking, "Did your mother write a book?" and the woman who related how she laughed and wept on the subway while reading the ice cream story.

Aah, the ice cream story. Suzanne says she can tell it.

One hot August day, shortly after the Kim family's arrival, the electricity went out in a relative's grocery store in Jamaica. Mrs. Kim decided to collect the ice cream before it melted, figuring that she could treat the kids of Sunnyside. Off she went on the 7 train, with little Elizabeth wailing by her side.

She balanced one large pot of ice cream on her head, grabbed another by the handle, and headed home—but boarded the express, not the local. Soon she and Elizabeth were many stops from Sunnyside, unable to ask for directions, while ice cream dripped down her head in streams of chocolate, strawberry, and vanilla.

It took her two hours to get home, where her panicked husband scolded her. But at least some kids in Sunnyside got something sweet.

As Suzanne wipes tears from her eyes, Mrs. Kim begins to speak animatedly in Korean. She tells her daughters to emphasize that life is not a movie, that there are no retakes. Then—in English—the Purple Lady says, "Just one chance."

JUNE 4, 2005

Breathing Life into a Park, Through Pipes

Bryant Park rises slowly from its slumber. Men left rumpled by the night stare into a new day's grassy abyss. Birds warble from shrubs and trucks harrumph from Sixth Avenue. It is 7:00 in the morning, and all that is missing is the bagpiper.

"He usually plays over there, on the gravel," says a guard, pointing toward the West Forty-second Street side of the park. "Over there."

People dressed for the office hustle past the hydrangeas, their iPod headsets blocking out the songs of birds. Walking among them, though much slower, is a bear of a man in dress shirt and tie. In one hand he holds a cup of coffee, and in the other a blue gym bag from which juts a fashion accessory that distinguishes him from the pack.

This is Rich Riemer: father, businessman, bagpiper.

He sits on a green bench, his usual spot, and assembles his instrument. He breathes into the blowpipe, filling the bag with air that previously resided in his large chest. He settles his fingers on the holes of the flutelike piece called the chanter. Standing now, he fills the park with the strains of a stirring Scottish march, "Scots Wha Hae."

People look up. Birds fly away. Good morning, New York.

Mr. Riemer, forty-four, lives in Clifton, New Jersey, and works as a pension and insurance consultant on the East Side. For years now he has commuted to the Port Authority and walked to his office through a morning-quiet Bryant Park. He has pondered over many things during these walks, everything from what college might suit his daughter, Joanna, to what he and his girlfriend, Stacey, might have for dinner that night—to the hope that someday he might play an instrument. Not just any instrument, by the way.

Why the bagpipe? Simple, he says. The "stunning" bagpipe riff he heard as a boy growing up on Long Island, in a 1977 song by Paul McCartney called "Mull of Kintyre." "I'd sing it for you," he says. "But I should probably spare you that."

The song haunted him through high school, four years in the Navy and twenty years of work and child-rearing, until finally, last year, he called up John Bradley, a bagpipe instructor on the Lower East Side, and said: Teach me.

He plays a bit of "Mull of Kintyre," and then a bit of "Amazing Grace," but even a bit of music from a bagpipe is a lot. It can fill a room; it can fill a park. The two lawn mowers now roaring across the park's field are reduced to whispers whenever Mr. Riemer performs a finger jig over his chanter.

"Look at this place, it's beautiful," he says of the park. "You can't do this in Clifton at six-thirty in the morning."

Some might argue that by transporting a bagpipe across state lines, Mr. Riemer should be charged with concealing a weapon, or maybe conspiracy to commit aural assault. But many in the park could then be charged with aiding and abetting, judging by the reception he receives during his performances.

A woman being led by a huge white dog smiles and gives a sweet good morning. A white-haired man, carrying a black briefcase and doing loops on the gravel path, smiles or nods each time he passes. A deliveryman sits down, a wrapped floral arrangement at his feet, and listens. A former marine stops to say thanks for playing the Marine Corps hymn.

"A lot of thank yous," the bagpiper says.

In New York, it seems, the musical aspirations of people like Mr. Riemer are shared; their desire to apply soothing melody to urban cacophony, understood. He puts himself out there and plays an ancient Scottish march, and so we step to it, a bit livelier than before.

He fills the bag again with his air, brings the blowpipe to his lips, and attempts Beethoven's "Ode to Joy." But he stops after only a few notes.

"Can't do it," he says, winded, his face a little flushed.

He says that his instructor, Mr. Bradley, can play for two hours straight without breaking a sweat. It takes a lot of work, he says, a lot of practice. In fact, he has practice this afternoon.

It is still early in Bryant Park, with morning fog clinging to the Empire State Building like torn gray fabric on a fencepost. Some of the rumpled men with troubled stares have moved on, replaced by people practicing tai chi. More of us have joined the march to offices.

Mr. Riemer stands to take another attempt at Beethoven joy. He gets through it nicely.

Good morning, New York.

JANUARY 4, 2006

Pictures of Exhibitions

The artistic influences of Marie A. Roberts are many. There is Giotto, with his genius for bringing religious subjects to life. Raphael, with his thorough command of composition. Masoccio. Toulouse-Lautrec. Van Gogh. Lionel the Lion-Faced Man.

And don't forget Baron Paucci, the World's Smallest Perfect Man. Or the fake Siamese twins known as the Milton Sisters. Or Ms. Roberts's Uncle Lester, master of Coney Island Boardwalk patter and alchemist extraordinaire, who concocted a powder of amazing restorative power, christened it Bitter Wonder, and peddled it to suckers. Step right up.

With Baron Paucci straddled on Giotto's shoulders, and Toulouse-Lautrec on Lionel's, they hover behind Ms. Roberts, arguing, encouraging, as she paints her distinctive sideshow banners. And when she is done, what appears on canvas is a kind of study in Coney Island religious, in which sword swallowers and tattooed ladies are elevated to the near spiritual.

Dozens of her paintings are on display at the Snug Harbor Cultural

Center on Staten Island until February 26. More often, though, they adorn the Coney Island Circus Sideshow building on Surf Avenue, promoting the fire-eaters and contortionists performing within. It took her a while to accept that her art would be exposed to the elements, but she has come to embrace the "controlled freedom" of sideshow banner work.

It just feels right, says Ms. Roberts, fifty-one, who wears round-rimmed black glasses that evoke another time, and speaks in sudden bursts that would have made Uncle Lester proud.

She grew up in a Brooklyn house that fairly glowed in the reflected light of a long-gone amusement park called Dreamland. Her firefighting grandfather battled the Coney Island blaze that dimmed the Dreamland dazzle in 1911, and her Uncle Lester became the outside talker for the Dreamland Circus Sideshow that rose from its ashes. His younger brother—her father, Kenneth—often helped out.

Ms. Roberts cherishes family photographs from that time. Here is Uncle Lester outside the sideshow ("Strange Curios From All Parts of the World"). Here he is with Baron Paucci during a Havana tour. And here's a group shot taken at Stauch's Restaurant in August 1923, with many of the performers wearing silly hats.

"That's Lionel," Ms. Roberts says, pointing. "That must be Jolly Irene. My father talked about Jolly Irene all the time. And here's Lester, next to Baron Paucci."

In her childhood home, the coded language of "carny" was spoken, the sideshow's monkey and snake were buried in the backyard, and Uncle Lester's trunk of old Bitter Wonder boxes sat in the cellar. But all she wanted was to be a regular kid.

After earning art degrees at Brooklyn College and Queens College, she set out to be an artist, which meant working at Macy's and answering phones for a professional healer before landing a full-time teaching job at Fairleigh Dickinson University. She moved to Greenpoint and began painting what she calls "narrative invented figure compositions."

About fifteen years ago, she returned to the south Brooklyn house she grew up in. After reading about Coney Island U.S.A., an arts organization that runs the Coney Island Circus Sideshow, she sought out its president, Dick D. Zigun. She showed him her photograph of Uncle Lester and the gang in their funny hats at Stauch's. He said that it was nice to think of Lionel the Lion-Faced Man having a good time. And she had an epiphany.

"It made sense," she says. "It's like nobody understood this other part of my life. None of my Manhattan friends got Coney Island. It was kind of like a perfect fit."

In 1997 she enlisted some of her students to help her create a series of banners for the sideshow's summer season. The first one she completed herself was "Madame Twisto," and in painting it, she says, she felt as though she were painting memorials "to my grandfather, my uncle, my family."

Since then Ms. Roberts has painted hundreds of vibrant banners, most of them six feet by five feet, a few of them bearing the phrase, "Congress of Curious Peoples." Her sideshow style has become so popular in certain circles that people commission her to paint family portraits. She recently completed a painting called *The Amazing Devinda,* whose amazing subject is a three-year-old girl.

In winter, she paints in a studio. But for several months of the year, she works in her backyard, where sideshow animals are buried beneath the grass at her feet. She summons Giotto and Lionel, reaches for her brush, and returns to dreamland.

SEPTEMBER 22, 2004

The Mind's Eye as a Window to the City

With another day at the office behind him, Kevin Coughlin wades into the streets of a city that sings an incessant, contradictory song. Hear this; no, this; no, this. Step forward; step back; for God's sake, watch your step.

He pauses a moment to let his guide dog, a yellow Lab named Ruger, renew its acquaintance with a nearby fireplug. Then man and dog begin their familiar journey home, heading north on Seventh Avenue.

"Forward," Mr. Coughlin says. "Good boy."

They walk past the colors that paint one day in late September 2004, colors that Mr. Coughlin no longer sees: the golden brown of an oversized pretzel; the yellow of a passing taxi; the reds, whites, and blues exploding on a Madison Square Garden marquee.

But Mr. Coughlin draws upon a storehouse of thousands of visual memories to see his city. He remembers the straight-edged look of the entrance to the Hotel Pennsylvania to his right, and to his left, the look of streams of commuters pouring down that Penn Station maw of a stairwell.

Using these remembrances, his other senses, and Ruger, Mr. Coughlin does what others find daunting even with the gift of sight: He navigates New York.

One February day seven years ago, Mr. Coughlin could not read the print of his morning newspaper. Within four days, he lost 85 percent of his vision; within four months, he was blind. A rare genetic condition, the doctors told him.

How could this be? One moment he was a healthy man of thirty-six who enjoyed hiking around Manhattan, looking up, down, and sideways; "I was someone who noticed everything," he says.

The next moment he was a healthy man of thirty-six who could neither see nor believe that he could not see.

"I can't even—it's difficult to put into words," Mr. Coughlin says. "I didn't cry until two years after my blindness."

He knew that he had to adjust. He found a home for a beloved dog that he could no longer manage and acquired a guide dog that he now adores. He devised methods to distinguish one shirt from another, and one-dollar bills from the fives, tens, and twenties. He eventually returned to the workforce, writing grant proposals for the American Foundation for the Blind.

"I had to move forward," he says. "My life had to go on."

Listening closely to the sounds of passing cars, sensing the movement of others—and trusting Ruger—Mr. Coughlin crosses Seventh Avenue and gets in line for the crosstown bus on West Thirty-fourth Street. He wears black shoes, black pants, and a black shirt, an outfit more practical than urban hip. The black clothes highlight the green of his eyes, which he refuses to shield behind dark glasses, as an aunt had once suggested.

"Maybe people would be nicer to you," she had said.

An eastbound bus arrives. Mr. Coughlin takes the first seat behind the driver, with Ruger tucked between his feet, and together they rock to the bus's lurch and sway. On previous rides, he has heard passengers talking about him as though he were not there, saying that he was too young to be blind, or too well dressed. No one speaks today, though, as he counts the five stops to Lexington Avenue.

He remembers what the Thirty-fourth Street of 1997 looked like, but allows for seven years of change. He imagines that Herald Square looks about the same, for example. And he keeps track of the Empire State Building, often asking friends on evening walks to describe the color of the lights that are setting the majestic building aglow.

Mr. Coughlin and Ruger get off the bus at Thirty-fourth and Lexington, in front of a flower market whose roses and tulips brighten the sidewalk, and walk north. He pauses for a few minutes to allow Ruger to sniff and pace about the sidewalk. Guide dogs need their dog time, too.

They enter a corner grocery, where green watermelons line the floor and red apples and purple plums glisten from boxes. One of the employees collects Mr. Coughlin's order of a pound of coffee and a blueberry yogurt. He fishes a five and a ten from his wallet to pay the bill.

They hesitate a bit at Thirty-sixth Street, where cars bound for the Queens-Midtown Tunnel jut into the crosswalk. It's much worse in the summer, he says.

Man and dog continue on in this loud city, toward the apartment he has lived in for a decade, with sight and without. He knows this neighborhood so well that he can see the spire of the Chrysler Building shimmering in the evening sun.

"Forward," he says.

Art Underfoot, and the Angel Who Guards It

The round-faced sleuth with the orange visor knelt to take a closer look at a circular patch of concrete. Where others might see only Manhattan sidewalk, she saw evidence of a form of art theft: the disappearance of yet another of New York City's glorious manhole covers.

She knew what was missing because she had once photographed it, a cast-iron cover adorned with a five-pointed star and a raucous sea of raised dots. It was the handiwork of the old Liberty Iron Works foundry on Tenth Avenue. It had been blithely trod upon for generations, and now it was gone.

"This is one of my real tragedies," muttered the woman, Diana Stuart.

No one could challenge her use of the possessive. Ms. Stuart has devoted the last decade to the adoration of manhole covers. She has whisked them clean like an umpire tending to home plate, photographed them by the thousands, cataloged their whereabouts, researched the long-gone foundries that struck them, led walking tours in their name, and lobbied without success to have them granted landmark status.

So associated is Ms. Stuart with their preservation that she holds unchallenged claim to a nickname that may not be as intriguing as the Woman in Red, but is not quite as unsettling as the Pigeon Lady. She is the Manhole Cover Lady.

Ms. Stuart, who is single, initially chafed at the nickname, sensing that its wink of eccentricity would do little for her social life. But she gradually decided to embrace the moniker as a mark of distinction in this city of millions.

Manhole Cover Lady? Why, that would be Diana Stuart, of course.

The Manhole Cover Lady maintains an air of mystery. She lives alone in a studio apartment, where her files and photographs— "highly organized," she says—leave no room for pets. She declines to reveal her age, which is about fifty, because she sees herself as "ageless." She also does not want her borough of origin made public. "Just say I'm a native New Yorker," she says.

But she makes no secret of her crusade to save the ancient manhole covers, coal-chute covers, and vault covers that dapple the city surface by the hundreds of thousands, some of them still-active portals to the netherworld. She estimates that a good 10 percent of the four hundred covers featured in her book—*Designs Underfoot: The Art of Manhole Covers in New York City*—have already been paved over or tossed away since its publication in April.

To prove that manhole covers equal art, Ms. Stuart conducted a private, head-down tour of Murray Hill, infusing her patter with the urgent tone of someone who seems at constant risk of missing her train. She strode with the confidence born of having walked thousands of streets, dodging cars and eluding undesirables, armed only with a camera, a notebook, and a whisk broom.

As she guided on this rainy morning, she pointed to covers whose raised features may have once had a practical purpose—providing traction for the hooves of horses—but are now the cast-iron expressions of whimsy from the nineteenth and early twentieth centuries. Ship's wheels and snowflakes, hexagons and honeycombs, chain links and flowers, all meant for more than just horses.

In front of 114 East Thirty-seventh Street, for example, she spotted a coal-chute cover of an anonymous foundry that sported a raised star, bubblelike, dots and a ring of diamond shapes. And on the southeast corner of Madison Avenue and Thirty-seventh Street, embedded like a jewel in the slate pavement, there glittered—well, not quite—a Jacob Mark Sons cover dating from 1878. Rows of mauve- and gold-colored glass insets, surrounded by an elaborate petal design, lent it a certain grimy class.

"Is it at risk? Yes, definitely," Ms. Stuart said, her face damp, her voice raised. "Someone could just come and pierce their equipment right through this."

Her pleas to the city's Landmarks Preservation Commission have yielded no support. Robert B. Tierney, its chairman, said that while he admired Ms. Stuart's commitment, manhole covers are impermanent fixtures by design. Giving them landmark status raises the specter of commission involvement every time Con Ed has to change a manhole cover.

"It may not be something that is a landmark priority," he said. "But that does not mean that it's not important. It's incredibly interesting."

Ms. Stuart, who feels as though she is racing against time, remains committed to her cause. She promotes her slim volume, which has brought her some fame but no money. She conducts her tours. She leads the Society for the Preservation of New York City Manhole Covers. She is, after all, the Manhole Cover Lady.

"OK," she said, again pointing to the sidewalk. "This is a very important cover."

AUGUST 6, 2003

The Best Lips Ever Asked to Zip

As Steve Herbst walks the crowded streets of this city, he possesses the strange knowledge that he can whistle better than anyone he passes. If you challenged him to a whistle-off, he would look you square in the eye and blow you away with a three-octave range. Mozart, Brubeck, Sondheim; you name it, he does it. The man can whistle.

But his is a loner's art. He practices until his dog, Sparky, is tired of walking; until his wife, Melinda, wonders what silence sounds like; until his colleagues at work ask him to close his door. And it is not as though he can jam with other whistlers in his East Side neighborhood.

"I'm not the only whistler in New York City," he said. "But name another whistler in New York City."

Whistling was once an enviable talent. Some of us used to swing to the sounds of the Big Band whistler Elmo Tanner, or nuzzle and coo to Fred Lowery whistling "Gypsy Love Song" on the stereo. The act of whistling may not have been considered ladylike, but if you were a man, and you could whistle—well, brother, pucker up.

But something happened. Society's appreciation for the art form turned to annoyance and, eventually, to, "Will you knock it off already?"

Whistlers came to be seen as odd. Fifty years ago, a man could stroll down Second Avenue whistling "The Surrey with the Fringe on Top," and no one would blink. If he did that today, some outreach worker would hand him a sandwich and ask if he needed to talk to someone.

Mr. Herbst, a whistler for fifty of his fifty-seven years, has given a lot of thought to the reasons for whistling's decline. He has decided that boom boxes and portable disc players and cellphones have encroached upon those moments we once reserved for ourselves. "People don't entertain themselves anymore," he said, as he demonstrated another talent: cracking knuckles.

"You have a whole generation, the baby-boomer generation, that basically doesn't know whistling," he said. "And the children that this generation has produced, they don't have anybody setting an example for them like my father did for me."

Mr. Herbst's father, Allan, whistled on the way to his job as a Wall Street trader, whistled down in his woodworking shop, whistled while driving his Studebaker. Young Steven took up the habit, and by the time he was ten, he could do something no other kid on his block could do: whistle his way through every section of Prokofiev's *Peter and the Wolf*.

He whistled and sang with the University of Pennsylvania Glee Club, but chose not to pursue a career in professional whistling in favor of one in recruitment advertising. Setting aside the whistler's life was not a difficult choice, he admitted. "There just didn't seem to be enough of a call for it."

Mr. Herbst continued to whistle at weddings and parties, though, and felt his competitive juices stir whenever he saw an international grand master of whistling performing on *The Tonight Show*. In 1994 he packed his bags, puckered his lips, and flew to Louisburg, North Carolina, for the annual International Whistlers Competition.

"I thought I'd go down and clean up," he said. "I came in fifth."

Mr. Herbst returned again and again to Louisburg, confident that his mastery of classical and popular, jazz and blues, would someday earn him the recognition he deserved. Why so persistent? "If you have the chance to be the world champion at something, that's worth taking a look at," he said. "Whistling is something I'm better at than almost anybody in the world—anybody you're going to meet."

Last year he finally won the International Grand Champion award, and this year he was named International Whistling Entertainer of the Year. He is proud of these accomplishments: trophies adorn a corner of his apartment, and his status as a grand champion is reflected in business cards stored in a gold holder.

But it is not all about ego. Mr. Herbst sees himself as an ambassador of whistling, and has adopted the motto "Whistling is an idea whose time has returned." He appears in local clubs, auditions for commercials (they usually opt for a clarinet), and released a CD of his whistled interpretations of Broadway tunes.

He also promotes the art form simply by whistling in public, out in the street. Sometimes people give him the fish eye and sometimes they thank him, saying they just don't hear much whistling anymore.

There are signs that whistling is on a rebound, though. The other day, Mr. Herbst walked along Second Avenue, loudly whistling a perfectly pitched "Bring Him Home" from *Les Misérables*. Not one person told him to knock it off.

NOVEMBER 1, 2003

Sweet Sounds Ease the Pain, Then and Now

The conversation has already sounded every note in the scale of her proud life, from the highs of those younger days in the theater to the lows of a son dying. Now it returns to more notes at the bottom of the scale: a second son seriously ill, again; rent in serious arrears, again. Again.

Sometimes, she says. Sometimes at night, she just gets weepy. That's the word she uses: weepy.

Well then, she is asked, would she play a little piano? Would she play "Come Sunday" by the Duke?

Of course, dear, of course.

Marjorie Eliot goes again to the piano, drawn to it as though it were a shiny black cistern of water. The fingers of mature hands reach out with familiar ease, ready to summon the holy music of Duke Ellington. "Come Sunday." Yes, come Sunday.

Lord, dear Lord above,
God Almighty, God of love,
Please look down
and see my people through.

Marjorie Eliot, slight and with black hair tinted an autumn orange, is a New York City institution, so declared by those who know her and by the nonprofit organization called City Lore: The New York Center for Urban Folk Culture. Three years ago it honored her as a living city treasure, and here is why:

Every Sunday she converts her apartment, on Manhattan's Sugar Hill, into an intimate concert hall. With dozens of guests sitting, transfixed, in those metal folding chairs normally found in church basements, guest musicians beat their drums, blow their horns, and play that jazz.

By no means are these loosey-goosey jam sessions. The musicians are expected to dress appropriately for the paid gigs. The performances begin precisely at four P.M., usually with Ms. Eliot singing a spiritual, as that seems fitting on a Sunday. Juice and salad are served between sets.

Nor does the transformation of her living room into a stage mean that she has no secrets. Ask her age, and she will say, "I'll just leave that out of the equation." Ask about her relationship with her estranged husband, the jazz percussionist Al Drears, and she will say, "Let's leave that alone."

But she gladly talks about these sessions. The idea came to her a decade ago, after one of her five sons, Philip, died at thirty-two. She lost him on a Sunday, and the only way to get through every succeeding Sunday, she realized, was through music. Music on a Sunday. Then, thankfully, Monday. The neighbors didn't seem to mind. And when the police came one time to answer a noise complaint, she said, "They hung and listened a bit."

The years passed, a blur of Sundays, with those in-between days providing the time for Ms. Eliot to exercise other talents, as an actress, playwright, and teacher. She established a children's theater, worked with students at Public School 128, and covered the rent with the money she earned by performing at nursing homes, hospitals, and colleges—though there were times when friends chipped in.

Her eldest son, Michael, forty-five, became gravely ill this year, and Ms. Eliot has spent her days accompanying him to doctors' appointments and sitting by his hospital bedside. Which meant declining those gigs at the nursing homes and colleges. Which meant that she fell so far behind in her rent that her landlord—good people, she emphasizes—sent an eviction notice.

Ms. Eliot said she saw one of the owners the other day, on her way out again to visit Michael. "I know I owe you," she told him, "but I'm crazy here."

Mary Aslan, the rental agent for the landlord, Golson Realty Corporation, said the notice of eviction was sent reluctantly. "This has been going on now for quite some years," she said. "I've stalled and stalled because she's an exceptional person, but there's nothing more that I can do."

Word of Ms. Eliot's travails reached Steve Zeitlin, the executive director of City Lore, and soon plans were set in motion to salvage this living city treasure. Tomorrow, on a Sunday, there will be an old-fashioned rent party in her apartment, featuring spirituals, saxophones, juice, and salad. It costs twenty dollars, with sets at two, four, and six P.M. in Apartment 3F, in the landmark building at 555 Edgecombe Avenue. Take the C train. Not the A train; the C.

Someone is bringing some chicken, and someone else promises a cheese tray. The chairs are already unfolded and set in rows, and there are extra paper towels for the bathroom. Still, Ms. Eliot is nervous, and finds calm only at times like this, at the piano, her fingertips lingering on the keys.

Come, Sunday, oh come Sunday,
That's the day.

APRIL 14, 2004

A Corner Gets Crowded with Dreams

Good morning, my friend, medium milk no sugar? Good morning, sir, large black one sugar bagel with butter? No problem. Hello, darling, small milk one sugar glazed? Am I right? Have a good day, my friend.

Sam Zaman deals in the language and commerce of coffee. He spends several hours a day hunched inside a narrow silvery cart, pouring coffee for a morning-long parade of people. They jut their faces into his tiny window, as if posing for passport photos, and speak in a specific New York idiom that conveys urgency without employing a single verb. Small black Sweet'N Low.

Every weekday at two A.M., the Afghan-born vendor leaves his wife and three children in Queens to conduct business in coffee dialect from an Eighth Avenue vantage point, just north of West Forty-second Street. At thirty-seven, he is a man in a box, about four feet by ten feet. In winter he freezes, in summer he sweats, and in all seasons he asks how many sugars.

He wears his city license around his neck, keeps his city certificate of approval on display, and tucks copies of city inspections somewhere up with the hot chocolate packets. "No violations observed," reads an inspector's recent scribbling about the cart of Mr. Zaman, who translates it to mean: "I am legal."

He says these words with an emphasis that rises from sixteen years of trying to make it in this city: selling ice cream on the streets, then books, then fruit, and now coffee and doughnuts. His only break from this outdoor routine was a brief cabdriving tour that earned him little more than a bad back.

Mr. Zaman is indeed legal, but no license from the city could ever protect him from the realities of its streets, where nothing is static and every inch is the foundation of someone else's American dream.

In recent months, for example, he has peeked through the sesames and plains that line his window to watch a storefront's transformation a few yards away. First there were just windows, then windows and chairs, and now windows, chairs, counters, and signs that promise pastries and "fine coffee."

A couple of weeks ago, Mr. Zaman says, someone complained to the police that his cart was illegal in some way. The complaint prompted a cop check that found nothing out of order, he says, and a conversation with someone from the new restaurant that went nowhere. "I told him, 'I don't bother you, you don't bother me,'" he recalls.

Mr. Zaman's new competition is not some faceless corporation, but John Giampilis. He, too, is a hardworking immigrant, a baker from Greece. He, too, lives in Queens. And while he has no children—not yet, he says—he does have a fiancée.

Mr. Giampilis, thirty-three, says that he is a part-owner of this twenty-four-hour restaurant, called Europan, and that he holds interest in a couple of other food places, including a Hot & Crusty and a Bread Factory. He hopes that his baked goods will attract some morning business, but expects that his Europan will be busiest at night.

As for the coffee guy out there, Mr. Giampilis says that the vendor is not allowed on the subway grates. "As soon as I open, they will take action," he says, referring to the city.

According to the Department of Health, there is no prohibition against parking "mobile food units" on subway grates. Mr. Zaman, meticulous keeper of city records, knew this, of course. But still he worries.

What he hopes for is that when Europan opens this week, two immigrants can coexist in peace. That consumers will weigh quality and cost and choose accordingly, between cart coffee milk no sugar for sixty-five cents, or restaurant coffee milk no sugar for ninety-two cents. That this corner of New York is big enough for two cups of coffee.

"I'm too far away from this guy," Mr. Zaman says, pointing past a garbage can to Europan's front door. "It's not like I'm next to him."

But with each passing day, this stretch of Eighth Avenue seems to get smaller and smaller, leaving less room for Mr. Zaman's silvery cart.

He nods with sad face toward another storefront a few feet away, where a sign promises an Auntie Anne's pretzel shop "coming soon." Although he doesn't sell pretzels, he does know of a city requirement that mobile food units be at least twenty feet from any entranceway to a building.

Mr. Zaman is thinking of getting a smaller cart. Maybe that way, he says, no one will bother him.

DECEMBER 3, 2005

The Mayor Who Ran, Ran, and Ran

The mayor of Central Park lives in an SRO on the Upper West Side. His one room has an unkempt bed, two small dressers that belong on the curb, lumps of clothes on the worn carpet, and a rusted hotplate that he means to throw out. The telephone permits him to dial only 911.

Decorations are spare. They include a dusty State Senate resolution from 1985 that honors him for his contributions to the park, and an autographed poster of Grete Waitz, the nine-time New York City Marathon champion, that brightens the peeled-paint wall. "Keep up the good work," she wrote.

The mayor, Alberto Arroyo, says he has lived here for nearly a quarter century because it reflects the simplicity he has sought for most of his nearly ninety years. He has taken a vow of poverty, he says, like St. Francis of Assisi.

"You've heard of St. Francis of Assisi?" he asks.

He wears clothes that should be cleaned or tossed. He eats one meal a day, usually the lunch served at a local senior center, as long as it is not the oxtail or the knockwurst. He survives on Social Security and a modest pension from his old employer, the Bethlehem Steel Corporation, but will not touch his savings because it is to be given away once he dies. And he lives here.

"Everyone wants the maximum," he says. "I want the minimum."

The mayor's true home, his Gracie Mansion, is Central Park, where he needs to be right now. Wearing a "mayor" cap over his sparse white hair and a coaster-size medallion around his neck, he pushes his four-wheeled walker toward the door. Slowly.

Mr. Arroyo was once a trailblazing runner. Back in the mid-1930s, when he was a young boxer from Puerto Rico with a radical sense of physical fitness, he began running on the 1.6-mile path that encircles the Central Park Reservoir. Now, thousands jog there every day.

"I am the first man to run in Central Park," he says, a claim that no one bothers to challenge.

But there is no question that in a city reluctant to wave hello, he became an identifiable, approachable character: the guy at the reservoir, the one with the white mustache, running, standing on his head, posing for tourists, forever sharing the many stories of Alberto Arroyo. How he stowed away on a ship; ran bare-chested in winter; defied a rapacious landlord to win rights for tenants; raised money to make this crushed-stone track what it is today; on and on.

Along the way he also became almost a spiritual presence, one with the park—"a constant," says George Hirsch, board chairman of the New York Road Runners club.

Mr. Arroyo stopped running a decade ago, reluctantly. Now he takes a good twenty minutes to walk the three blocks to the park, and another ten to reach the reservoir's path.

He shuffles counterclockwise on the trail, the better to fulfill his ambassadorial duties.

As he moves north, nodding and saying hello to runners—"Hi, Mayor," they call—he recites stories that he has told too many times before.

Still, when he tells them, it is as though one of the old London plane trees at the reservoir were given voice.

Mr. Arroyo says he was there, for example, when a man removed his clothes, neatly folded them on the shore, and swam into the reservoir to drown. He was there when the police hung yellow tape around the spot where Robert Chambers left the body of young Jennifer Levin. He was there when Jacqueline Kennedy Onassis began looping the reservoir many years ago, and there when she visited the park a few days before she died, in 1994.

By then they had become acquaintances. Mr. Arroyo remembers many things she said to him, especially this: "Call me Jackie."

He continues along the path, talking about Jackie, and St. Francis, and Alberto Arroyo. "My time is up," he says. "People tell me, 'You're going to live another ten, twenty years.' Baloney. But nobody should be afraid to die because you keep living. You just go from one apartment to another."

Mr. Arroyo sits on a bench dedicated to him near the South Gate House. It is the desk to his open-air office. People jogging by call out to him, while a boy one bench over slips carefully out of school clothes and into running shorts.

Sunlight is giving way to shadow. The boy runs off, but the mayor says he will stay until dark.

OCTOBER 29, 2005

Up in 4-B, the Crime of a Lifetime

Wah-Hop Eng is eighty-seven years old. A half century ago, he came to New York by way of China and Hong Kong, and moved into an old red building at Third Avenue and East Eighty-ninth Street. From that narrow, two-bedroom apartment, his American life unfolded.

He worked in a laundry, a Chinese restaurant, and a grocery store. He and his wife, Yuk Ying, raised two children, Peter and Ava. Their children went to college and moved away. His wife died in 2003. And Mr. Eng was alone, save for an older brother in the same building. Yes, an older brother.

In June, Mr. Eng went on an extended trip. He visited his daughter in Toronto, and then his son in Massachusetts. Meanwhile, back in New York, a neighbor saw two men carrying furniture down the stairs early one morning.

"They weren't being particularly careful with these items," the neighbor recalled yesterday. "Slamming them against the wall."

One Saturday in mid-August, Mr. Eng boarded the bus for home. When he arrived at his fourth-floor apartment, he could not get in.

Gone was the heavy-duty lock that his son had installed, and in its place, a lock in which his key would not fit. Then, he later told the police, one of the new landlords, Dominick Galofaro—a man who wasn't born when Mr. Eng first moved in—bum-rushed him out the door, saying: This is not your house. Go back to Boston.

A shaken Mr. Eng spent the night with his brother. The next day his son came down from Massachusetts and dialed 911. With his passport and with his mailbox key, the little bald man easily proved to the responding police officers that he was Wah-Hop Eng, the tenant in 4-B.

A few minutes later Mr. Galofaro opened the door to reveal—nothing.

Gone were the beds and cabinets, the televisions and fans, the lamps and phonograph. The rare records he had carried with him when he left China. The silver coins he collected while working in the laundry. His stamp collection; his eighty-year-old ginseng wine; his medicinal herbs.

Gone, too, were traces of his wife. The videotapes and old family photographs. The pearl earrings, diamond rings, jade bracelets. The fur coat and silk skirts and dressing gowns and things that may still have carried her scent.

The landlord was charged with felony counts of grand larceny and burglary. He did not speak to the authorities, but his lawyer, Sam Schmidt, gave them the following explanation:

Dominick Galofaro shares ownership with his brother, Salvatore, who runs a food store in the same building and is more familiar with its operations. While Salvatore was in Italy, Dominick and the super traced the source of a leak to the rent-controlled apartment of Mr. Eng, who the super said was living in Massachusetts. They broke the lock, opened the door, and found an apartment filled with an old man's stuff.

"The apartment seems unattended to," Mr. Schmidt explained. "So he has people move the furniture into the basement."

Dominick Galofaro did not check the building records, which would have shown that Mr. Eng was current in his $158-a-month rent, and that he had left his son's telephone number in case of an emergency. "He understands this was the wrong way to go about it," Mr. Schmidt said. "This was a mistake."

"Mistake" falls short somehow. Remember those belongings moved to the basement? Gone, gone, gone. And the Galofaros have offered no explanation.

"He certainly has an inkling," said Mr. Schmidt, referring to Dominick Galofaro. "But he's not going to make any allegations."

Of course. Why would he?

Prosecutors dropped the burglary and larceny charges for lack of any evidence, and Dominick Galofaro pleaded guilty this week to illegal eviction, a misdemeanor. He will be sentenced soon to probation and community service.

Mr. Eng has filed a $13 million lawsuit against the Galofaros and is living with his son, who says his father is too frightened to return to the apartment.

Mr. Schmidt said that the man had rarely lived there anyway, and that his fear was "ridiculous," since his brother lived in the building. He added that the landlords had offered to pay restitution, and that Mr. Eng's list of missing items was not particularly substantial—monetarily speaking.

Funny, isn't it, how the life possessions of a man could vanish in Manhattan, just like that. Records and coins, photos and videos, furs and jewelry. Those things of his, those things of hers.

OCTOBER 27, 2004

True Laughter That Flickers but Never Dies

George Mazzey, the grand sheik of Staten Island, summons the faithful to his tent three or four times a year. His wife always attends, and his sister, and his brother-in-law. After that, well, put it this way: No need to open a second bag of chips—although an eleven-year-old grandson may be worthy of membership one day.

Once assembled, these members of the March of the Wooden Soldiers tent of the Sons of the Desert, the official Laurel and Hardy appreciation society, watch a movie. Could be *Saps at Sea* or *Pardon Us* or *Way Out West,* the grand sheik's favorite. After that, the floor opens to discussion that usually focuses on the national convention just past, or fast approaching.

It certainly is not like the old days. Back then, back in the 1970s, a pretty good crowd would be waiting for Mr. Mazzey to fill a blank screen in their lives with something distracting, something—funny. A reel selected from his vast collection, a 16-millimeter projector clicked on, and soon a flickering light would summon from the black-and-white past another fine mess involving two derby-topped misfits.

"Everybody used to have a great time," says the grand sheik, sitting in the living room that his wife, Karen, long ago declared a Laurel-and-Hardy-free zone.

His words, free of regret or betrayal, convey that he understands how tastes can change over the years. Not his, though. Stan and Ollie's idiotic efforts to deliver a piano up a flight of stairs tickle him still, for the hundredth time, the thousandth.

But why? Why has a man of sixty-two devoted most of his free time to celebrating two clowns? Does he find grace in how they are forever trying, failing, and trying again? Is he comforted by the enduring, though sometimes violent, friendship between two block-heads?

Maybe it is his lantern jaw, so Laurel-like that he often dresses up like the comedian at Sons of the Desert conventions. Or maybe it is the many jobs he has had, working-class jobs worthy of Laurel and Hardy: beach-club waiter, apprentice embalmer, longshoreman, volunteer firefighter, bank guard, and, now, locker room supervisor at the Richmond County Country Club. About all he has not done is call out "F-r-e-s-h f-i-s-h" from a beat-up jalopy (*Towed in a Hole,* 1932).

Mr. Mazzey declines an offer to get Laurel-and-Hardy deep. Stan and Ollie, he says, have just always been there, no matter that the fat one died in 1957, and the thin one in 1965.

Long ago, after seeing *The Music Box,* the 1932 short in which the two clowns engage in that Sisyphean struggle with a piano, a very young George asked his mother about this Stan and Ollie. She answered as though she were talking of beloved relatives. "'Me and your father used to go into the theater and see them,'" he recalls her saying. "'They're very funny.'"

"After that, I just got into them," he says.

When he was eighteen he bought a projector and an abridged version of *A Chump at Oxford,* the first in what would become a collection of 192 Laurel and Hardy movie features and shorts. Around that time he longed to speak to his hero, Laurel, so he enlisted a telephone company employee—his sister, Adrienne—to find Laurel's number in California.

Soon young George was fumbling with change and stalling the operator until he was patched through. The call lasted maybe thirty seconds, but Mr. Mazzey remembers the thrill of hearing that voice. "You know it's him," he says.

He leads a tour of his memorabilia-crammed Laurel and Hardy room—"Ah, the room," Mrs. Mazzey says—then opens a binder stuffed with keepsakes: the one letter that Laurel wrote to him; the congratulatory telegram that Laurel's widow sent when the Mazzeys married; the photographs from decades of Sons of the Desert conventions. He says he has been the head of the March of the Wooden Soldiers tent now for, for . . .

"Honey," he calls to the kitchen. "How long have I been grand sheik?"

"Eight to ten years," comes the answer.

Mr. Mazzey is now selling off his reel collection. None of his three grown children have the interest, and his wife wants some of the clutter cleaned up. Besides, he has most of the films on DVD now.

Which means that when not minding other people's lockers, or tending to domestic chores, the grand sheik of Staten Island can again watch two old friends sing, dance, and clown in *Way Out West,* 1937. His favorite scene: the end.

"Finally, their troubles are over," he says. "And they start singing again."

JANUARY 31, 2004

A Riddle Once Wrapped in a Tortilla

The modest call for help appeared in the gray roster of classified advertisements in *The New York Post*, tucked between an ad for a 1992 Nissan Maxima—"runs great, sunroof"—and a foreclosure notice. Perhaps because it was set all in capital letters, the plea smacked ever so faintly of desperation:

> REWARD! LOST GOLD X-SHAPED EARRING.
> TUESDAY, JANUARY 20TH, PM. IN A TAXI
> BETWEEN 1049 PARK & 65TH ST. AND PARK.

Rising above that hint of panic, though, was the suggestion of an unshakable hope against impossible odds: that on an island of 22.6 square miles and 1.5 million people, an object no larger than a half dollar would not only be found but returned to its rightful owner, all through a newspaper advertisement that was even smaller than the object in question.

"All the old clichés apply," said Mary McLain Carter, who placed the ad. "Hope springs eternal. There's always luck involved. Things like this."

The other day Ms. Carter paused from packing for another Mexican vacation to discuss the missing earring, and why it matters so. Viola, her powder puff of a Pomeranian, dashed about the peach-and-gold decor of her Upper East Side apartment, which is more a kind of Manhattan base than it is a year-round residence.

She summers in Newport, Rhode Island, and considers home to be her place in Dallas, where people are more apt to recognize the significance of her middle name, Milam—as in Benjamin Milam, hero of the Texas Revolution. "He's my ancestor, yes," said Ms. Carter, with the slightest and most refined of drawls. "On my mother's side."

Anyway, the earring. During a vacation in Acapulco about fifteen years ago, her husband, Rudulph Ellis Carter—Foxy, for short— presented her with a pair of 18-carat gold earrings designed by Paloma Picasso. They were a birthday gift, and they came wrapped in a breakfast tortilla.

Which birthday? "Let's say, fifteen years ago, when I was twenty-five," said Ms. Carter, who is quite eligible for AARP membership.

A friend in another room began to laugh. Ms. Carter called out, "Oh, hush!" And the Pomeranian darted here and there.

The clip-on earrings were not identical; one was a fairly standard X, while the other one—now missing—had sort of a distinctive swirl. They were expensive, but not that expensive; in the hundreds of dollars, not the thousands.

Their true distinction and value came from the fact that they were a gift from Foxy, who had won a certain woman's heart during a cocktail party in his East Side townhouse a quarter-century ago now. He had been an officer with the foreign service for many years, and had served as a political adviser in the United States Mission to the United Nations.

"He was very, very attractive," said Ms. Carter, now wearing oversized dark-blue glasses that matched her dark-blue top, and a tan scarf thrown almost carelessly over her shoulder. "And very bright."

The earrings became her preferred accessory as she traipsed the world beside her restless husband. "We lived like assassins," she said.

They traveled a lot because Foxy had taken up croquet in retirement. To say that he had "taken up" the sport might be an understatement, though, since he eventually became president of the United States Croquet Association.

New York, Mexico, Newport, Dallas, and New York again, so it went—"I carried his mallet," she said dryly—until dear Foxy died at the age of sixty-eight, in 1994. Those X-shaped earrings rocketed in value. She wore them everywhere, always sporting the one with the slight swirl on her left lobe—not that the earrings were ear specific.

"It depends on which is more comfortable for the individual," she said, "as ears are different."

She had them on, as usual, during that East Side bridge party several evenings ago. But as soon as she got home, she noticed that her left earring was missing. She hurried back to East Sixty-fifth and Park, where the taxi had dropped her off, and began rooting about the snow, searching for a speck of gold in mounds of city white.

Telephone calls to her dinner hostess and to the Taxi and Limousine Commission were just as fruitless. She placed her small, hopeful advertisement in the *Post,* and called Tiffany's to inquire about replacing the lost earring. It can be done, she said. "But it won't come in a tortilla."

As the conversation drew to a close, she was asked about the animal-shaped gold knocker that adorns her front door. Was that the face of a Pomeranian?

"No," said the woman with one earring. "It's a fox."

SEPTEMBER 18, 2004

Hire the Guy with a Head for Baseball

Mr. Met does not have the ability to speak. This could be related to his hydrocephalic condition, or to fear among his handlers that if he ever brought foam tongue to palate, he might sound like Anna Nicole Smith, or some tapped-out denizen of a Flushing boardinghouse who gargles with gin.

Whatever the reason, it is probably best that he remain mute. For if Mr. Met could speak, he might release a bansheelike wail that lasts through the day and well into the night, long after the lights at Shea Stadium had stopped illuminating the latest crime committed in the name of baseball.

The sleepless children of Queens would ask: "What's that sound, Daddy? It's making me sad." Their fathers would answer: "That's Mr. Met, my child, crying for us all. Now let's sing that lullaby you used to like."

And, with voices trembling, they would sing: "Meet the Mets, meet the Mets, step right up and . . ."

If you were to get inside Mr. Met's head—there's plenty of legroom—you would see memories that would have you howling as well. Just four years ago, the Mets won the National League pennant, earning the right to be thrashed by the Yankees in the 2000 World Series. But it seemed that the Mets had channeled the spirits of championship seasons past and would again be challenging the Yankees for the attention, if not the universal affection, of this city's baseball fans.

Wait till next year, shouted the gesticulating white-gloved hands of Mr. Met, who could take pride in knowing that as far as team mascots, he owned this town. That's MISTER Met to you, George.

The next year, 2001, the Mets were barely average. In 2002 they were bad. In 2003 they were downright embarrassing, losing twenty-nine games more than they won. Which brings us to these closing days of the 2004 season.

Up in the Bronx, the Yankees are once again strutting toward the playoffs, led by a grinning shortstop whose teeth seem preternaturally white. And in Queens, the Mets are once again losing, led by a pitcher whose front teeth were knocked out in a traffic accident while en route to Shea.

Up in the Bronx, the Red Sox–Yankees series this weekend is getting more press than the presidential campaign. Meanwhile, the Mets . . .

Who?

The Mets. Meanwhile, the Mets are in Pittsburgh. Their only incentive for winning is that they do not want to finish last in their division. In other words, they hope to finish fifth.

What happened? According to the hollering that filters through the spittle-flecked microphones of sports-talk radio, the reasons are many: injuries, bad trades, little hitting, less defense, questionable managing, a meddling front office. It is fitting, almost Metlike, that the manager, Art Howe, was fired this week, but will continue to manage until the end of the year, as if out of some solemn commitment to failure.

Clearly, what the Mets need is a manager who is able to command respect in the clubhouse and rouse fans with a quick dance on the dugout roof. Someone whose actions speak louder than words. Someone like Mr. Met.

After more than forty years with the organization, no one has been as complete a company man as the six-foot-ten mascot wearing Number 00. Remember Lady Met, who temporarily distracted Mr. Met with her two-big-heads-are-better-than-one tease? Sent packing on the 7 train.

How about the time they decided Mr. Met's head was, uh, misshapen? "His head was too large, and he literally could not get through doorways," recalls Dave Howard, the team's executive vice president of business operations. "When we wanted him to go to events and to suites, it didn't quite work. So we went back to the drawing board."

Not one peep from brave Mr. Met.

Mr. Met also exudes a happy-within-himself aura that the Mets have begun to exploit. In addition to visiting hospitals and schools, he now makes appearances at bar mitzvahs, birthday parties, and decidedly unromantic weddings.

This weekend, for example, he will light up a lucky someone's birthday party in Brooklyn. And last week he arrived by limousine to a gaudy Midtown affair, although he had to sit on the vehicle's floor so that his head could fit.

Last, Mr. Met has charisma. He enchants those children who do not cry at the sight of him. And when he invited retirees to walk the base paths after a recent game, Mr. Howard says, "there was a bottleneck at first base of senior citizens wanting their picture taken with Mr. Met."

Mr. Met, the perfect manager for this organization: smiling on the outside, howling on the inside.

Name Is Gotti, but Principle Is Peter

Not so long ago in this city, the Gotti surname carried clout, as in one to the head. It said give me your money. It said, maybe you did not hear me, give me your money. It said, whack, thank you for your money. In short, Gotti said sociopath.

No question. Back then, the Gotti bloodline dominated the sixth borough of Thugdom. John Gotti, the patriarch and the head of the Gambino crime family, would order murders the way the rest of us order lunch—Yes, I'll have the Louis DiBono, please, shot—and then joke that the only family he ran was the one with the wife and kids back in Howard Beach.

"Ha-ha-ha," everyone would say. "You are so funny. And handsome, too." They would then bid leave with backs to the door, in proper deference to a mad king with a gun.

Oh, but he was a proud man, and a stickler for detail. When he learned that some induction ceremonies had strayed from Mafia guidelines—that saint cards were not being burned, or trigger fingers pricked—he demanded a wholesale do-over. Suddenly, mothers of veteran killers throughout Brooklyn and Staten Island were denied use of their own paneled basements. Such was the clout of the Gotti name.

Those days came to mind while in a Manhattan courtroom on Thursday, as yet another Mafia informer, Anthony Rotondo, shared reminiscences from the stand: of a time when John Gotti was feared, rubouts were de rigueur, and the mob had its hooks in everything from catering halls to the latest Kids "R" Us. His words occasionally carried the hint of a boast.

A few yards away, maybe listening, maybe not, sat the marquee defendant, the acting boss of the Gambino crime family, a pot-bellied man in an oversized suit who sort of looked like Rodney Dangerfield's homely kid brother. In fact, he was John Gotti's older brother Peter, whose defense against this latest round of racketeering charges is that he is known to be a dope.

Peter Gotti, sixty-five, is a retired sanitation worker who became a made member of the Mafia through a ritual more steeped in tradition than even the mob's induction ceremony, a ritual known as nepotism. He has no nickname, perhaps because none has ever occurred to him, or perhaps because John Gotti's Brother says it all.

Because he has no reputation for violence, or thought, it seems that only the Peter Principle can explain his ascension in the ranks. His brother John died in prison in 2002, and his other brother, Gene, and his nephew, John Gotti Jr., are in prison now. So is he, serving nine years on a previous racketeering conviction. And here he is, on trial again.

Peter Gotti argues that he is being persecuted because of his surname (the very name that allowed a certain sanitation worker to live large for so many years). Somehow, though, his niece Victoria—John Gotti's Daughter—has parlayed the same name into a moneymaker, through a disturbing reality television show called *Growing Up Gotti*.

The show transforms her father the dead sociopath into a kind of benevolent spirit. See the "Manscaping" episode, for example, in which one of her teenage sons honors his grandfather by getting a large tattoo on his back. Or the "Godmother" episode, in which Victoria is inspired to counsel others after visiting her father's grave.

Growing Up Gotti has yet to include an episode in which Victoria Gotti's three gel-dipped boys microwave some popcorn and curl up to listen to government tape recordings of dear old Grandpa, dear foul-mouthed Grandpa, in full homicidal rage.

They could listen to the greatest hits of the Ravenite Social Club, including the time that Grandpa said, "Every time we get a partner that don't agree with us, we kill him." Or the time that Grandpa said of Louis DiBono, "He's gonna die because he refused to come in when I called."

After John Gotti's imprisonment, prosecutors say, Peter Gotti ordered the killing of Salvatore Gravano—the informer whose testimony helped convict the mob boss—as a statement that he was going to "come out of the long shadow" of his brother. But Mr. Gravano was arrested on drug charges before the plot could be carried out, they say, leaving Peter Gotti with nothing more than the murder-conspiracy charge he now faces.

His mistress recently killed herself, his marriage just ended, and his days of collecting tribute on the waterfront are long gone. He sits in court listening to old comrades tell secrets. During a break he pops a candy into his mouth and says it's his only pleasure in life.

His name is Gotti. That's right: Gotti.

DECEMBER 22, 2004

Sister Mary, the Mother to a Multitude

Sister Mary de Sales, ninety-one, checks her wristwatch again. Yes, it might be best to head down to the chapel on the first floor. A priest friend was saying Mass at noon, and here she was on the fourteenth floor, at a time of day when the elevators at the New York Foundling Hospital move so slowly.

Sister de Sales "retired" in 1997, but to separate her from this city institution after a half century would have been like separating her from the Sisters of Charity, whom she joined when Hoover was president. So she has stayed on, working in the Closed Records section, making unofficial rounds and dashing off now and then with three other nuns to play the twenty-five-cent slots in Atlantic City.

"It's just for the fun of it," she says. "And to get out."

Yes, Sister. Now back to the Foundling.

The elevator descends through the Chelsea building, past the maternity residences on ten and nine, past the crisis nursery on eight. Sister de Sales stops at seven to show off Blaine Hall, where fifteen children—abused and now in city custody—are being evaluated. Sister Teresa Kelly, who oversees the program, says the children are in class right now, and aren't those colorful comforters on their beds nice? Recent donations.

On the other side of doors that are often banged on by children, Sister de Sales and Sister Teresa live in a mostly empty "convent" with Sister Marilda Joseph, who at the moment sits in a chair with a crossword puzzle. Dressed in the black habit and bonnet that many others in her order abandoned decades ago, she confides that she has trouble keeping the habit's white collar stiff. No starch, she says.

The nuns of this city, going, going—going to Atlantic City?

At least Sister de Sales is, on occasion. She says that a sister who is still able to drive will take this gambling-nun posse for a midweek stay at the Showboat, or some other casino where they can get adjacent rooms, eat, and see a show. Sometimes they lose a little at the slots, sometimes they lose a little more.

But, as the good nun likes to say, "What is, is."

Sister de Sales worked through the Roosevelt years as a grammar-school teacher in Brooklyn. Eventually, though, the order decided that she should earn a master's degree in social work and dedicate herself to its foundling hospital, on the Upper East Side.

For many years she was the assistant director in the adoption department, working to match abandoned children with adoptive parents. She then became the tough-minded director of the maternity residence, and she remembers the whispers about the Foundling at the time: "Don't go to the Foundling because they make you crochet a blanket for your baby."

"I'm a great crochet person," she says, with no hint of apology. "And I just felt that they should be doing something for their baby."

Sister de Sales has been there. There in 1958, when she and others carried scores of babies out of the old building and into a new one ("275 Infants Move to New Hospital," shouted the *Times*. "The Sisters of Charity Take Their Charges Across 3rd Ave. in an Hour").

There in 1988, when the Foundling moved again, to Chelsea, where it continues to provide preventive and foster-care services to the children of the city.

There for the calls of frantic unwed mothers, of would-be parents, of adults trying to piece together their past. There for personal involvement in what she estimates to be more than fifteen hundred adoptions or placements in foster homes.

She remembers many specifics, too, from the newborn girl found in a telephone booth in 1965 to the nine-year-old girl who left with foster parents the other day, wearing the scarf that Sister de Sales had crocheted for her.

Dozens of her children keep in touch. One is a newspaper editor, another works with children up in Washington Heights. One, a police detective, stopped by a couple of years ago, carrying Christmas gifts for children. She approached the security guard and asked:

"Is Sister Mary de Sales still living?"

Finally, finally, the elevator reaches the first floor. A very small nun makes her way to the chapel for that Mass at noon. She is the last of the Collins family of the Highbridge section of the Bronx, her mother, father, sister, and brother all gone. So many of her Sisters of Charity gone, too.

But that is OK. She plays her slots, crochets her scarves, helps her children.

Speaking of which, here comes one now, through the doors, someone whose adoption she helped to arrange some forty-six years ago. The priest.

MARCH 13, 2004

Starsky and Calvary

The Jackson Triplex in Queens had three features clicking away the other afternoon. In one theater, the thriller, *Twisted*. In another, the comedy, *Starsky and Hutch*. And in the middle, in the premier house, that blockbuster, *The Passion of the Christ*.

Perhaps only Joe Rivierzo could fully appreciate the interesting juxtaposition. Tucked away in the projectionist's booth, far up and all the way back, only Mr. Rivierzo experienced the cinematic blend of

Ashley Judd earnestness, Ben Stiller wackiness, and the crucifixion of
Jesus as seen through the blood-misted lens of Mel Gibson.

Mr. Rivierzo has watched snippets of *The Passion* here and there
from a porthole in the booth, but he has no plans to see the entire
movie, considered inspiring by some and anti-Semitic by others. His
girlfriend has already seen it, he explained, and besides, "I'm not that
religious."

He is more reverent about the vital role of the projectionist, the
last in a long chain of talented people responsible for the creation of
movie magic. "And nobody knows we're up here," he said.

Mr. Rivierzo raised his voice to be heard above the clack and hum
of his concrete-floored workplace, where reels of film as wide as hula
hoops twirled at ninety feet a minute through three projectors to create distinctly different movie experiences—from the comic antics of
two cops to the persecution of Christ.

There is a monkish quality to Mr. Rivierzo's workday. He slips his
rail-thin body into a tan jumpsuit and climbs thirteen steep steps to a
narrow room with a small refrigerator, a bathroom, a cuspidor, and
timetables for three movies. There he stays for the next twelve hours,
making sure that the films unwind in perfection, the projectors whir
uninterrupted, and the sounds and images remain clear, distinct.

He considers it his duty to jut his head through the porthole at the
start of every movie to hear what the audience is hearing. He knows,
for example, that a roomful of winter coats can muffle sound effects
and require adjustments to the Dolby system.

Mr. Rivierzo's lot in life seemed preordained. His father and
grandfather were projectionists, and when young Joey decided to join
the union twenty-six years ago, he thought his pedigree ensured him
of work in a top-flight theater.

" 'Put him in a porno house,' " he recalled his father telling a
union official. "I looked at him like he was on fire. He says, 'You're
not going to ruin my reputation.' "

Mr. Rivierzo smiled at the memory, then shot a stream of semi-
sweet chewing tobacco into that cuspidor. His father, Lou, died at
eighty-seven a few years ago. He was a good man, he said, and the best
projectionist he ever saw.

Lou's son is forty-six now, his years of projecting pornographic
movies well behind him. He serves as an executive board member for

Local 306, the movie projectionists' union in New York, and works for a "sweetheart" of an owner, Manny Diaz, at this quaint theater in Jackson Heights, where the ushers wear red vests.

Each day he senses the isolation known to his elders, an isolation that his father often likened to prison time. The solitude has its purpose, though. Little things—a scratch on the film, a garble in the sound—are noticed quickly. Little things.

For example, in recent days Mr. Rivierzo has started the four P.M. showing of *Twisted,* then walked to the other end of the booth to prepare *Starsky and Hutch* for its 4:10 showing. When he returns to *The Passion* in the center of the room, the Century projector is always illuminating the same scene.

"It's the scene where they're putting the crucifix into the ground," he explained, as if previewing what was about to appear on screen. "They dig a hole, like a fencepost, they lift the crucifix and drop it in. That's the scene I see, only because of the way the shows are stacked."

And with the Dolby-enhanced sound, he added, "It goes right through you."

With the two other movies under way, Mr. Rivierzo turned up the sound system and peered through the porthole. "Watch," he said. "They drop it in—watch!—and I've got the four-ten going."

BAM!

"See?" he said. "You feel it?"

As Jesus died and was resurrected on screen, Mr. Rivierzo sat on an upturned crate, talking about life. Before long, it was time for the 4:50 showing. He stood up and walked over to the projector.

"We're going to light the candle," he said, peering through the porthole. "My old man used to say that: 'We're going to light the candle.'"

He pushed a button, and the passion began again.

OCTOBER 4, 2006

A Barber's Emotional Tug-of-War Between Hair and Heir

Giovanni the barber had a decision to make. It kept him awake at night. It denied him the comfort he tried to give his customers in the nook of a barbershop he owned on the Upper East Side. Should he or shouldn't he? Yes or no?

Normally he would never hesitate to discuss life's challenges with his clients, his extended family. They might not know that his last name is Cafiso, but they do know the story of the slight, bald man who for so long has snipped their hair, patted their cheeks with witch hazel, and released their improved selves back into the world.

How at nine he began a four-year barber's apprenticeship in the Sicilian town of Pozzallo. How at fifteen he started working on a cargo ship as a busboy. How at twenty-one he entered the United States illegally on a ship called *Yolanda,* met a young woman named Rosa, married, became legal, bought a house, and raised six children.

How for forty-five years, six days a week, he has stood before mirrors in which his reflection was not the one that mattered.

But this time Giovanni could not bring himself to discuss his quandary. For several months he talked with customers about everything but—World Cup soccer and the Yankees and the old days—as celebrated clients looked down from glossy headshots above the mirror with expressions that asked: So what are you going to do?

Giovanni had little time even to consider the question. Some clients wanted their hair cut at six-thirty or seven in the morning, which meant that he often left his home in Rockland County before five o'clock. Sometimes he timed his commute so that he arrived as last call at neighborhood bars opened up parking spots near his shop, on East Eighty-first Street.

He rarely left before seven in the evening, and worked on Saturdays and Sundays. Only on Mondays did he remove himself from the scissors and Clubman talc.

He is sixty-seven now, and his life's regrets center on all the time he spent at work and not at home. So many parent-teacher conferences missed, so many school plays not seen, all because he had to cut some Wall Street executive's hair, which earned him money, which paid for the food and the clothes and the house in New City.

The children, grown now, still tease him about his absence. They once made him sign a contract promising to retire—nonbinding, of course, an expression of love more than anything else. The document hung on the refrigerator for years, its terms ignored.

Almost five years ago, one of his daughters gave birth to a baby girl named Giovanna, but was too ill to care for her. Giovanni and Rosa are raising the child, and her photograph sits alone, in a place of honor, on a shelf in the barbershop.

For the last three years, Rosa has taken their granddaughter to Sicily, to Giovanni's homestead, for the winter. When they are gone, he often sleeps on a loft bed in an eight-by-eight room at the back of his shop so that he is available for his early-morning clients. Still, the arrangement has the feel of solitary steerage.

One night last month, sleep would not come again for Giovanni. He thought of his children's teasing that he had been an absentee father, and he thought of his granddaughter. Then the answer came to him like a slap of witch hazel to the face: He would retire immediately and move to Sicily with his wife and Giovanna.

He roused his wife and told her to buy him a one-way ticket. Finally, she said.

Giovanni so feared becoming emotional that he first told customers he was going on vacation in mid-October. But they were family. So, one by one, he told them that tomorrow would be his last day. Many said they were happy for him and sad for themselves.

In Giovanni's barbershop yesterday, the scissorslike hands of the clock ticked down the hours. The phone rang with people calling for last-minute appointments and farewells.

"Jerry, I'm sorry I no tell you," Giovanni said to one caller, his voice breaking. "I didn't want to cry. I know you so many years. I am going to Sicily, yes."

Giovanni hung up the phone and returned to cutting the hair of a longtime customer named Doug Isaacson for the last time. The snip-snip seemed in harmony with the soft background music. Pieces of Mr. Isaacson's dark hair fluttered to the ground, soon to be swept up by Giovanni. An ordinary moment suddenly seemed sacred.

The two men hugged, and Mr. Isaacson headed for the door. But Giovanni called him back because he had forgotten to brush away some hair. There.

"*Ciao,*" the barber said.

JANUARY 21, 2004

A Long Road to Old Age in a Cubicle

The space that Sofiya Avrukina takes up in her adopted country is one room in Brighton Beach, with a sink, stove, refrigerator, and sofa bed. Walk six paces this way, you hit the wall; twelve paces that way, and you're out the door.

Normally, Ms. Avrukina would have been out the door by now. Gone to that adult day-care program in Canarsie, where the meals are free, the camaraderie is forced, and the workers don't mind if she, a widow of eighty-three, tucks a tiny milk carton or a fistful of sugar packets into her overcoat before boarding the shuttle for home.

But she stayed in this morning because the handymen from the Metropolitan Council on Jewish Poverty were coming to install a grab bar above her tub; that way, at least, she would have something to hold on to. Maybe she will ask for other things while they are here. It would be nice if they spoke Russian.

Ms. Avrukina is small but sturdy, with gray hair that she keeps battle-ready short. She is one of those old Russian women you will see on the coldest, most unforgiving days, walking into the wind along the boardwalk, as if daring the elements to knock them down because nothing else has.

She closes a Russian novel, marking her place with a "Food Stamps for Immigrants" pamphlet, and agrees to explain how she wound up alone in Brooklyn. Valeriya Beloshkurenko, the council's director of home services, translates, occasionally muttering, "Typical, typical"—typical of the elderly Russian immigrant experience.

In 1941 the Nazis came to Ms. Avrukina's small village, outside Minsk, and laid waste to all that she knew. On bent, arthritic fingers, she counts off the family members who were killed: her sister Genya; her sister Bronya; and Mendel, her brother, who "was forced to dig his own grave."

There is a knock at her door, an occurrence that she describes as rare. Standing at the threshold are the handymen, Sergey and Nahum, God-sent angels so large they seem to take up a fifth of the room. "You speak Russian?" she asks. "Wonderful."

She leads the men to the cramped bathroom, and soon the telling of her life story is competing with Sergey's hammering.

Family members who survived the Nazis scattered, including Sofiya, the youngest. In 1943 she was reunited with her mother and a sister in Birobidzhan, Stalin's Jewish Autonomous Region. Then on to Maykop, where she married, raised two children, and became a dentist. Those years were filled with cooking, dancing, and family. At least that is how she remembers it now, here.

After her husband, who was not Jewish, died twenty years ago, Ms. Avrukina began to feel less safe as a Jew, and her sister Rachelle was calling from the Bronx, begging her to come to America. Finally, two years ago, she agreed, taking with her a grown son, his family, and four thousand dollars.

What happened next has Ms. Beloshkurenko, the translator, nodding in recognition. Money spent; sister dies; son becomes too busy for his mother. Ms. Avrukina found herself in Brighton Beach, America, covering her six hundred dollars rent and other monthly bills with food stamps and modest government assistance.

For a while, memories of what she left behind conjured musings of suicide. But now, she says, she finds comfort in her frequent walks along the shore, where the ocean air is "like medicine for my emotional condition."

Ms. Avrukina may be a tough old woman, but she still harbors worries familiar to the elderly. She never unfolds the sofa bed that she sleeps on because it was here when she moved in, and she fears the dirt that lies within. She wants her locks changed because, who knows, the prior tenant probably still has keys.

These fears are why Sergey and Nahum are here. Working for a program called Project Metropair, they travel from one apartment to the next, replacing locks, installing grab bars, even lowering peepholes for people who are not as tall as they used to be. Sometimes, the tenants are happy just for the company.

Later today, Sergey and Nahum will visit a man named Abraham, who needs his windows caulked. But not before the simple needs of Sofiya Avrukina are met: a new lock; a smoke detector; a carpet for the worn floor.

Ms. Beloshkurenko asks if she needs anything else.

An electric fan.

Anything else?

A small stepladder, so that she can reach the cabinets above the sink.

Ms. Beloshkurenko jots the information down and rises to leave. Soon the handymen will be gone too, and an elderly Russian woman in a Brighton Beach cubicle will be eating her dinner of oatmeal, alone.

MARCH 9, 2005

When Change Rains Down, You're Going to Need a Hat

Arnold Rubin knows hats. A plaque attesting to his stature in the field of felt and fur adorns the only wall space in his store not obscured by homburgs and fedoras. It announces to all that he was named Hat Retailer of the Year in 2001 by the Traveling Hat Sales-men's Association of America.

"For excellence in the retail headwear business," it says.

A lot has happened since then, beyond the hat salesmen's decision to change their group's name to the Headwear Association. The state decided to revitalize a stretch of Eighth Avenue, a little south of Times Square. *The New York Times* decided to build a new headquar-ters on Eighth Avenue, a little south of Times Square. Someone in-voked those magical words, "eminent domain," and presto: say goodbye to several small businesses on Eighth Avenue, a little south of Times Square.

Among them, Arnold Hatters, also known as Knox Hats, which had been at 620 Eighth Avenue for more than forty years and whose owner could trace his Times Square hat-selling lineage to 1926.

New York is ever evolving, the urban planners say; change is its nature. But paying the practical cost of that change are not the urban theorists above, but the locksmiths and hatters below. Mr. Rubin had worked to build a presence at that location, and had personally chased pimps and crack dealers away from his store's entrance—save for those few interested in seeing, say, a Biltmore grand beaver homburg in a 7 1/4.

Now, at sixty-eight, he had to start all over.

For four months in late 2003, this city's choral cacophony did not include the voice of Mr. Rubin and his two grown sons, Peter and Mark, as they renovated a new store farther down Eighth Avenue, just south of Thirty-seventh Street. Finally, late that December, Arnold Hatters reopened, shouting its motto in full throat:

"Much is said by what you wear on your head."

Some citizens have heeded that advice, though not as many as when the old store used to benefit from Times Square and Port Au-thority foot traffic. Business is off about 40 percent, which means that choice words are still reserved for the *Times* and the state. But the Ru-bins refuse to dwell too much on the past. They have hats to sell, thousands of them.

There are the top hats, favored by costume designers, drivers of horse-drawn carriages, and the worshipful masters, or chief officers, of Masonic lodges. And the fedoras, including the zoot and the Bogart models. And the homburgs, including that Biltmore model preferred by tradition-minded pimps. And the straw boaters, two-inch brim for seventy dollars, three-inch brim for seventy-five dollars.

"They're predominantly for the theater trade," explained Mark Rubin. "And the occasional barbershop quartet."

As store hours drew to a close Monday evening, a young man asked to see something in a black porkpie. Studying this fresh head like a phrenologist, Mark Rubin estimated the size, reached for a box, and led the man to a three-sided mirror. Soon the customer was preening before the glass, perhaps seeing in himself a cross between Popeye Doyle and Miles Davis.

"I'll take it," he said.

As Mark Rubin steamed and brushed the porkpie, his father showed off some of the ancient tools of a dying trade. Here was a wooden hat block, the size of a human head. Here was an old metal steamer that softens felt and allows the hatter to reshape the crown of the hat. Here were two silvery brim cutters, one to remove one-sixteenth of an inch from a brim, one to remove one-eighth of an inch.

Soon Arnold Rubin was speaking in the obscure language of the hatter. A porkpie hat is also known as a "tight telescope." Traveling hat salesmen are called "drummers," because of the round boxes they carry. A "snake" refers to an additional crease in the crown, while "double snake" refers to a complicated crease that looks like the letter Z.

"If you see someone with that, they've been wearing hats for a long time," he said.

When Arnold Rubin first joined the family trade, his uncle Sidney all but ordered him to wear a hat. So he made his selection. "It was a raw-edge, Western-style homburg called the 'Americana,'" he recalled. "It was never a very successful hat."

Over the years, as old buildings disappeared from the city, so too did many hats; fedoras with teardrop crowns gave way to baseball caps. But Arnold Rubin is a hatter, and proud of it. When he closed his store Monday night, he went out into the city wearing a beret.

Does She Know Any Songs by Carpenters?

Only the luckiest of us ever experience it: that singular moment when the clouds of self-doubt part and you suddenly find the answers to nagging metaphysical questions about who you are and why you were put on this earth. Natalia Paruz is among the few so blessed.

She vividly remembers her epiphany's where and when: Austria, a decade ago. Her fledgling career as a dancer had ended when a taxi struck her outside Lincoln Center, and now, after months of rehabilitation, her parents had taken her on a change-the-subject vacation to the setting of one of her favorite movies, *The Sound of Music.*

One day, while she was watching a vaudeville-like show intended especially for tourists, a man stepped onto the stage. He began to play the saw. Young Natalia nearly swooned.

"I was totally wowed," she says.

After the show the awestruck teenager went backstage to find the saw player surprisingly free of groupies. She asked if he would teach her how to play the saw; he said no. She asked again, saying that she would pay for the lessons; he said no. But he gave her some advice: When you go home, pick up a saw, imitate what I was doing—and you'll figure it out.

Ms. Paruz says she now realizes that the man was not behaving like your typical, stuck-up saw player. "I know he wasn't just brushing me off," she says. "This is the tradition for learning to play the musical saw."

Once home in Astoria, Queens, she began to practice on a rusty saw owned by her landlady, who for some reason had been using it to cut wood. She then went to a local hardware store, where she tested the tonality of various saws before choosing one: a Stanley Handyman. "It had about two octaves on it," she says.

Ms. Paruz gradually learned to coax music from the saw by placing its wooden handle between her legs, running a bow over its steel edge, and carefully bending its body. The greater the bend, the higher the note, she says, adding, "It's really amazing how a piece of steel can sound so human."

She got a job selling souvenirs at a Broadway theater, and during her breaks she practiced on her saw in the parking lot. One night a man heard her playing and gave her five dollars. Thus a New York busker was born.

Over the years, she made adjustments. After a police officer gave her a $150 ticket on the ground that her saw's teeth made the tool— that is, instrument—a weapon, she began searching for toothless saws made especially for music. That led her, eventually, to buy a customized saw from a Monsieur Grau, a retired clown and handyman in France.

"By the way," she says, "he also taught me how to play the bicycle pump."

Ms. Paruz is now the Saw Lady, the best-known saw player in New York (though there is another one out there named Moses). She is that wispy redheaded woman seen in the Times Square subway station, or the one at Union Square, summoning haunting music from quivering steel.

She has made many television and radio appearances, and has performed at various festivals and events, including a few in Tel Aviv with the Israel Philharmonic Orchestra, Zubin Mehta conducting. She has a Saw Lady hat, a Saw Lady Web site, a Saw Lady Christmas CD—and even a regular Saw Lady column in a publication called *The Saw Player News*.

Ms. Paruz, thirty, runs her Saw Lady franchise from a room in the Astoria house she shares with her husband, Scott Munson, a musical composer. On the wall hangs a photograph of Marlene Dietrich playing her favorite instrument, a saw. On the bookshelf sits a thick volume called *Treasures of Mechanical Music*. On a visitor's lap purrs a thick cat, one of five roaming about. And in every other corner rest pitched cowbells in merciful silence.

Cowbells: Ms. Paruz's other instrument of choice.

It seems appropriate to ask Ms. Paruz, whose mother was a classical pianist, why she didn't take up the piano, or the cello, or the flute, or the harp, or the flügelhorn even. Other instruments just didn't "catch me," she says.

She reaches for the saw made especially for her by a retired clown from France and begins to play "Avé Maria." The saw trembles, as if in awe of a fortunate woman doing what she was meant to do.

MARCH 11, 2006

Sweet She Ain't, and She Has the Stories to Prove It

The Inner Circle, a troupe of current and former City Hall reporters with not enough stage fright, will present its annual follies at a Midtown hotel tonight. Hundreds of people who like to be in on the joke will watch as journalists lampoon the bluster and blunder that can sometimes define civics in this city.

If the script keeps with tradition, someone will escort to the stage a small woman with cat's-eye glasses and braided white hair kept in a bun by translucent combs. She will deliver a brief, naughty line, accept the laughter, and toddle away from the spotlight.

Many in the audience will not recognize this woman, Edith Evans Asbury, and will probably whisper, "Oh, what a sweet old lady," because we tend to believe that once we reach a certain age, we become little more than Kewpie dolls eligible for senior discounts.

Sweet? Hah.

Old? At ninety-five, with failing ears, failing eyes, and a regimen of pills for every day of the week, she'll let this pass.

But lady? Hah.

Ms. Asbury can often impersonate a sweet old lady, but a more apt description might be: queen mother of the pointed question. She was a newspaper reporter, after all, among the best in this city; a relentless investigator, an astute observer, a role model for women when newsrooms might as well have had MEN engraved on the doors.

She retired twenty-five years ago but still writes an occasional self-deprecating essay about her long career. And she still attends many media functions like the Inner Circle because—because she is Edith Evans Asbury. And though she never says as much, her presence barks out the question:

Anyone else here ever interview Amelia Earhart? Anyone?

Ms. Asbury lives in a very warm Greenwich Village apartment with a home-care aide and a whippet of a dog that uses her hearing aids as chew toys. Books crowd her living room, including many by the second of her three husbands, Herbert Asbury, the prolific author who wrote *The Gangs of New York*.

Two hours spent with Ms. Asbury in this hothouse of memories is a mad dash to smell every single flower. So much is not touched upon, from the time she interviewed Earhart to the time she angered Mayor John V. Lindsay so much that he slammed his phone down and broke it. So many stories.

"Oh that's a long story," she said at one point. "There was a Nazi spy, and, oh . . ."

What emerges is one continuing story, of a young woman who knew what she wanted. And that was to be a newspaper reporter.

She began at the *Cincinnati Times-Star* in July 1929. She moved to Knoxville, Tennessee, married a man, divorced that man, outgrew the newspaper there, and spent her vacations in New York, asking newspapers to hire her.

During one of these New York visits, she sent a resignation telegram to her editor in Knoxville. "Have chance of job here," she wired, which was true only in the broadest of terms, and quite daring, considering it was in the midst of the Depression. She also sent that telegram collect.

Ms. Asbury found a succession of jobs, including one at a new magazine called *Life*. But when she was laid off, she demanded to see the top editor, who gently suggested that she return to Knoxville.

In recalling this moment, her voice rose in anger. "No! No!" she shouted, stamping her foot at the thought of the seventy-year-old memory. "I will not go back to Knoxville!"

Ms. Ashbury did not go back to Knoxville.

She would go on to work for the *New York Post,* the Associated Press, and the *World-Telegram and Sun.* In 1952 she joined *The New York Times,* but only under the condition that she work as a reporter in the city room, and not in the women's department.

She soon asserted herself as one of the paper's indispensable reporters, bullying and charming her way into story after story, many of them investigations into slumlords, city hospitals, and the small and many ways in which the poor are victimized. After deadline she could smoke and drink and talk tough with the best of them—though, she says demurely, "I was not a cusser."

She recalled with glee how someone once summed her up: "You're the kind of reporter who, when they slam the door, you knock on it."

Those who might coo at the sight of Ms. Asbury on stage tonight should know that she was once famous for not suffering fools, especially editors who treated her as a second-class woman, and not as a first-class reporter.

Sitting in her warm apartment, feeding goodies to her dog, she recalled one editor who never treated her fairly. One day he died on the job.

"And I was delighted," said this sweet old lady.

AUGUST 27, 2005

Forever in Peace (and War) May He Wave

War. Rising oil prices. The Pitt-Aniston breakup. Sometimes the world is too much with us, and life so crazy, that we need to seek out someone who seems grounded, comfortable in his own skin. Someone like the man who dresses as a Fourth of July pinwheel and stands on a Cross-Bronx Expressway footbridge, waving two American flags and tweeting his whistle at the traffic rumble below.

His name is Luis; just Luis. When asked where he was born, he says, "I forget." When asked where he lives now, he says, "Everywhere," then adds, "Put Queens." And when asked his age, he says:

"When people ask, 'How old are you?' I say I am living in the present only. Yesterday I forgot, and tomorrow maybe never come."

Luis turns to the traffic to impart a blessing with his flags, and an eastbound truck blows its horn as it passes underneath. This is the Cross-Bronx equivalent to a church service's exchange of peace. Peace be with you, says Luis; and also with you, answers the truck.

If your daily routine includes hours traveling the major roads of New York City, chances are quite good that you, too, have received the blessing of Luis. Seven days a week—"Sometimes eight," he says—he stands near the Long Island Expressway in Queens, or Second Avenue and Fifty-ninth Street in Manhattan, or here in the Bronx, waving his flags and blowing his whistle.

For those who have seen him only as a red-white-and-blue blur on the horizon, here is what he wears. A blue cap with five small American flags that jut from the top and occasionally jab those in close proximity. A sign that says I LOVE MY LIFE. A pair of extremely oversized sunglasses that suit him somehow. A tie, a blazer, a knee-length blue overcoat, another sign saying RELAX—FREE AIR, and a peculiar kind of lapel pin, consisting of four small mirrors glued to the face of an old wall clock.

What is the meaning of the, uuh, mirror-clock accessory?

"You are very intelligent," he says. "Congratulations."

The mirrors, he says, are meant to direct positive sunrays to his people who are passing below. "They have concerns," he says, struggling to speak above the traffic's roar. "Money, job, whatever."

As for the clock, he says, it reminds him that he follows no schedule but his own. That after working for twenty-seven companies—"hotels, restaurants, more, more, more"—and raising six children, he is his own boss, his own chairman of the board. "And this," he says, pointing to the footbridge pavement, "is one of my offices."

He began his ministry many years ago, so long ago that he had only one flag back then. It has its own set ritual now, with location changing based on his schedule, which is subject to change.

Yesterday, for example, he packed water, apples, slices of plain bread, and his flags and arrived at the Cross-Bronx at eight A.M.—an hour later than he would have preferred, but the subway threw him off schedule. Then he began to perform what he calls his "duties": a series of elaborate flag waves, intended to raise the spirits of those navigating the asphalt river below.

Flags held with arms outstretched and parallel to the ground: "Respect." Flags raised high above the head: "Up, up, keep it up." Flags waved in breaststroke fashion: "Speed, speed, faster, faster."

From below comes a long honking response. Luis smiles. "People understand my system," he says.

A man crosses the footbridge, making sure to keep his distance from small, gray-haired Luis. Another passer-by simply salutes. Then comes Bob Reilly, cane in hand and on his way to feed pigeons in a nearby park.

"This is the best man in the world," he says of Luis, now busily signaling to the passing trucks and cars. "You don't see nobody like him."

Luis pauses from his duties to attempt an answer to the why of his endeavor. ("Excellent question; you are very smart.") A distillation of that answer goes something like this. He wants to send positive waves. He wants to remind people that the air is free and life is good. He wants to celebrate the United States of America.

Finally, those people below, with their horn beeps and hand waves, give him purpose, meaning. "They're helping me," he says.

Other questions that earlier came to mind, ones that would have sidled up to the matter of compos mentis, now seem inappropriate. As if anticipating the question, Luis proffers one of his flags and commands this poor pilgrim to join him in facing the traffic and sharing in the duty.

"Up! Up! Up!" he shouts, his arms raised high.

His ever-flowing congregation honks in response: And also with you.

Epilogue

NOVEMBER 15, 2006

On a Corner Midstream in the Rush

With an evening rain lashing, a stream of people burble and bob toward the stairwells draining down to Penn Station. Some of those being carried along use umbrellas as shields against the wet and the city. Others hunch their bodies in clear resistance to their surroundings and to any notion of rainwater as a blessing.

Clumps of people clog street corners whenever the floodgates go up; that is, whenever the traffic lights turn green to unleash cabs and cars down Seventh Avenue. But when those lights flash red, the people float again upon the released current, across and down to trains and subways departing. The weekday ritual of the Midtown evening rush reflects life in this rushed city, where facial expressions and body language impart the clear message to get out of my way, I've got to be somewhere else, and fast. All the more reason, then, to pull oneself out of the river, miss that departing train, and pause for a moment.

Immediately, another corner in this city of a million corners—a corner usually dismissed as a way station—reveals itself in ways as engrossing as any novel by Dickens, as cinematic as any movie by

DeMille. Full-throated and fully charged, brusque and vulgar and sentimental to the brink of maudlin, it is all New York.

The leaden clouds above hang low, as if held in drooping place by skyscraping tent poles. Their rain, misty one moment, copious the next, lacquers Seventh Avenue in a way that transforms the reflected lights into quivering spills of paint, reds and greens and blues constantly being disturbed by shooting taxicab yellows.

Meanwhile, a symphony plays; the drumbeat of raindrops on umbrellas, the whish of tires on wet pavement, the whistles of beckoning doormen outside the Hotel Pennsylvania, the ringing of the Salvation Army man's bell—a ringing uninterrupted by another ringing, that of his cell phone. He takes the call, but keeps right on ringing.

Above it all rises the bellow-song of a heavy man failing to keep dry under a mangled umbrella that looks like a splayed crow. He is singing on behalf of the homeless, or so he sings, his voice rumbling up from that great stomach to prick a city's conscience: Even a penny helps, ladies and gentlemen, help feed the homeless, help out today, New York.

Moments unfold. Here comes a man asking if anyone has Knicks tickets, which marks him as someone interested in crimes against basketball; within hours, the Knicks will lose again. Here stand two grisly palm-card guys talking shop as they brandish cards for another strip club. ("Him and this guy Victor." "Yeah, yeah, he used to work for V.I.P., and then Stilettos.")

Here falls a well-dressed woman, and her dinner spills from a bag and onto the sidewalk. I hand her back her errant roll, and who knows why, but I say I am sorry.

Who knows why, but I see through the veil of rain a glowing white sign on Thirty-second Street for the Church of St. Francis of Assisi, which reminds me of the church's morning breadline, forming at seven o'clock, feeding dozens and vanishing by seven-thirty—a daily miracle.

Who knows why, but I think of the train tracks behind me, and of a man I know who for years slept beneath the platform of Track 15; he is sober now, and back among us.

Who knows why, but standing in the midst of this New York color and shout, I realize that the river of people streaming past reflects more than just the city's rushed nature. It is the ever-flowing life's blood sustaining New York: the saints and con artists, the fallen and redeemed, the immigrants from Missouri and from Mexico, the work-weary people who succumb to a subway's gentle rocking.

On this just-another-Monday-in-Manhattan, I think of how extraordinary the city is even at its most mundane, and how proud I am to be a child of it, and how silly it is to harbor any proprietary sense about a place so old and so immense, simply because my Irish mother and New York father met at a church dance in Brooklyn long ago.

In truth, I pause beside the flow of the city to say goodbye to this column about the city, for this is my last "About New York." They tell me I will be launching a national column in a couple of months. Still, the loss I feel is keen.

But before I rejoin that ever-flowing river, before I catch a train with return ticket clutched in hand, let me say this: It's been a privilege. Thank you. Now get outta here.